BAY AREA INTERURBANS

Legend:
- SP
- KEY
- 40 LINE
- NWP
- P.R.Y.
- P & SR
- SN
- SFN & C

WITHDRAWN
WORN, SOILED, OBSOLETE

PACIFIC OCEAN

SAN FRANCISCO BAY

Locations: Alamo, Danville, Moraga, Berkeley, Oakland, San Leandro, Hayward, Alameda, Yerba Buena I., Treasure I., Angel Island, Alcatraz, Waldo Pine, Sausalito, San Francisco, Daly City, Colma, Holy Cross Cemetery, Baden, Tanforan, Millbrae, Burlingame, San Mateo, Palo Alto, Cupertino, San Jose, Campbell, Saratoga, Los Gatos, Congress Springs

D1791585

Interurban Railways of the Bay Area

Interurban Railways
of the
Bay Area

by Paul C. Trimble

FRESNO  1977

INTERURBAN RAILWAYS OF THE BAY AREA

Copyright © 1977 by Paul C. Trimble, all rights reserved. No part of this book may be reproduced or utilized in any form or by any means without permission in writing, except in the case of brief quotations embodied in critical articles and reviews.

Library of Congress Card Number 77-085687

ISBN 0-913548-47-2

Printed in the United States of America

Valley Publishers
Division of Book Publishers, Inc.
8 East Olive Avenue
Fresno, California 93728

To the memory of my father, Sinclair G. Trimble,
who rode the interurbans and taught me to appreciate
them, and in honor of the Bay Area Electric Railroad
Association, whose members have done so much to
preserve the heritage of the interurbans,
this book is respectfully dedicated.

"Somewhere in this world there must be a good transit system, although I would never dare call any of its patrons as my witnesses to the fact. Some systems have been recognized by the whole industry and have been visited by strangers from other countries, yes, other continents, for information and enlightenment. But in their own city the sad truth is that there is none so poor as to do them reverence."

—Irving S. Fairty, General Counsel for the Toronto Transportation Commission, from *Railroad Magazine*, February 1953, Vol. 6, No. 1

Table of Contents

AUTHOR'S PREFACE x

PROLOGUE xii

Chapter One
EVOLUTION OF THE INTERURBAN 1

Chapter Two
THE BIG RED CARS, Interurban Electric Railway 7

Chapter Three
THE LAST TO GO, Key System 25

Chapter Four
THE BIG SUBS, Market Street Railway Company 49

Chapter Five
THE FOUR RAIL TRACKS, Northwestern Pacific Railroad 67

Chapter Six
THE BLOSSOM LINE, Peninsular Railway 83

Chapter Seven
THE BIG WHITE CARS, Petaluma & Santa Rosa Railroad 95

Chapter Eight
THE COUNTRY'S LONGEST INTERURBAN, Sacramento
   Northern Railway 113

Chapter Nine
WINE COUNTRY AND GEYSERS, San Francisco, Napa &
   Calistoga Railway 133

Chapter Ten
THE WATER ROUTES 145

Chapter Eleven
OTHER LINES 165

Chapter Twelve
THE SURVIVORS 173

Chapter Thirteen
EPILOGUE 175

APPENDICES AND BIBLIOGRAPHY 185

Preface

Growing up in San Francisco, I did not find it difficult to develop a love affair with railway transit vehicles and ferryboats. After all, here was a city which boasted no less than four streetcar tracks on its main thoroughfare, two cable car systems, interurban lines, and ferryboats paddling across the Bay to greet the transcontinental trains of three class 1 railroads. All this was spiced with the Southern Pacific's Third and Townsend Streets depot which hosted three name trains (*Coast Daylight*, *Lark*, and *Starlight*) as well as others of lesser vintage. As a youngster I would walk several blocks out of my way in order to ride a streetcar or a cable car when a motor bus would have been more direct.

By the time I was out of school, all the interurbans, most of San Francisco's streetcars, and all but three cable car lines had been abandoned. The only sources left to me to nourish my affection were, for the most part, between the covers of books and magazines. Ultimately, this led to a study on my own, the original purpose of which was to catalogue all the interurbans which once served the San Francisco Bay Area.

In order to accomplish this, I first had to define what an interurban was, and whether some of these so-called interurbans were worthy of the name. For the most part, an interurban was so-called for no other reason than the ownership's advertising as such. Sometimes they were called interurbans because the rolling stock compared favorably with other lines (particularly in the Midwest) whose definition was beyond question.

In 1911, a book was published entitled *Electric Railway Dictionary*, by Rodney Hitt, which was to serve as a bible of electric railways for many years. In his *Dictionary*, Mr. Hitt catalogued types of cars, manufacturers, parts of cars, electrical equipment, motors, fareboxes, and a host of accessories for streetcars and interurbans. Included was a glossary which was the first attempt to standardize terms and definitions. In spite of some excellent scholarship, Mr. Hitt's definition of streetcar, suburban car, and interurban car failed to pigeonhole properly the eight electric railway systems which offered intercity service in the Bay Area. Perhaps this was because the area's transportation needs and development were—as they are now—unique. However, for the record, let us quote from Mr. Hitt's *Dictionary*:

"Street Car. A term used to designate surface cars used only in city passenger service as distinguished from cars used in suburban or interurban service."

"Suburban Car. A car used for short runs into suburban and country districts. Usually fitted with cross seats and more powerful motors than city cars, but not designed for the high speed of interurban cars. *No sharp lines of distinction are drawn between city and suburban cars or between suburban and interurban cars.*" (Italics mine—P.C.T.)

"Interurban Car. Any electric car used in long distance speed service, as distinguished from city and suburban cars. Interurban passenger cars are built in lengths up to 65 feet of very heavy and substantial construction, closely resembling steam railroad coaches. Various types are illustrated...."

As the reader will see upon perusal of the text, pigeonholing some of these lines will be difficult at best, so for purposes of this volume, my own definition is offered:

"Interurban Car. An electrically powered railway passenger car, usually heavier and larger than conventional city streetcars, operating principally over a right-of-way between one city and another."

Granted that the above definition of the idiom will not satisfy every traction *aficionado*, the reader is asked to make his judgment in light of the context.

For, after all, eight different railways are under discussion within these pages. First, there is the

Southern Pacific and the Interurban Electric Railway, which is the story of a major railroad. The Key System is the story of an interurban with attendant streetcar and ferryboat service. The Market Street Railway is the story of a city streetcar system with an attendant interurban line. The Northwestern Pacific is the story of a narrow gauge steam road which was electrified. The Peninsular Railway is the story of mixed streetcar and interurban service. The Petaluma & Santa Rosa Railroad is the story of an interurban line which operated river steamboat service as well. The Sacramento Northern is the story of the merger of two roads—both of which were substantial interurbans in their own right—to form the nation's longest interurban line. The San Francisco, Napa & Calistoga is the story of an interurban whose survival as an independent railway depended upon its freight service to a naval yard, eventually being purchased by the U.S. Navy itself. Clearly, this was variety!

Yet, because of this variety, a composite of the interurbans of the United States, with their pluses and minuses, can be illustrated within the following pages. While the original purpose was simply to incorporate, within one book, information on those eight railways, it has led to questions which, in light of today's automobile-related problems, demand answers so that students of public transit may better come to grips with the background of the evolution of intercity transit—from steam railroads to electrics, abandonment of the electrics, automobile use, failure of automobiles for mass transit, and restoration of electric train services such as is the case with BART.

In closing, I would like to express my gratitude to those persons and organizations without whose contributions, however small, of photographs, editorial assistance, and background, this book would never have become a reality. If anyone has been omitted, it is purely accidental.

For assistance in illustrations and caption material, I am indebted to: Virginia Dennison and Sharon Rodriguez of the Alameda-Contra Costa Transit District; Suzanne H. Gallup, Reference Librarian, and the Bancroft Library, University of California at Berkeley; Randolph Brandt; George Campbell; Fred P. Codoni; Commonwealth Club of California; Harry Cook, Barbara Fong, and John E. Wright of the California State Toll Bridge Administration; Edward Fratini of the Sonoma County Historical Society; Golden Gate Bridge, Highway and Transportation District; Tom Gray; Ray Hannah; Stephen D. Maguire; David Mitchell; John Muzio; Robert Rockwell of the San Francisco Municipal Railway; Vernon J. Sappers; Charles D. Savage; Jo Ann Shelburne; Charles A. Smallwood; Paul Gordenev of the Western Pacific Railroad Company; Wilbur C. Whittaker. Special thanks go to San Francisco artist Albert Tolf for the use of his historical cartoons.

For editorial assistance I am indebted to: Robert G. Anderson, Sr., Putnam Barber, Charles H. Givens, Paul Gordenev and Dudley Thickens of the Western Pacific Railroad Company, Newton K. Gregg, Ray Hannah, Addison H. Laflin, Jr., David Mitchell, Benson Munger, Jr., John Muzio, Vernon J. Sappers, Robert A. Sederholm of the Southern Pacific Transportation Company, Charles A. Smallwood, and Wilbur C. Whittaker.

For reference assistance I am indebted to: the Bay Area Electric Railroad Association; Hon. Peter Behr, California State Senate; Fred Biagi, Jr., Melanie Clark of the San Francisco Port Authority; Fred P. Codoni; Dr. William N. Davis, Jr., Chief of Archives, California State Archives; Addison H. Laflin, Jr.; Marin County Public Library; Orange Empire Railroad Museum; Sonoma County Public Library; State of California Toll Bridge Administration; Pauline Tigue of the California State Automobile Association; the late Jack Trotter; Ward Walkup; David A. Young of the Library and Archives of Washington University of St. Louis, Missouri; Jeffrey Wetmore; William T. Wooten.

In addition, special thanks go to members of my family, without whose patience, understanding, and encouragement I could never have finished this work.

Paul C. Trimble

Novato, California

Prologue

On the coast of California lies the world's largest land-locked harbor, a harbor separated from the Pacific Ocean by a narrow strait—only a mile wide — known as the Golden Gate. The southern portion of this harbor, called San Francisco Bay, extends over thirty miles to the south. To the north and northeast are San Pablo Bay and Suisun Bay, respectively. Blessed with a mild climate, a natural seaport, and a gateway not only to the goldfields of the '49ers but to what is today the most productive agricultural area in the world—the Great Central Valley—the San Francisco Bay Area is comprised of nine of California's fifty-eight counties. At the tip of the peninsula separating San Francisco Bay from the Pacific Ocean is San Francisco, bounded on the west, north, and east by salt water and on the south by San Mateo County, thus left with a land area of only approximately forty square miles.

Surrounding the Bay's waters is a mixture of marshlands, mudflats, and relatively level farmlands, leading into the gentle hills which develop into the Coast Range Mountains; the Coast Range is the western rim of the Great Central Valley, the Sierra Nevadas being the eastern.

Transportation in this region during the eras of Spanish colonization, American settlement, the Gold Rush, and the years preceding the Civil War had been dependent upon the availability of waterways, the availability of dray or riding animals, or the availability of one's own feet. This plainly was not sufficient for the pioneers who were in a position to help develop California to the point where its nickname "the Golden State" would mean much more than the mere gleaning of that precious yellow metal.

Opportunity would avail itself only with the coming of the railroad, for wagon roads, while usable during the dry months of the year, were limited in scope since an animal, whether horse, mule, or ox, could only pull so much tonnage before its days of service were over. During the rainy season, with the rims of the wagon wheels sinking into the adobe clay, travel was severely curtailed. A proliferation of sailing vessels on San Francisco Bay did afford a means of transportation, but heavy fogs, insufficient wind, and a decided lack of speed rendered this form of transportation erratic, and in some cases inconvenient as well, as the cargo had to be brought to the boat landing prior to loading, thus once again necessitating the use of roads and animal power for heavy lading.

But not only freight was involved. The movement of passengers was just as vital, for until the automobile was attainable by the masses, public transportation of people ranked on a par with freight moving. Unless there were means for railway passenger travel, there would not only be a restriction of commerce, but of the exchange of human values essential to prevent a society's stagnation.

The railroad, unlike water vessels, could be directed to travel not only to the towns and cities surrounding the Bay, but actually through the towns. The high iron neutralized the problems of the winter mud, and concentrated steam power was more effective than animal power. The problem with railroads, however, was the high cost of construction, brought about by having to ship rails and locomotives from the mills and factories in the East as well as by land purchases, grading, and the building of terminals and shops.

Throughout the years between the Civil War and the turn of the century, railroad construction in the Bay Area would proceed haphazardly at best, because of these expenses. Many were the railroads that were incorporated, but few were the ones that did anything more than lay a few miles of track. Fewer still were those that were to survive to perform their intended function.

Looming in the background of all railroad construction in California, however, was the mighty Southern Pacific and its predecessor, the Central Pacific Railroad.

For all that has been written about the corporate background of the Southern Pacific, two items have to be considered: it served to unite the eastern and western shores of North America, and within California itself it formed not only the basis of a railroad, but of a total (for that time) transportation *system*. Besides linking the state with its steel rails, the railroad's right-of-way provided a path for the telegraph wires. Moreover the Espee maintained a sizeable fleet of riverboats and ferryboats which filled in the gaps caused by waterways.

As a consequence, many short lines came under S.P. ownership not merely because the Big Four of Crocker, Hopkins, Huntington, and Stanford were acquisitive—which they were—but because the resources of the parent road could be drawn upon to help maintain service in lean times. Further, the S.P. management was able from its central headquarters to coordinate its subordinate short lines' services for maximum efficiency and profit.

There is no question that the corporate policies of the Big Four made them extremely wealthy men, and in this case wealth can be equated with power. That in itself was both an inducement and a hindrance to the building of competing railroads, since there was wealth to be made once the competing line was built, but a short line railroad (which most interurbans were) could not offer anything approaching a total transportation system. And, in the end, it was to aid in the demise of the interurbans in the Bay Area.

By the time of the Gay Nineties, men such as Farmer, Davenport, Daft, van Depoele, Edison, and Sprague were making electrically powered railways a reality. No longer would the vehicles of locomotion have to be shipped out west from New York and Pennsylvania, with the ultimate result that West Coast carbuilders such as Carter Brothers, Holman Car Company, and the Hall-Scott Motor Car Company would come to take their rightful places in the Parthenon of railroading.

While travel by land was progressing, a system of river steamers and ferries was evolving, and when the day came for the electric railroad to make its debut, several lines were already well enough established to form the all-important links with San Francisco. The combination of ferry and/or river steamer travel connecting with the railways of the day gave the San Francisco Bay Area a variety of travel which was unique in North America in the years preceding World War II.

A trip out of the city for San Franciscans, in those years before the automobile had firmly implanted intself in the everyday lives of the American public, was a true adventure. Consider these trips: First, the streetcar or cable car ride down to the Ferry Building at the foot of Market Street, San Francisco. Then a choice of ferries or riverboats. The Northwestern Pacific's sparkling white ferries would take you to Sausalito where connections could be made with the speedy electric trains out to Fairfax, San Rafael, San Anselmo, or to Mill Valley where you could connect with the Mt. Tamalpais and Muir Woods Railroad. Or you could decide to take instead the Monticello Steamship Company's boats which would dock at Vallejo, connecting you with the San Francisco, Napa & Calistoga's electric interurbans. These trains would speed you through the Napa Valley, providing a view of some of California's world-famous vineyards. The trains also stopped at the State Hospital at Imola and the old soldiers' home in Yountville on their way to Calistoga, where you could enjoy the hot springs.

Another option would be to take the Petaluma & Santa Rosa Electric Railroad's river steamers from San Francisco, across San Pablo Bay, then up the Petaluma Creek to Petaluma where connections could be made with the P. & S.R.'s interurbans to Sebastopol, Santa Rosa, or Forestville.

The Southern Pacific Railroad's ferries offered two choices. After crossing the Bay you could either connect with their famous transcontinental trains (indeed, you could well be riding the same ferryboat as the most noted celebrities of the day) or their monstrous seventy-one-foot long interurbans which would speed you throughout the communities of the East Bay.

In competition with the Southern Pacific were the ferries of the Key System. The Key's ferries, after crossing the Bay, would dock at the end of a three-mile-long pier, and upon disembarking the passenger could either take one of the Key's handsome orange interurbans to the East Bay cities or the Sacramento Northern's fast interurbans through the Oakland Hills, past Walnut Creek to Bay Point (now Port Chicago), and then across Suisun Bay on the S.N.'s car ferry *Ramon* from Mallard to Chipps Island and on to Sacramento. After a short stopover in Sacramento, the train would embark on the last leg of its journey, the trip to Chico, a total of about 180 miles—the longest interurban trip in America.

San Francisco also had an interurban line which ran from the heart of downtown down the Peninsula to San Mateo, running through open countryside and racing the S.P. along portions of parallel track.

Fifty-five miles south of San Francisco were the speedy electric interurbans of the Peninsular Railway, serving Santa Clara County commuters and picnickers for almost two generations until the automobile had successfully alienated affections between the people and the railway. Steam trains of the Southern Pacific, from either Oakland, San Francisco, or other points, connected with the Peninsular, which was another Espee property.

With electric reading lights, with platform men instructed in the fine points of both operating rules and public relations, and minus the noise and smoke emanating from a steam locomotive, the interurban was able to utilize rights-of-way for high speed travel and then, like a chameleon, switch to city street running in order to bring passengers closer to their destinations. Moreover, the electric cars could travel distances which heretofore could not be matched by either horsecar or cable car, and thus transfers from one car to another were reduced to a minimum. Because there was competition, fares were kept in check. For transbay travel, light meals and snacks were available aboard the ferries. Regular commuters on the interurban-ferry systems not only became attached to the particular line and train number which they rode, but occasionally regarded their regular seats on the interurban or ferryboat as their own personal property, and interlopers were often met with a stare which could make the Mona Lisa frown.

Occasionally the interurbans would meet untimely fates. They would be destroyed in a fire in a tinder box of a wooden carbarn. They would be engulfed in a fire on a pier over the waters of the Bay. They would crash. They would be involved in grade-crossing accidents when people thought the vaunted strength of the cars would allow them to stop on the proverbial dime. They would be destroyed when their days of service were at an end. A few fortunate specimens would have guardian angels in the form of railfans and railfan clubs which would spare them from the scrapper's torch to preserve them for posterity.

The most fundamental reason for the decline of the interurbans—and this was a national pattern—was that with few exceptions they were money losers. Even in their halcyon years they were sometimes money losers, and the long and repetitious record of bankruptcies and corporate reorganizations was a most unfortunate aspect of the interurbans when contrasted to their general excellence in construction and operations.

There were several underlying reasons for the poor financial health of the interurban railways. For one thing, the automobile hit the middle-class American market just as the interurbans were finishing their last wave of construction, thus reducing their chances of retiring construction bonds, and these roads were often undercapitalized in the first place. Another reason advanced for the interurbans' decline was that they were forced to carry the most expensive of all passengers: commuters.

But now, largely because of commuters and their automobile-related problems, America is seeking a return of her long-lost interurbans. San Francisco, Seattle, Baltimore, Atlanta, St. Louis, Pittsburgh, Washington, D.C., and Los Angeles are either building or planning electrically powered railway systems to replace the interurbans which were once allowed to die for lack of patronage and sufficient revenue. The interurbans of the future will not be the wooden cars with wicker seats of yore, but will be sleek vehicles of aluminum and glass, capable of great speed. The traditional motorman and conductor will be replaced by computers. Individual and colorful names such as Key System, Napa Valley Route, and Sacramento Northern will be replaced, in many areas, by the seemingly ubiquitous name of Metropolitan Transit Authority. Thanks to funding from the Federal Government, designs of the new railway vehicles will become standardized, and individual car styles will be a thing of the past. On one score, however, the heritage of the interurban will reign triumphant: the most efficient form of moving large numbers of people at one time is in an electrically powered railway car.

Chapter One
Evolution of the Interurban

From the time of the arrival of the first man on the continent of North America until the first steam railroad train there were exactly three means of transportation available: foot, boat, and animal power. All this was to change when a Scotsman by the name of James Watt mastered the harnessing of steam energy, and with the subsequent development of a stationary steam engine for water vessels, it was only a matter of time before it would be applied to the railways which heretofore had to settle for animal power.

Some of the earliest railways in North America had utilized what has come to be known as a horsecar, a lightweight vehicle usually mounted on four railway wheels and pulled by horses or mules. Actually, they were unsatisfactory since they required large stables of animals whose usefulness was lost after about three to four years, their travel distance was limited, and they posed a constant threat to public health from the proliferation of urine and feces on city streets. Moreover, they didn't go very fast.

With the development of the stationary steam engine, attempts were made to utilize steam as an animal substitute on city streets. Again, widespread dissatisfaction ensued. The steam dummy, or locomotive, clearly had no business running down the middle of a street, in spite of attempts by builders to disguise them as railway cars, for they were noisy, belched smoke and cinders, and their low steam pressure level reduced their effectiveness for stop-and-start running.

Pause for a moment and ask why the dwellers of the cities continue to patronize these contraptions. The answer is that the focal point of civilization is transportation. The peoples of the ancient world knew this, and in recognition the Roman Empire constructed roads of such durability that some remain in use to this day. As people gain mobility, they are able to expand commerical and cultural intercourse with others and increase the delivery of foodstuffs and other necessities of living to a city. This in turn allows the city to enlarge, both geographically and in population.

Perhaps the best form of public transportation in the pre-electric age was the cable car. It was relatively quiet, was not hampered by excessive grades, did not employ animals, and provided an economical use of fuel, since only the cable-driving plant used any machinery. The cable cars, propelled by means of a grip taking hold of an endless wire rope running underground, were simplicity in themselves, and were found in many of the major cities of the United States, including Chicago, Kansas City, Los Angeles, New York, Oakland, Omaha, Seattle, and their birthplace, San Francisco.

Yet they posed one major drawback insofar as city growth was concerned: they could only travel as far as a cable could reach without causing undue wear and tear on it. This led the inventors back to attempts to produce an efficient, clean and speedy self-propelled railway vehicle. A number of ideas were attempted, including compressed air, battery, soda, and naphtha propulsion. None worked well, if at all.

Meanwhile, urban population was increasing, and growth patterns demanded some form of transit from the farthest reaches of the city to the inner core within a time span of less than an hour. The problem was accentuated by the need of farmers to find an alternate means of transportation to the steam powered railroads whose monopolistic practices, bereft of public regulatory agencies as we know them today, had aroused public enmity. The obvious answer, in retrospect, was the interurban.

Unlike the goddess Minerva, the interurban did not spring full-blown into life without a long

The Market Street Railway Co. which appeared on the signboards of the horsecar shown above was a corporate extension of the Central Pacific Railroad, later the Southern Pacific. Typically, the eastern terminus of this horsecar line was the Central Pacific's ferry sheds.

period of development. Perhaps the earliest traces of the electric interurban could be found in the year 1834 in the Brandon, Vermont blacksmith shop of Thomas Davenport. Davenport had experimented with a number of battery-powered railway vehicles, paving the way for the Edinburgh-Glasgow (Scotland) Railway which used an iron-zinc sulfuric acid battery to achieve a speed of four miles per hour. However, not until the development of the dynamo, or generator, in 1860 could electric railroading be taken seriously.

In 1867, Moses G. Farmer invented a car which could be operated with a motor and dynamo, and from then on, inventors such as Leo Daft, Charles van Depoele, and Thomas A. Edison would continue to work and develop until the way was paved for Frank J. Sprague to perfect the concept of multiple unit operation, or having two or more motors—even on separate cars—operate under one control.

At first, electric railway cars were developed for city street running, but as lines began to extend beyond the practical operating limits for animal and cable powered vehicles, it was understood that it would only be a matter of time before electric railways would connect not only neighborhoods, but even towns and cities. It is a matter of debate as to which was the first interurban in the United States for the simple reason that the differences between a street railway car, a suburban car, and an interurban car have never been clarified. However, it is agreed that the first line to run over a private right-of-way, using electric power, and employing a larger car than those generally used by city streetcar lines, was the Oregon Power and Railroad Company, which ran trains between Oregon City and Portland, Oregon, beginning in February of 1893. Almost ten years later, the San Francisco Bay Area would see the beginning of the interurban services which would continue for some fifty-six years.

Despite advances in the technology of the electric cars, the carbuilding industry was hardly keeping pace. Many of the carbuilders started out as carriage makers and builders of railroad cars for the steam roads, and there was but gradual change in design from period to period. The earliest steam railroad passenger cars, appropriately called carriages, were, in fact, makeshift stagecoaches.

Next came the elongated cars with either longitudinal or cross seating. This was the basic design of the city horse car, and it was to last, in modified form, well into the twentieth century. A platform at one or both ends provided working space for the driver as well as a receptacle for entering and/or alighting from the car. Since air conditioning was unknown, a portion of the roof was raised and fitted with celestory windows which could be opened to provide air ventilation.

This window arrangement would continue to be used on some lines until after World War II.

Except that they were longer and could carry more passengers, the trailers on the city steam dummies matched those of the horsecars. The dummies, in an apparent effort to disguise themselves, were often built to resemble shortened passenger cars, complete with siding and windows.

In warmer climates, the so-called open car was used. This car had the same floor, roof, and seating arrangements of a conventional city car of the period, but had no sides. Thus passengers would not be forced to ride inside a stuffy car on a hot day. On some lines smoking was permitted in the back seats of an open car.

When the cable car was introduced, there was little, if any, change in basic carbody design. The first cars, in San Francisco, employed a dummy, or grip, car. This car had bench seats around the working area of the operator, or gripman. Hitched to the gripcar was a trailer. While San Francisco cars rarely used more than one trailer per grip car, other cities, notably Chicago, did. Trailers could be either open or closed cars, depending upon the ownership.

The first breakthrough in street railway cars appeared on the Market Street Cable Railway Company of San Francisco in the early 1880s when a new design for cable cars was used, this time combining the gripcar and the trailer into one unit—a type of car found today on the Powell Street cable cars in San Francisco. This design was followed by the California Street Cable Railroad Company when they attached two grip sections to a closed section—one on each end. This type of car, favored in California because of its generally mild-to-warm climate, became known as the California type, i.e., having an open section at each end of a closed section.

The California type gave the owner the option of reversing the car at the end of the line by using a switchback track, a wye track, a loop, or in at lease one case, a turntable, and found early favor with electric streetcar operators, the only disadvantage being exposure to the elements during cold winters or heavy rains.

Meanwhile, fully enclosed street railway cars had never completely vanished from the scene, and remained in use, albeit mostly on either horsecars or early electric cars, with minor refinements being added from time to time. Occasionally an end platform would be enclosed, either by gates or folding doors, providing safety to passengers and offering protection from the weather to the platform men. Occasionally they would be partially enclosed, thus placing them halfway between an enclosed and a California-type car.

When Frank J. Sprague had perfected the concept of multiple unit operation, the stage was set for the interurban. Since these cars had to travel over city streets as well as their own right-of-way, they had to be able to negotiate tight

The grip car, or dummy, and trailer arrangement for cable cars was developed in San Francisco and would be the pattern for cable cars throughout the United States until the Market Street Cable Railway designed a combination car which would be the forerunner of the California Type car. The Geary Street cable line was another property of the Central Pacific.

This photo, taken in 1886 at the corner of Ellis and Market Streets in San Francisco, shows the progression from a little four-wheeled horsecar into a thirty-five-foot long cable car with open platforms at either end. The electric interurbans were still a generation away for Californians.

curves. Since they would be on rights-of-way, they should be capable of traveling at high speeds. High speeds meant heavier construction than previously used on cable car and early electric car roadbeds as well as the carbodies themselves.

Thus interurbans came to assume the best features of both steam-powered rail cars and city streetcars. Many adopted the railroad-type roof, which was a raised section in the center with the celestory windows, but the ends curved downward to join the end bulkheads. Some cars retained the deck roof, which provided for the celestory windows but did not curve downward at the end, and was encircled by the lower part of the roof. As ventilators became more advanced, some cars used the arch, or turtle-type roof, which was simply an arch, rounded on the ends, which covered the entire carbody.

These cars were often divided into smoking and non-smoking sections, with space often partitioned for the motorman. The motorman's section often carried light freight such as express packages, newspapers, baggage, and mail.

The interiors of the cars were often adorned with polished wood, inlaid and sometimes carved into the handsome filigree so popular in the Victorian Age. The brass—handles, luggage racks, screws, and other hardware—was polished regularly, as were the brass buttons on the trainmen's uniforms.

Seats were of wicker or rattan. In later years, and on first class accommodations, leather or a sturdy but comfortable fabric was used. On double-ended cars, the seats were built to be reversible by folding the backrest from one side of the bench to the other.

From a passenger viewpoint, one of the major improvements of electric railway cars was the replacement of oil or gas lamps by electric lights.

Until the early years of the twentieth century, most street railway cars, suburban cars, and city streetcars were built of wood. Later, steel predominated, partially to increase traction on the rails but mainly for safety. In a crash the steel cars were less apt to crush the passengers. A serious accident which splintered a wooden car on the Pacific Electric Railway in Los Angeles, killing and seriously injuring a number of passengers, caused the railway to cancel an order for new wooden cars and have steel ones built instead.

Later, lightweight metals would be used instead of steel, but this carbody design was to remain in force on city streetcars and interurbans until the 1930s, when such innovations as the P.C.C. car and the Key System's bridge units would be outshopped from the few remaining carbuilders.

Electric current collection from the trolley wire would see very few changes over the years, once the trolley pole was perfected. The trolley pole was mounted on top of the car, and at its end was a harp which held a grooved wheel, called the trolley wheel, in place. The trolley pole was held upright, causing the trolley wheel to rest against the wire, by either springs or pneumatic pressure. In later years the wheel was replaced with a shoe which slid along the trolley wire, but fitted to the same type of poles.

A second method of current collection was by means of a pantograph, which resembled a diamond-shaped framework with a rod running across the top which slid along the trolley wire. They were collapsible, and had two advantages over the trolley pole: they rarely came loose from the wire and they permitted the car to run in a reverse direction without having to stop and change the trolley pole. (A variation of the pantograph, though rarely used in the United States, was the bow collector, which was nothing more than an elongated metal loop which rested against the wire and was spring mounted a la twin trolley poles.)

A fourth method of current collection was the use of the third rail. By far the most efficient for the transmission of high-voltage electricity, it was also the most dangerous to man and animal alike. Running alongside the tracks would be a third rail, and a shoe would extend from under the carbody (most often on the wheeltrucks) and spring rest against the rail. Needless to say, it had to have an insulated cover inside the train station, at cattle crossings, and anywhere else where it might pose a hazard. Occasionally, city street railways, in an attempt to rid the community of disfiguring overhead wires, put a third rail below ground, and an arm would reach down through a slot in the street—usually between the rails—into the underground conduit to make contact with the rail.

The trolley wire was the umbilicus which connected the cars on the line to the equally mysterious carbarn, an ediface which was often off limits to outsiders. The carbarn was the heart of the trolley line, for here was where the crews reported to work, the cars were stored when not in use and were serviced and repaired, the day's receipts were counted, and the electric generators were often located, where odorless, colorless, and silent electricity was sent out over the wires to feed through either the antenna-like trolley pole or the ungainly frame of a pantograph and on to the motors of the interurban cars.

In those years prior to the Second World War, the electric interurbans rolled over the Bay Area's nine counties, and with polished brass, emaculate paint, and fierce-sounding gongs, they carried with them all the poise and flair of the French Guarde Republicaine or John Philip Sousa's Marine Band.

Across the dash, or front, of these mighty cars was a series of windows, and behind one of those windows sat the motorman. The motorman controlled the speed of the interurbans. He guided them over the switches and braked them to a halt. He sounded the gong at crossings. Needless to say, the level of respect he received from small boys ranked with that of a ship's

The two early San Francisco streetcars shown here at 16th and Folsom Streets closely resemble the California Street cable cars of today, and this design—having two open ends and a center enclosed section—was to be known in the carbuilding trade as a California Type car.

(Collection of the author)

captain or an airplane pilot. In the center of the dash was usually a large headlight. Sometimes the headlight was removed for servicing during the daylight hours, but never removed were the awesome looking pilots, or cowcatchers, as the non-railroaders called them.

Unlike many interurban railroads in the United States, those in the Bay Area were usually built by first-class construction, and would come to use some of the heaviest and longest interurban vehicles anywhere in North America. They would suffer financial reverses, corporate takeovers, passenger service declines, and eventual abolition. But their importance at a time when the only public means of travel from one part of the Bay Area to another was often at the whim of the steam railroads can never be underestimated.

The various regions of the Bay Area adopted the electric railway for as many reasons as there were lines and service areas. In some cases, it was to provide competition with the Southern Pacific. In others, it was because there was no other form of adequate public transit. At times it was to promote a real estate development, paving the way for more commuters. At others it was in conjunction with much-needed railway freight service which had failed to materialize due to undercapitalization of short line steam railways. And in one case, a steam-powered suburban service converted to electric interurban in order to compete with another interurban!

The population of the Bay Area's counties totaled 658,111 in 1900 and would climb to 925,708 by 1910. A growth area needs and demands public transportation, and the automobile at that time was only a plaything of the wealthy. Indeed, only five years earlier, in 1895, there were only four gasoline-powered vehicles in the United States. (Amazingly enough, two of them collided in St. Louis, causing injury to both drivers.) And so it happened that the void in transportation came to be filled by the electric interurban railways.

Central Pacific No. 1272 was photographed sometime between 1891 and 1898 at the corner of Shattuck and Virginia while in service on the Berkeley Local. No. 1272 was built in 1873 and was the first locomotive product from the Sacramento Shops of the C.P.R.R. In 1910 she was sold to the Central California Traction Company aid in construction of that interurban road.

Chapter Two
The Big Red Cars

Anticipating the construction of the San Francisco-Oakland Bay Bridge, the Southern Pacific on November 14, 1934 formed a wholly-owned subsidiary corporation, to be known as the Interurban Electric Railway, to operate its network of electric interurbans in Alameda County and across the bridge into San Francisco. The corporation issued 20,000 shares of stock at ten dollars per share, all being held by the Southern Pacific. This short-lived corporation's interurban service folded on January 18, 1941, after less than two generations of service.

The Espee's history of electric rail transit in the East Bay had dated back to June 1, 1911, when it ended a history of steam-powered rail transit dating back to August 2, 1863. While there have been others, such as the Northwestern Pacific, the S.P. interurban lines are among the few that were electrified after having been steam powered.

The exploits of the Central Pacific's (later Southern Pacific) Big Four of Charles Crocker, Mark Hopkins, Collis P. Huntington, and Leland Stanford are well documented in other railroading chronicles, and for the most part bear no repeating. However, the business and political influence of one Collis P. Huntington cannot be overlooked. It was Huntington who lobbied so successfully in Washington for additional funding in the form of government loans which were so necessary to complete the transcontinental railroad. It was Huntington who secured the locomotives and rails during the critical Civil War Years. It was Huntington who saw to it that ships were available to bring the necessary railroad equipment 'round the Horn. And it was Huntington who exerted the influence, not only over his three partners but over legislators as well, to see the greatest feat of railroad construction to a successful conclusion. Lastly, it was Collis P. Huntington who foresaw such riches in California that he would settle for no less than a monopoly of transportation in the Golden State.

To complete the transcontinental railroad, a western terminus had to be established, and the big question of the day was whether to terminate at Sacramento, Oakland, or San Francisco. There was even a consideration of terminating at San Jose, then the state capital. Sacramento was eliminated because it meant a transfer for the passengers to a river steamer to reach San Francisco, which was then the major city in the West. Oakland did offer a seaport, but again the passengers had to ferry across San Francisco Bay. The state capital was being moved to Benicia, but the Central Pacific continued to toy with the idea of bringing their trains around the southern part of the Bay through San Jose and then directly into San Francisco. In the end, the C.P. opted to route the trains into Oakland with appropriate ferry service. To accomplish this, it absorbed the Western Pacific, which ran from Sacramento to Stockton to San Jose. (This Western Pacific, incidentally, has no relationship whatsoever to the present railroad of the same name.) A cutoff through Niles was constructed, and the dream of a railroad from the Atlantic to the Pacific became a reality.

Huntington and his partners had never displayed any hesitation about acquiring any other railroad line, and the vast network of today's Southern Pacific bears testimony to that. At the same time, the Big Four never displayed any hesitation about influencing politicians. While Stanford actually went on to become Governor of California, and later served a term in the U.S. Senate when senators were still chosen by state legislatures, Huntington eschewed the political limelight and chose instead to exercise his superb knowledge of the nineteenth century political

Passenger-baggage combo No. 602. The white flags indicate she is running extra, or a non-scheduled trip. (Stephen D. Maguire Collection)

process in the legislative cloakrooms.

However, it was not merely in the political arena that Huntington proved himself the master, for he was promoting a totally new concept in transportation. This was the idea of a total transportation system in which the C.P.R.R. would operate not only the mainline railroad, but short lines, riverboats, ferries, steamships, and street railway systems to provide feeder service as well. Even the railroad's mainline provided a route for the nation's telegraph wires.* Naturally, the Central Pacific would own or control all this, and to put such a concept into action required political weight to secure the necessary franchises as well as adequate finances. The establishment of such an idea in public transportation in an area where service was sporadic suited the intent of the Big Four to secure a transportation monopoly in California.

(Note that the decline of the Central Pacific's political influence coincided with a number of other factors such as the advance of the rails of the Atcheson, Topeka & Santa Fe into California, the rise of the populist movements in the Golden State, and the success of competing local lines such as the Key System.)

In order to effectively maintain their avowed intention of rail monopoly, it was necessary to establish community and suburban transit to support the main lines. In San Francisco, the Southern Pacific would come to own one of the earliest steam dummy lines, and members of the Big Four—including their families—would have ownership in the Market Street Cable Railway, Geary Street, Park & Ocean Railroad, California Street Cable Railway,** Omnibus Railroad & Cable Company, and the Ferries & Cliff House Railway. All these lines conveniently terminated at or transferred to the Ferry Building (to meet the S.P. ferries) or the Southern Pacific Depot (to meet the S.P. trains).

The same pattern would manifest in Oakland, Alameda, Berkeley, and surrounding communities. Through mergers and acquisitions, the Central Pacific, and later the Southern Pacific, came to own all the local steam lines in Alameda County.

The first train service in Oakland was a short line which ran from Broadway to the Oakland Pier on Seventh Street. The road, called the San Francisco & Oakland Rail Road Company, was incorporated on October 21, 1861, and began

Prior to World War II, this westbound I.E.R. train was photographed emerging from the Northbrae Tunnel in Berkeley. This trackage was shortly to become an extension of the Key System's F Line. (Stephen D. Maguire Collection)

service on September 2, 1863. In 1870, it was merged with the San Francisco & Alameda Rail Road Company. The S.F. & A. had been incorporated on March 25, 1863, and had commenced

---

*Today, when many U. S. railroads are losing money, the Southern Pacific is prospering while continuing to offer the public a total transportation concept, utilizing trains, trucks, pipelines, air freight, and transportation leasing.

**When informed by his chief engineer that the Cambria Steel Co. of Johnstown, Pennsylvania refused such a small and unorthodox order as rails for the California Street Cable, Huntington is said to have replied, "They'll roll your rails or they will roll no more for the Central Pacific." Cambria quickly got the point and the order was filled with dispatch.

service on August 13, 1864. Later the successor of this road also gained control of the San Francisco, Alameda & Stockton Railroad Company, a line which began runs from Alameda Wharf to San Leandro on August 25, 1864. On March 2, 1865, the San Francisco & Alameda extended its line to Haywards, as Hayward was then known. The entire holdings of the S.F. & A. passed into the San Francisco, Oakland, and Alameda Railroad in June of 1871 and the Central Pacific Railroad two months later.

One of California's more colorful narrow gauge steam roads began service from Alameda's Park Street to Newark on March 20, 1878, eventually reaching Santa Cruz on May 15, 1880. Originally called the Bay & Coast Railroad Company, this road was the godchild of Silver King James Fair. On May 23, 1887, it was reorganized as the South Pacific Coast Railway, and on July 1 of the same year passed into control of the S.P. In 1906, the S.P. widened the track to standard gauge, sending still serviceable narrow gauge rolling stock to the Northwestern Pacific in Marin and Sonoma Counties.

On January 22, 1882, the famed Oakland Mole was opened for service, and thenceforth all S.P. passenger train-connecting ferries to Oakland would use the Mole's ferry slips, confining the use of the Oakland Long Wharf to freight. Other S.P. ferries would continue to use the longer "Creek Route" up the Oakland Estuary to the foot of Broadway.

During the years 1895 to 1901 a large scale excavation took place, a project which would create an island out of Alameda, rather than the jut of land it was. Bridges over the channel were constructed, which would be used by the Espee's

The above photo shows a Southern Pacific local train on Berkeley's Shattuck Avenue in 1910. The train, which is leaving University Avenue and heading for the Oakland Mole, is belching enough smoke and dirt to do horrors to milady's Monday wash and today's air pollution controls would probably prohibit the entire operation. To the right and alongside the Espee's tracks are the tracks of the Key Route. (Roy Graves Collection, Bancroft Library)

trains to connect with other parts of the county. Meanwhile, the S.P. continued to serve the Alameda Mole with the ferryboat service it inherited from the South Pacific Coast Railway—a service which would continue until completion of the San Francisco-Oakland Bay Bridge.

On the eve of electrification, the pattern of trackage of the Espee's interurban lines had been established, and only minor modifications would be made in the conversion from steam to electric.

In the early years of Espee electrification in the East Bay, passenger-baggage combo No. 600 was photographed heading a three-car train. The rectangular windows on the forward bulkheads were later to be replaced by round windows. (Stephen D. Maguire Collection)

When electrified in 1911, the five basic lines were as follows:

Line 2—Oakland Mole to Dutton Avenue, San Leandro, via 7th Street.

Line 3—Oakland Mole to Thousand Oaks Station via 16th Street, Stanford Avenue, Adeline Street, Shattuck Avenue, Henry Street, and the Northbrae Tunnel and private right-of-way to Thousand Oaks Station on Solano Avenue.

Line 4—Alameda Mole to Fernside Junction via Main Street, Central Avenue, Encinal Avenue, and Fernside Boulevard.

Line 5—Oakland Mole to Thousand Oaks Station via 16th Street, Doyle Street, 9th Street, and Solano Avenue, Berkeley.

Line 6—Alameda Mole to Fruitvale Station via Main Street, Pacific Avenue, Marshall Way, Lincoln Avenue, and Tilden Avenue.

In addition, the Southern Pacific and Interurban Electric Railway operated express lines such as Line 7 (Dutton Avenue) and Line 9 (Shattuck Avenue).

The above lines were complemented by local lines which used both the Big Red Cars and the "dinkeys," or streetcars. The local lines were as follows:

Oakland Local—Cedar and 16th Streets to Franklin and 14th Streets via Cedar Street, 18th Street to Market Street, 19th Street, Curtis Street, 21st Street, Brush Street, Jones Street to Telegraph Avenue, 21st Street, Franklin Street to 14th Street.

Oakland Streetcars—Same route as the Oakland Local trains except the streetcars continued from 14th and Franklin Streets to Webster Street and along Webster Street to the waterfront.

Berkeley Local—Sometimes called the "California Street Line," the trains ran from Calais and Stanford Avenue to Thousand Oaks Station via Calais to Dwight Way, California Street, Rose Avenue, Davis Street, Monterey Avenue, Colusa Avenue, Solano Avenue to Thousand Oaks.

Ellsworth Line—Adeline Street and Woolsey Street to Ellsworth Street and Allston Way via Woolsey to Deakin Street, private right-of-way to Ellsworth Street, Ellsworth to Allston Way.

In 1902, Francis M. "Borax" Smith consolidated all of his street railway holdings in the East Bay into the San Francisco, Oakland & San Jose Railway, together with establishing his own ferryboat service to San Francisco. The meeting point of ferries and interurbans was the Key Pier, a long wharf which reached some three and one-quarter

The opening of a new railway line was always a good reason for a celebration, and the first electric train on the 7th Street Line in Oakland on November 7, 1911, was no exception as the photograph taken at the corner of 7th and Broadway in Oakland shows. The conductor standing on the buffer plate on the end of the car is Bob Guance. Sixth from the left is "Belly" Norton, Assistant Superintendent of the electric lines. Next to Norton is R. E. Hewitt, Master Mechanic for the electric lines. Other celebrants are members of the West Oakland Improvement Club. The train's consist was four cars—two motors and two trailers. (Vernon J. Sappers Collection)

miles from the shoreline to deep water. This shortened the ferryboat ride considerably, and Smith's fast electrics sped over the wharf to reach the East Bay communities.

The Espee's ferries had had their East Bay slips at the Oakland Mole, which in itself was a one and one-quarter-mile-long pier. Prior to the opening of the Oakland Mole in 1882, the ferries used the Oakland Long Wharf. This was a longer distance from San Francisco via ferry than that to the Key Pier and consequently a transbay trip via S.P. ferry, then a transfer to the local steam trains which the Central Pacific/Southern Pacific had been acquiring over the years, took some twenty to twenty-five minutes longer than it took a S.F. O. & S.J. Ry., or Key Route, passenger to get to the same place.

Once aboard a Southern Pacific steam-powered local, the passengers would find themselves riding behind a machine which belched smoke and cinders. The insides of the cars were poorly

The year was 1913, and the city of Oakland was showing civic maturity. A new city hall was under construction, the big electric trains of the S.P. were pulling into the Franklin Street Station which was between 13th and 14th Streets, the local streetcars of the Key Route were prominent, and it was evident that the age of the automobile had dawned although an occasional horse and wagon could still be seen. The Tribune Tower would rise where the newsstand is. (Alameda-Contra Costa Transit District)

lit by oil lamps (which in themselves were dirty). And the steamers were noisy. Comparing those trains with the relatively quiet, clean, roomy, and electrically lit Key Route trains, local traffic soon opted for the latter. And they did so in such numbers that within a mere thirteen days after opening, the interurbans had increased their carding to no less than sixty-seven trains daily and on a thirty-minute headway. The mighty Southern Pacific was facing such serious competition that in less than thirty years after electrification it would withdraw its interurbans from the East Bay altogether.

In 1900, Collis P. Huntington, a giant of American railroading, died, and Huntington's Southern Pacific shoes were filled the following year by another giant, one Edward Henry Harriman. Harriman was no slouch when it came to being a railroad tycoon, and combining his control over the Southern Pacific and the Union Pacific, he began a new era in western railroading, and the S.P. in particular. Additional track was laid, the Lucin Cutoff across the Great Salt Lake was opened, and a general modernization program began. Harriman's imprint on the Espee was so profound that certain coaches and locomotive designs used on the S.P. and the U.P. were called "Harrimans."

Thus in 1911 an order went to the American Car and Foundry for the first of the Big Red Cars—some nineteen years after Alameda County's first electrified railway. The Big Red Cars were to be powered by electricity, and they were to seat as many as 116 passengers. Although Harriman had died two years prior, the programs of progress and renovation which he had instilled in the S.P. carried on to his successors. About this time the Pacific Electric in Los Angeles—another S.P. property—began its modernization, and in 1918 the S.P. began heavy electrification of its interurban service in Oregon. During this period it also acquired control of the Peninsular Railway in San Jose and half interest in the Northwestern Pacific.

Prior to 1911, the conventional voltage for railways using overhead trolley wire had been at 600

11

Fitted with eclipse fenders—sometimes called "streetcar cowcatchers"—these cars of the Espee fleet were used for local train services in Oakland and Berkeley. Photo taken at the Franklin Street Station. (Ray Hannah Collection)

The S.P. built its streetcars like its interurbans—steel and rugged. They were later assigned to the Key System although used very sparingly by the Key. (Stephen D. Maguire Collection)

Wilbur C. Whittaker photographed these two S.P. cars at the Alameda Mole and caught a perfect comparison between the rectangular windows of the trailers and the round windows of the motorized cars. (Wilbur C. Whittaker)

volts, d.c., which resulted in heavy power losses along the line unless supplemented by feeder stations and feeder lines. However, the S.P. used a high voltage system on an overhead wire. Rated at 1200 volts, d.c., the S.P. not only reduced power losses, but actually reduced the amperage to about one-half of a 600 volt, d.c., system using the same load! While this high voltage system had been developed in 1907 by General Electric, the Southern Pacific was the first railroad to use it.

The second major development in electric railroad operation to be introduced by the Southern Pacific was the mechanism for activating street traffic signals by the motorman of an electric railway car. First used at the corner of Shattuck and University Avenues in Berkeley, it would be found on street railways of other cities and would become a godsend to streetcar motormen in later days when automobile traffic would demand precedence on city streets through sheer force of numbers.

The new cars were painted green, then later the more characteristic red found on S.P.'s electric lines and were lettered "Southern Pacific Lines." With the advent of service on the San Francisco-Oakland Bay Bridge, they retained their red color scheme, but underwent a program of relettering to read "Interurban Electric Railway," which reflected their new corporate registry. By the time of final abandonment, not all cars had been relettered, and except for a few changes in car numbering, conversion from waist-high gates to full gates covering the loading vestibules, and the altering of the end windows from rectangular to round (which had been done long before I.E.R. days), there were few noticeable outward changes.

There was no question about it: The "Big Red Cars" were big; the monsters were over seventy-two feet long (over twice the length of one class of San Jose's interurbans) and weighed in at over thirty tons. Until the arrival of similar cars from the carbuilders to the Northwestern Pacific in

Four trains totaling eleven Big Red Cars wait for the next ferryboat to come into Alameda from San Francisco. By the number of cars this could be the beginning of the afternoon commute rush. The gingerbread-laden Alameda Mole was a legacy of Silver King James Fair's narrow-gauge South Pacific Coast Railroad. (Alameda-Contra Costa Transit District)

1929, they were the largest interurbans in the Bay Area. In later service on the Pacific Electric, they—along with the cars from the N.W.P.—would be known affectionately as "the Blimps."

Between 1912 and 1930, the S.P. supplemented its East Bay interurban service with local streetcars. However, these streetcar operations never equalled the volume of service offered by competitor Key System, and in 1930 the cars were sold to the Key and the S.P. ended its streetcar services in Oakland and Berkeley. At the same time, the Key System realigned some of its lines to avoid duplication of routes. Moreover, in 1933 both companies reached agreement to honor each other's commuter tickets where services overlapped.

In 1934, as has been noted, the Interurban Electric Railway was formed, and the Big Red Cars bore their new owner's name on their signboards. With the opening of the San Francisco-Oakland Bay Bridge, the Big Red Cars rerouted their lines, but slightly, for instead of using the Oakland and Alameda Moles, the trains went out to the 26th Street Junction in Oakland and thence

The high gates on these two Southern Pacific trains connecting with the ferryboat *Berkeley* at the Oakland Mole indicate that they were being readied for operations on the Bay Bridge, and their use of the Oakland Mole was on the wane. (Lorin Silleman photo/Tom Gray Collection)

to the Bridge and to downtown San Francisco.

Because of the anticipated volume of traffic on the bridge from no less than three railroads (I.E.R., Key System, and Sacramento Northern), and in order to accommodate a planned peak-hour load of 17,000 people in and out of San Francisco per twenty minute period, the bridge's

Ken Kidder snapped this photograph of the interior of the Oakland Mole where over the years millions of passengers transfered between the ferries to and from San Francisco and S.P. trains to and from all points, including the Big Red Cars bound for Oakland, Albany and Berkeley. (Ken Kidder photo/Tom Gray Collection)

It was unusual for a passenger-baggage combo to run on the Alameda Lines, but Will Whittaker managed to catch one anyway on the Webster Street Bridge heading for San Francisco in 1939. (Wilbur C. Whittaker)

In days when the electric railways were prominent, suburban and interurban stations such as Melrose Station in Oakland were vital transportation arteries. Photographed in September of 1939, this five-car train is heading for San Francisco via the Bay Bridge. (Stephen D. Maguire Collection)

The above is a photo of a railfan photographing a train crossing the Fruitvale Bridge in I.E.R. days. Even in declining days of electric operations the S.P. maintained the roadbeds in good condition. (Alameda-Contra Costa Transit District)

If there were any doubt that the S.P. regarded the Big Red Trains as part of its total railroad operations, this picture dispels it in a hurry. Pictured in 1940 at the East Oakland Station, the Westbound #2 Line train appears to be racing a freight drag headed by steam locomotive No. 2828, a consolidation-type loco built in 1908. (Wilbur C. Whittaker)

A Big Red Train at Berryman Station on Shattuck Avenue when automobile traffic was such that people appear to be standing in the middle of the street with no apparent fear of being run over. (Wilbur C. Whittaker Collection)

On Berkeley's Shattuck Avenue one could find two interurban companies competing for patronage, and Wilbur C. Whittaker caught this beauty. The three-unit Key System train is westbound for San Francisco while the Big Red Train is eastbound for Thousand Oaks Station.

Eastbound on Adeline Street, this four-car train of the I.E.R. stops at Ashby Avenue. This train will then go out Shattuck Avenue en route to Thousand Oaks. The afternoon shadows and a full carload in No. 346 indicate that the train is probably a commuter with as many as 400 passengers. (Stephen D. Maguire Collection)

signal system was designed to allow for ten-car trains to run thirty-five miles per hour on a headway of sixty-three and one-half seconds.

The General Railway Signal Company's "NX" electric interlocking system was used at both ends of the Bay Bridge. This was necessitated because the heavy flow of traffic could not have been handled in a speedy and efficient manner by the old hand lever method of controlling switches and track turnouts. What the "NX" system actually did was have the towerman push one button of a diagram indicating the entrance to a given route and a second button which indicated the exit, thus allowing the traffic to move smoothly and quickly through a crowded corridor.

The "NX" control panels were large consoles which showed the complete track layouts as well as track occupancy. Moreover, each route of the I.E.R. and the Key System—Sacramento Northern trains used Track 6 in the San Francisco terminal which meant that the I.E.R. and the Key shared the other five tracks—was designated so that the towerman could coordinate not only safe arrivals and departures but adherance to posted time schedules as well.

The I.E.R. cars were equipped with train control and cab control equipment which came from the Union Switch and Signal Company, and complemented the "NX" interlocking system, controlling train movements between the bridge and the 26th Street Junction in Oakland.

These automatic controls worked thusly: the engineer* working a train in the bridge area would receive a permissive speed signal which would show a speed of 11, 17, 25, or 35 miles per hour. The speed allowed the train would be based on the volume of traffic ahead. A train adhering to posted speed showed a white light. If a train exceeded posted speed by as little as .5 miles per hour, a warning signal appeared, and if

---

*Since all trainmen for the S.P./I.E.R. worked under steam railroad type labor contracts between union and management, rather than streetcar type contracts, the train operators were titled "engineers," rather than "motormen," the more common term found on electric railways.

Authorized speed	Speed above which white light shows	Speed above which warning signal is sounding	Speed at which emergency brakes are applied
35 mph	35 mph	36 mph	37 mph
25 mph	25 mph	26 mph	27 mph
17 mph	16½ mph	17½ mph	18½ mph
11 mph	10¾ mph	11¾ mph	12¾ mph

The end of the line for the Berkeley trains was at Thousand Oaks Station. The man at left is probably a commuter strolling home after a traffic-free ride from San Francisco. (Charles D. Savage photo/Tom Gray Collection)

A pair of motorized units rolls over the private right of way in the Northbrae section of Berkeley in this pastoral setting. (Tom Gray Collection)

This single-car train was photographed by Charles D. Savage on the Solano Avenue section of the I.E.R.'s 9th Street Line in Albany. This train will terminate at Thousand Oaks. (Ray Hannah Collection)

the engineer failed to slow his train within two and one-half seconds, the power would be cut automatically and the brakes would be applied in emergency. This was accomplished by sending a 100-cycle signal current through the rails with a uniform series of interruptions in each block (specified section of track.) The number of interruptions were 180 interruptions per minute for "clear track ahead;" less than "clear track" was denoted by 120 interruptions per minute and occupancy of the second block ahead by seventy-five interruptions per minute. Occupancy in the first block ahead was denoted by a steady or no current. Receivers at the motorman's or engineer's end of the train picked up the signal current, filtered and amplified it, and the rate of interruptions in the current automatically activated the proper permissive speed signal.

When the interurban trains left the cab-controlled territory—in the case of the I.E.R. it was at the 26th Street Junction—an additional code of 240 interruptions per minute cancelled the cab signal and switched on a violet light which showed the letters "NS" and from then on the train could proceed under its own restrictions until it once again made contact with the bridge's cab control network.

Power came to the S.P./I.E.R. interurbans from two sources: outright purchase of electricity for bridge operation and its own Fruitvale powerhouse for East Bay runs. Furthermore, the Bay Bridge was equipped with an emergency battery system so that in case of power failure the signal system would continue to operate.

The Fruitvale powerhouse was equipped with two 550 kw. turbo-generator units operting three phase and at a frequency of twenty-five cycles. The power generated was then transmitted to three substations: one in Berkeley, one at the Oakland Mole, and one in the Fruitvale powerhouse itself. The West Oakland substation (Oakland Mole) was equipped with 1500 kw. two-unit coverter sets. The Berkeley substation was similar. As for the Fruitvale substation, it was set up with one 2500 kw. motor-generator and three 1500 kw. two-unit rotary converter sets.

Despite their popularity with the public—22,000,000 passengers in 1920—the Bay Area's love affair with the automobile ultimately doomed the big red interurbans. The increasing competition of the auto ferries caused a drop in ridership to 14,000,000 by 1936. The opening of the Bay

Bridge to auto traffic in 1936 further cut into the ridership until records showed drops to 12,000,000 in 1937, 11,000,000 in 1938, and a meager 9,900,000 in 1939. With the Depression still on, that was more than the Southern Pacific could bear. In December of 1939, the Espee, together with competitor Key System, made application to heavily reduce service with new schedules. The Interurban Electric Railway was by now justifying its position by showing losses of $1,000,000 per year.

Transit authorities and the riding public do not always see eye to eye. For example, the "expert" sees in a heavy traction motor the power to do a given job; the neighbors complain of noise. The "expert" regards "owl," or midnight to 6:00 A.M. service, as wasteful and economically infeasible; the rider sees transportation home after a night shift. The "expert" sees competition as duplicate trackage of doubtful necessity, dual lines serving the same areas, and lack of planning. The rider views competition as lower fares, attempts to serve the public, and frequency of service. The "experts'" contentions were factors in the impending abandonment of the I.E.R.

As early as 1920, Edward Hungerford wrote in the *Electric Railway Journal* that competition between the S.P. and the Key System was leading to surplus service which, in his opinion, was wasteful. It was his belief that "the rapid transit services at the east side of San Francisco Bay shall be permanently and securely merged." If by merger Mr. Hungerford meant the coordinated services of A/C Transit and BART, then he was indeed a prophet.

February 26, 1940 brought two events: the reduced schedules and further application with the Public Utilities Commission of the State of California, only this time for permission to abandon all interurban service. On July 4th of the following year, the last red car rolled down Berkeley's Shattuck Avenue and the Interurban Electric Railway was dead.

Dead from a car-labeling standpoint only, for portions of the I.E.R. continued to appear, much like a gravely wounded animal which refuses to die. The Key System continued some I.E.R. service with the use of its trains and buses, and

The Interurban Distribution Center. In the center foreground a Key System train can be seen leaving the Bridge Yards. It will pass under the freeway and the Southern Pacific tracks in what was called the Key System subway. The train will then pass the series of sheds which comprise the Emeryville Yards and Shops, and from there to Yerba Buena Avenue and due points in the East Bay. While trains of the Sacramento Northern Railway will follow those of the Key System, trains of the I.E.R. will veer to the right until they reach the S.P.'s 16th Street Station. (State of California Toll Bridge Administration)

This January 7, 1939, photograph shows the "NX" system of controlling three different interurban railways over the San Francisco-Oakland Bay Bridge. This panel controlled all of the switches in the bridge yard on the main line tracks and tracks leading to—as well as set out tracks—the main line. This board also controlled the entrance of the train in the bridge yard until it reached San Francisco where the automatic sorting switch would route the trains into the terminal on the assigned track. "NX" was an abbreviation for entrance and exit. (State of California Toll Bridge Administration)

September 8, 1939—this control board illuminates the train route destination sign downstairs on the main concourse of the Transbay Terminal so that passengers can observe if their train is in and on what track. The operator also announced each train through a public address system as the train arrived in the terminal. (State of California Toll Bridge Administration)

some I.E.R. track was annexed to the Key. The demands of World War II caused portions of remaining I.E.R. trackage to continue to be used for the war effort, and it might well be said that part of the Interurban Electric Railway has come to life with BART. The Big Red Cars themselves, however, fully justified their builders' art by finding new lives on other roads, notably the Pacific Electric Railway in Los Angeles.

Taken to the Pacific Electric's shops, the behemoths of the bay were equipped with trolley poles rather than their old pantographs. Other non-visible alterations were also made and they soon found themselves carrying a full share of P.E. patronage. Originally sent to the P.E. under ownership of the United States Maritime Commission during World War II, the ex-I.E.R. cars reverted to P.E. ownership after the war.

Others of the I.E.R. fleet found new life in Utah, Washington, and in as distant localities as Camp Lejune, North Carolina.

In fairness to the automobile, it should be pointed out that the Interurban Electric Railway was beset with two other financial "drags" which worked solidly against it. First, the Southern Pacific's East Bay interurbans came under its Western Division, and all crews held seniority rights in that division. Thus, all I.E.R. trains operated on steam railroad-type labor union contracts, and minimum manpower requirements always exceeded the requirements of the rival Key System. Even one additional man cut heavily into revenues which were already in a state of decline.

The second financial drag on the I.E.R. was more or less indirect, yet its effect was just as brutal. That was the Toll Bridge Authority's reduction of the auto toll on the Bay Bridge from sixty-five to twenty-five cents. And this at a time when patronage had to be encouraged rather than discouraged.

An often overlooked factor concerning the I.E.R. can go a long way toward explaining why its interurban lines failed while the Key System continued, and that was that the Interurban Electric Railway had no streetcar or motor bus feeder service. The S.P.'s diminutive streetcar operations had ceased after 1930, and as the suburban home area began to spread farther and farther away from the interurbans' station stops, there was more and more reliance upon the automobile. While the Southern Pacific, once again employing the concept of a total transportation system, had recognized the emergence of the automobile as a major means of transportation as early as 1908 when it added the automobile-carrying ferry *Melrose* to its fleet, this did not aid its interurban operations in the long run.

Why was the entire bridge operation not con-

A three-car I.E.R. train completes its journey from Thousand Oaks Station in Berkeley as it approaches the Transbay Terminal in San Francisco. In view of today's volume of automobile traffic on the Bay Bridge it seems incredible that there was but one car on the off ramp! (Ken Kidder photo/Tom Gray Collection)

demned by rights of eminent domain at that time for all three railways (I.E.R., Key System, and S.N.) to continue under public ownership? After all, an integrated signal and automatic train control system was already installed. Off ramps in San Francisco could have connected to the S.P. depot which was just seven blocks away, and could have provided through service to the Peninsula and San Jose. With war clouds on the horizon it should have been obvious that rail transportation would be a necessity in the war effort.

Yet it must be recognized that in those years public ownership of heavy industries, including railroads, was not a popular concept, and persons advocating such plans were often the targets of innuendos pertaining to socialist or communist sympathies. Because of such shortsightedness, BART is under construction today to provide much the same service by electric rail to the East Bay. The rails on the Bay Bridge are long gone and as a consequence an underwater tube has had to be constructed, and BART is under public ownership.

There can be little comparison between the I.E.R. type of operation and that of the rival Key System, for while the I.E.R. was strictly an interurban service, operating as part and parcel of a 16,000-mile railroad system, the Key System was a combination of local streetcars and buses, interurban trains and ferryboats, as well as minor freight switching duties.

Therefore the Southern Pacific presented its case for abandonment, citing severe losses in ridership in favor of the automobile; a strictly economic case. Pleas to retain the Big Red Cars (and in later years, the ferryboats) on the basis of friendly platform men, tradition of services, and preference of electric railway equipment rather than gasoline-powered buses rang hollow in the face of million-dollar-per-year deficits.

Interurban Electric Railway Rolling Stock

Carbuilders included the American Car and Foundries, Pullman, and St. Louis Car Company. However, all trucks were supplied by Baldwin, with the exception of the six 1926 cars from St. Louis which used St. Louis trucks. The latter,

incidentally, were the only I.E.R. cars from that company.

All motorized cars used pantograph current collectors. Originally the I.E.R. cars had square windows on the foreward bulkheads, but after rebuilding they were characterized by the "owl" look of the two portholes so commonly found on Southern Pacific electric cars. Sliding, hand-operated gates prevented passengers from falling out the side entrance steps. Later, for bridge operation, the gates were enlarged to cover the entire openings. In 1930, the cars were equipped with heaters. Their adequacy in carrying large numbers of passengers with sufficient speeds may be measured by the fact that they were geared for a top speed of 42.5 miles per hour.

When the Big Red Trains pulled into the new Transbay Terminal during the rush hour, hundreds of people disembarked at once, and the Terminal has been a beehive of commuter activity to this day. The five cars pictured here could account for as many as 580 passengers if every seat were taken! This train is on Track 3 on January 20, 1939. State of California Toll Bridge Administration)

A company photograph for the Southern Pacific tells the sad story of the decline of the Big Red Cars. To the left of the car heading out on the Encinal Avenue Line in Alameda is the advertising board for the automobile ferries which says "CHEAPEST WAY TO CROSS THE BAY." (Southern Pacific photo/Tom Gray Collection)

Passenger Motors

Class: 58-EMC-1
Builder: American Car and Foundries
Year: 1911
Length over platforms: 72′4½″
Weight: No. 1 end, 61,500 lbs., No. 2 end, 61,880 lbs.
Motors: Four G.E. 207-A, 140 h.p. each
Trucks: Baldwin
Body: Steel (partitioned), arch roof

Class: 58-EMC-1
Builder: American Car and Foundries
Year: 1911
Weight: No. 1 end, 60,600 lbs., No. 2 end, 62,020 lbs.
Body: Steel (non-partitioned), arch roof

Class: 58-EMC-1
Weight: No. 1 end, 60,600 lbs., No. 2 end, 62,020 lbs.
Body: Steel (non-partitioned), arch roof
(All other data same as 300-330 series.)

Class: 58-EMC-2
Builder: Pullman
Year: 1913
Weight: No. 1 end, 62,440 lbs., No. 2 end, 63,220 lbs.
Body: Steel, arch roof

Class: 58-EMC-1
Builder: American Car and Foundries
Year: 1911
Weight: No. 1 end, 60,600 lbs., No. 2 end, 63,220 lbs.
(All other data same as 300-330 series.)

Class: 58-EMC-1
Builder: American Car and Foundries
Year: 1911
Weight: No. 1 end, 61,820 lbs., No. 2 end, 61,560 lbs.

300-330 Series
Numbered 300-330 on S.P. roster. Seated 116. Nos. 300-312 to Toll Bridge Authority. Nos. 313-330 to Pacific Electric. Later Nos. 313, 315, 316, 320, 324-326 were de-motorized and sent to Union Pacific. Nos. 313, 315, 325-326 were sold back to P.E. and restored to electric runs. Aberdeen (Maryland) Proving Grounds received three cars believed to have been 301-303.

331-335 Series
Numbered 331-335 on S.P. roster. Later all cars went to Pacific Electric. Seated 116. No. 332 is now at California Railway Museum. (Other data same as 300-330 series.)

337-339 Series
Numbered 337-339 on S.P. roster. Later all cars went to Pacific Electric. Seated 116.

340-349 Series
Numbered 340-349 on S.P. roster. Seated 111. No. 344 is now at Orange Empire Trolley Museum, Perris, California.

350-351 Series
Numbered 459 and 439, respectively, on S.P. roster. Seated 116. Later they were sent to Pacific Electric.

352-361 Series
Rebuilt from combination motors. Numbered 606, 608-616, respectively, on S.P. roster. Seated 116. All cars to Toll Bridge Authority. No. 358 later went to Bamberger Electric in Utah.

With a seating capacity of about 340 persons, it seems like a small crowd to be getting aboard this I.E.R. train in Oakland, bound for San Francisco. This type of patronage did not help the Big Red Cars' cause when it came time to petition for abandonment.

Class: 58-EMC-3
Builder: St. Louis Car Company
Year: 1924
Length: 72′4½″
Weight: No. 1 end, 62,060 lbs., No. 2 end, 63,100 lbs.
Trucks: St. Louis
Body: Steel (partitioned), arch roof

362-367 Series

Numbered 362-367 on S.P. roster. Seated 108 passengers. All cars to Toll Bridge Authority.

Class: 58-EMC-1
Builder: American Car and Foundries
Year: 1911
Weight: No. 1 end, 61,500 lbs., No. 2 end, 61,880 lbs.
Body: Steel (non-partitioned), arch roof
(All other data same as 300-330 series.)

368-377 Series

Numbered 604, 605, 617-624, respectively, on S.P. roster. Nos. 368-375 to Pacific Electric. Nos. 376-377 to Toll Bridge Authority. Seated 116 passengers.

Class: 58-EMC-4
Builder: American Car and Foundries
Year: 1911
Weight: No. 1 end, 61,240 lbs., No. 2 end, 61,580 lbs.
Body: Steel (non-partitioned), arch roof
(All other data same as 300-330 series.)

378-387 Series

Numbered 435-437, 445, 438, 456-458, 336, and 607, respectively, on S.P. roster. Seated 116. No. 387 to Toll Bridge Authority, remainder to Pacific Electric. No. 379 is now on exhibit at Traveltown, Griffith Park, Los Angeles, California.

Non-operating Trailers
400-434 Series

Class: 58-ETC-1
Builder: American Car and Foundries
Year: 1911
Weight: No. 1 end, 35,880 lbs., No. 2 end, 34,980 lbs.
Body: Steel, arch roof

Numbered 400-434 on S.P. roster. Seated 116. Nos. 400-414, 416, 418-419, 421-424 to Toll Bridge Authority. Nos. 433-434 to Pacific Electric. Sent to Portland, Oregon, to be used by Spokane, Portland & Seattle Ry. in shipyard service, were Nos. 417, 420, 425, 427, and 430. Nos. 433-434 to Bremerton, Washington Navy Yard and Camp Lejune, North Carolina.

Operating Trailers
440-444 Series

Class: 58-ECTC-1
Builder: American Car and Foundries
Year: 1911
Weight: No. 1 end, 40,580 lbs., No. 2 end, 39,220 lbs.
Body: Steel, arch roof.

Numbered 440-444 on S.P. roster. Seated 116. Nos. 440, 444 to Portland shipyard duties.

446-455 Series

Class: 58-ECTC-1
(All other data same as 440-444 series.)

Numbered 446-455 on S.P. roster. Seated 116. Nos. 447, 448, 449, 450, 451, 454-455 to Portland shipyard duties.

Combination Motors
600-603 Series

Class: 58-EMCB-1
Builder: American Car and Foundries
Year: 1911
Length: 68'0½"
Weight: No. 1 end, 56,020 lbs., No. 2 end, 63,620 lbs.
Body: Steel, arch roof

Numbered 600-603 on S.P. roster. Seated 88. All cars to Toll Bridge Authority. Later to Pacific Electric as P.E. Nos. 496-499. P.E. 498 is at Orange Empire Trolley Museum, Perris, California.

625-628 Series

Class: 58-EMCB-2
Builder: Pullman
Year: 1913
Length: 68'0½"
Weight: No. 1 end, 57,320 lbs., No. 2 end, 64,900 lbs.

Numbered 625-628 on S.P. roster. Seated 83. All cars to Pacific Electric Railway.

Baggage Motors
700-701 Series

Class: 58-EMB-1
Builder: Pullman
Year: 1913
Length: 63'8½"
Weight: 106,080 lbs.
Body: Steel, arch roof

Numbered 700-701 on S.P. roster. Sent to Pacific Electric immediately after abandonment of I.E.R. Renumbered P.E. 1465-1466. Retired by P.E. in early 1950s.

Streetcars

Builder: Pullman
Year: 1912
Length: 44'8"
Weight: 62,400 lbs.
Body: Center entrance, steel, arch roof
Current collector: Pantograph

Cars numbered 800-811 by S.P.; never on I.E.R. roster. Nos. 810-811 were sold to Pacific Electric in 1913, returned to East Bay in 1919. All were sold to Key System in 1930, scrapped by Key in 1933. Seated 56 passengers.

Note: Exact disposition of all I.E.R. cars is unknown. Ex-I.E.R. cars are believed to have operated on the Santa Fe. Four unidentified cars went to Bamberger Electric for the war effort at the Ogden, Utah arsenal.

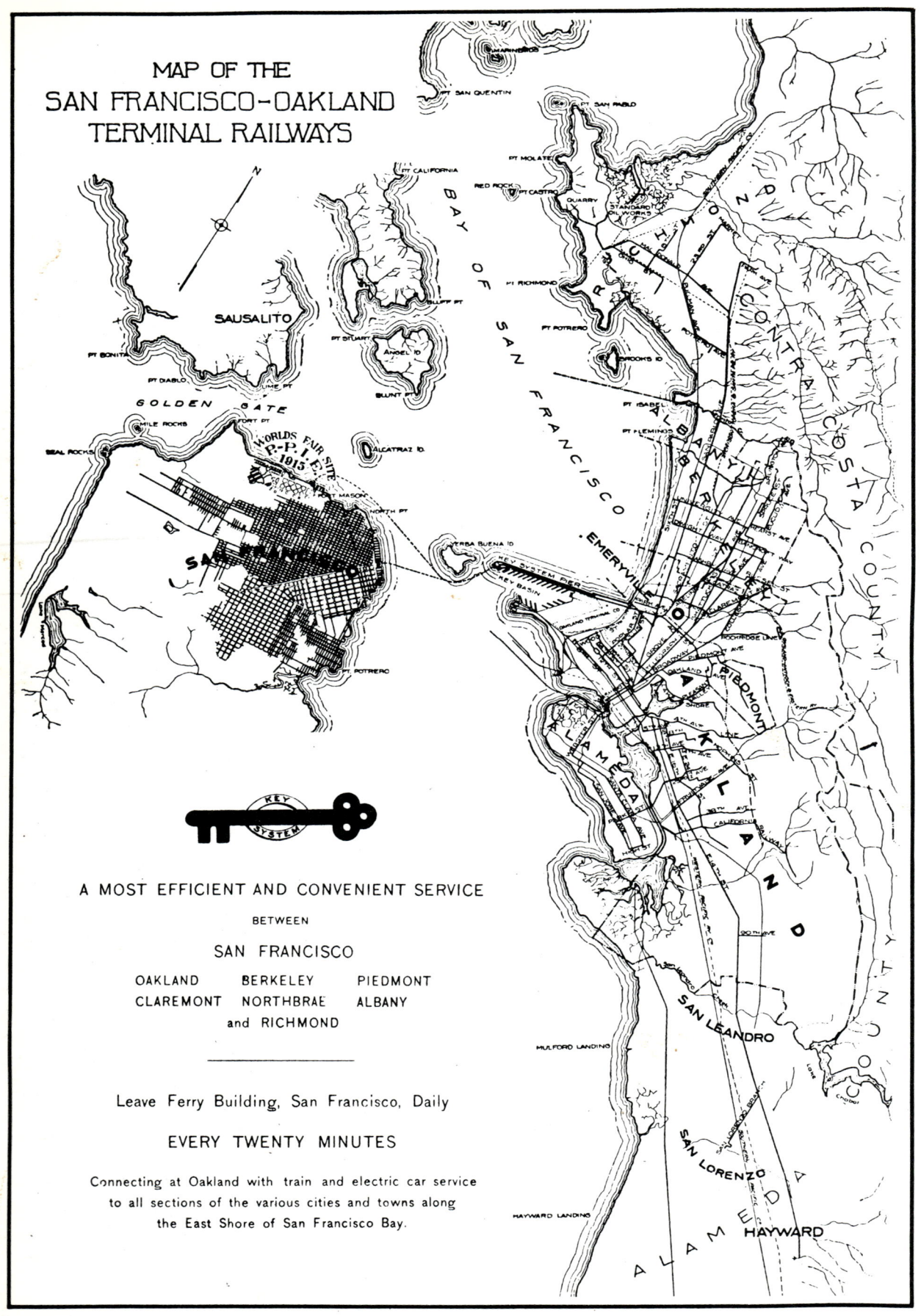

This 1913 map shows the Key Route's interurban lines and streetcar service as well. (Courtesy of John Muzio)

Chapter Three
The Last to Go

Key System

One thing that makes chronicling interurbans so interesting is that there was such an endless variety of lines and equipment that virtually every road could claim to be unique in some way, i.e. the first this, the only that. One almost reaches the point where one hesitates to cite a "for instance," in anticipation of being found in technical error! Yet the Key System had, we believe, at least its share of noteworthy claims, among them being the last interurban railway in Northern California, an absence of trunk-line freight traffic, one of the few roads to ever adopt its advertising slogan for a corporate name, and probably the first electric interurban railway to be resurrected from the dead—more than fifteen years after its final pantograph was dropped.

The Key System, as defined by the term "suburban service," was welded together under the name of San Francisco, Oakland & San Jose Railway in 1902 as Francis Marion "Borax" Smith consolidated all streetcar operations in the East Bay under his control. Smith, who had acquired his nickname because of his vast fortune—estimated at $30,000,000—which he gained from borax discoveries, began his move toward consolidation and eventual competition with the powerful Southern Pacific in 1893. At that time the S.P. had extensive street railway holdings in California as a complement to its transcontinental rail service, holdings which included street railways in the East Bay, San Francisco and Los Angeles—all the outgrowth of Collis P. Huntington's grand design for monopoly of all land transportation in the Golden State.

Streetcar line after streetcar line fell to the purchasing powers of "Borax" Smith, who had more than a few grand designs of his own, not the least of which was a combination real estate and railway empire (not uncommon in the era of street railway development). His first acquisition was the misnamed California & Nevada Railroad, which never reached farther east than Orinda. Then line after line began to come into the Smith orbit until, late in 1901, the last independent, the Oakland, San Leandro & Haywards, became part of Smith's Oakland Transit Consolidated,° giving the O.T.C. a total of 120 miles of track in Oakland, San Leandro and Hayward.

Before going further, a list of the predecessors of the Key Route might well be in order. They were: Oakland & Berkeley Rapid Transit Company, 1889;°° Central Avenue Street Railway Company, 1892; Consolidated Piedmont Cable Company, 1890; Piedmont & Mountain View Railway Company, 1896; East Oakland Street Railroad Company, 1892; Oakland Railroad Company, 1864 (electrified in 1892); Alameda, Oakland & Piedmont Electric Railway Company, 1892; Highland Park & Fruit Vale Railroad Company, 1875 (electrified in 1893); California Railway Company and its predecessors, and the Oakland, San Leandro & Haywards Electric Railway, 1892. The latter, incidentally, was the first railway to employ the "piggyback" method of moving freight. Express wagons were loaded on flat cars and hauled to their destinations. For service directly into downtown San Francisco, the same express wagons were then loaded onto the transbay ferries. This service lasted only from 1894 to 1895.

Smith's plans called for an underwater tube to Goat (now Yerba Buena) Island, using the island for a ferry pier. However, the United States Government refused permission°°° and Smith

---

°Nicknamed by patrons the "Syndicate Railway."
°°Dates given denote the beginning of operations.
°°°Coincidentally, the Southern Pacific was also thwarted in its efforts to construct a trestle to Goat Island for its ferry-train connection.

25

This car was built in the Key System's own shops in 1925. Cars of this series saw services on all lines, and the 12th Street Line became their special province. Of a center entrance type, No. 681 has what is called a deck roof. (Stephen D. Maguire Collection)

quickly changed course, this time using a long trestle extending from Oakland's shoreline over the shallow waters of San Francisco Bay for three and one-quarter miles until deep water was reached. (Much of the water of San Francisco Bay is very shallow and heavy dredging is an ongoing project in order to accommodate seagoing ships.) This pier would give Smith's newly formed San Francisco, Oakland & San Jose Railway the connection to his own ferryboat fleet. On October 26, 1903, No. 505 headed the first train of the S.F.O. & S.J. Ry. Reducing the traveling time from San Francisco to Oakland to thirty-five minutes (twenty minutes off S.P. schedules) and charging a ten-cent fare, the new electrics so proved their popularity that by 1912, there were 101 miles of track in the new interurban system.

Despite the name and several attempts, the railroad was never to reach San Jose. Actually, railroads in the United States had a penchant for names which suggested great distances in spite of the often limited expanse of their trackage.

If Pennsylvania Station in New York was "an affront to the Vanderbilts," the Key Route Pier, ferries and trains could logically be termed "an affront to the Southern Pacific." For the first time, the Espee had serious competition in its own backyard. It met this challenge and met it well by electrifying its Alameda County lines with large and fast equipment operating with its own ferryboat fleet in 1911.

In 1902, "Borax" Smith formed two corporations: Oakland and San Jose Railway and the San Francisco and Piedmont Railway. However, within a few months these roads were merged into the San Francisco, Oakland & San Jose Railway—a title which was to last until 1908. The name was then altered to read San Francisco, Oakland & San Jose Consolidated Railway. At the same time, the Oakland Traction Company was formed to operate the Key Route's local streetcar lines. Oakland Traction Company was the shortest-lived of all the Key's official names, for in 1912 the name was changed again, this time to San Francisco-Oakland Terminal Railways and the name "San Jose" ceased to grace the signboards. On December 15, 1923, the bankrupt railway underwent a general reorganization and the road adopted its slogan for its logo for the first time, using the name Key System Transit Company. Barely six years later—December 11, 1929—

Nos. 561 and 563 running southbound in North Berkeley from Richmond to Oakland. The Shipyard Railway, built during World War II, is long gone, but the two cars survive at the California Railway Museum. (Stephen D. Maguire Collection)

another reorganization took place. Under the title of Railway Equipment and Realty Company, four subsidiary corporations were formed: Key Systems, Ltd., which operated the passenger trains: Key Terminal Railway, Ltd., which operated the ferryboats and freight operations; East Bay Street Railway, Ltd., which operated the

Through a curious series of events, these five ex-Sacramento Northern cars found themselves working on the Key System's F Line-Berkeley. On April 8, 1946, they are traveling eastbound (Stephen D. Maguire Collection)

March of 1944 saw the five-car consist known by patrons as the *City of Berkeley* going westbound on Shattuck Avenue, Berkeley, from University Avenue. (Stephen D. Maguire Collection)

Key System No. 119 heading a train of five bridge units in Berkeley in 1943. This train had a capacity of over 500 passengers. (Stephen D. Maguire Collection)

streetcars; and East Bay Motor Coach Lines, Ltd., which operated the buses. In 1938, the Key Terminal Railway, Ltd., was changed to Key System and handled passenger service only. At the same time, the Key System, Ltd., had its name changed to Oakland Terminal Railroad and was assigned the freight switching duties only. In 1942, the O.T.R.R. was sold to the Western Pacific and the Santa Fe and had its name changed to Oakland Terminal Railway.

Smith's consolidations had provided Alameda County with a good unified street railway and an interurban network. With the pier extending out onto the Bay's waters, it resembled the shape of a key. Because of this, the company promoted the key as its symbol, first being labeled the Key Route, and later the Key System. Throughout the various ownerships which were to follow, the key remained the promotional symbol and the 1923 name of Key System Transit Company more or less made official the name the patrons had been using anyway.

The Key System operated eight lines in its interurban network, lettered A, B, C, E, F, G, H, and K, which were as follows:

A Line, Oakland-12th Street. Established April 1, 1909. Ran from the Key Pier along Yerba Buena Avenue to Louise Street, Louise to Poplar Street,

This vintage postcard shows San Francisco, Oakland & San Jose Railway No. 515 on the transfer table in the Key Route's Emeryville Shops. The postcard says, "MODERN CAR USED IN KEY ROUTE TRAIN SERVICE," and in those days before two world wars these cars were indeed modern.

1903—one of the first trains of the San Francisco, Oakland & San Jose Railway. No. 505 was also on the head end of the Key Route's maiden run on October 26, 1903. (Alameda-Contra Costa Transit District)

Poplar to 12th Street, 12th Street to 3rd Avenue, and along 3rd Avenue to 18th Street. After March 29, 1941, the A Line left 3rd Avenue at East 14th Street and continued out East 14th to 105th Avenue, until former I.E.R. tracks were re-routed, four weeks later, to allow Key System units to leave East 14th Street at 46th Avenue and terminate at Havenscourt Boulevard and Bancroft Avenue. Line abandoned on April 20, 1958.

B Line, Oakland-22nd Street. Established May 6, 1906. Ran from the Key Pier along Yerba Buena to Louise Street, Louise to Poplar Street, Poplar to 22nd Street, 22nd to Grand Avenue, Grand to Trestle Glen Road, Trestle Glen to Underhills Road. Line abandoned April 20, 1958.

C Line, Piedmont-40th Street. Established June 1, 1904. Ran from the Key Pier along Yerba Buena Avenue to 40th Street, 40th to Piedmont Avenue. Later extended to Oakland and Grand Avenues via Pleasant Valley. Line abandoned April 20, 1958.

E Line, Claremont. Established April 1, 1908. Ran from the Key Pier along Yerba Buena Avenue to Linden Street, Linden to 55th Street, 55th to Claremont Avenue, Claremont to Claremont Station at Domingo Avenue. Line abandoned April 20, 1958.

F Line, Berkeley. Established October 26, 1903. Ran from Key Pier along Yerba Buena Avenue to Linden Street, Linden to Adeline Street, Adeline to Shattuck Avenue, and Shattuck to University Avenue. On March 26, 1933, the F Line was cut back from University and Shattuck Avenues to Adeline Street and Alcatraz Avenue. On March 29, 1941, the line was extended back to University and Shattuck, and thence along Shattuck over the former Interurban Electric Railway's rails to Henry Street, to the Northbrae Tunnel, and through the tunnel to The Alameda. Line abandoned April 20, 1958.

G Line, Westbrae. Established June 11, 1911. Ran from Sacramento Street and University Avenue in Berkeley to Santa Fe Avenue via Key Route Boulevard. Line abandoned July 25, 1941.

H Line, Berkeley-Northbrae. Established June 11, 1911. Ran from Key Pier along Yerba Buena Avenue to Linden Street, Linden to Sacramento Street, Sacramento to Monterey Avenue, and Monterey to Colusa Avenue. Abandoned July 25, 1941.

K Line, Alcatraz Avenue-College Avenue. Established July 1, 1909. Ran from Adeline Street and Alcatraz Avenue to Bancroft Way and Telegraph Avenue via Alcatraz, College Avenue, and Bancroft Way in Berkeley. The K Line experienced a number of designations, variously being labeled the L Line, the G Line (letter exchanged with the Westbrae Line), and at one time being numbered 31. Line abandoned September 29, 1946.

Shipyard Railway. This line was operated by the Key System for the Maritime Commission during World War II to shuttle workers to the Richmond Shipyards. It ran from Yerba Buena Avenue and San Pablo Avenue along San Pablo, Heinz, 9th Street (over ex-I.E.R. rails) as far as Gilman Street, thence over private right-of-way to Potrero Avenue in Richmond, along Potrero to Cutting Boulevard, Cutting to the Shipyards.

The G and K Lines were serviced by the Key's streetcars. In order to enable them to run under

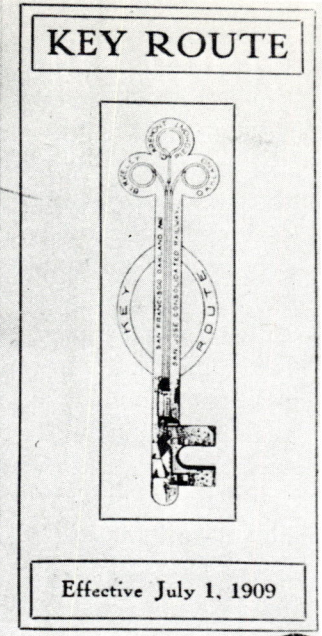

Known as "Lehighs" by Key Route employees, these cars were used as streetcars as well as interurbans. Their nickname derived from their purchase in 1904 from Lehigh Valley Transit Co. in Pennsylvania. (Vernon J. Sappers photo/Bancroft Library)

This cover from a 1909 Key Route timetable shows how the names Key Route and Key System arose. The ferry slips represent the notches of a key, the Key Pier represents the stem, and the trains running to Berkeley, Claremont, Piedmont, and Oakland represent the handle. (Alameda-Contra Costa Transit District)

the interurbans' overhead (normally the interurbans used pantographs and the local streetcars used trolley poles and hence differences in overhead wiring systems), these cars were equipped with pantographs in addition to their trolley poles. No Key streetcars were used on the Bay Bridge, however.

The Key System from its very inception had adopted the concept of trains consisting of two or more cars, although cars did occasionally run solo. This concept remained in force until the final abandonment of the rails. Another practice which remained throughout was the use of pantograph collectors; they were used by all of the Key's interurbans except when running on the Bay Bridge, where third rail shoes were used.

The story of the Key System would be incomplete without mention of that remarkable facility, the Key Pier. On June 30, 1916, the Key System completed construction of a solid fill pier which replaced the original pile pier built by Borax Smith. While the original had extended in a straight line over the water, the new pier would adjoin the original trackage on shore and once over the water would break into two reverse curves before reaching the Key Pier Terminal. The original pier was cut down to a stub some 400 feet long and used for car storage. This practice was ended and the stub torn down in 1932 when car storage facilities were provided on fill land adjacent to the Key System's rails.

By the year 1924, the Key Pier was one of the world's busiest railway terminals, handling more than 800 trains daily! Not even Penn Station in New York could boast that kind of traffic.

The Key System installed a most elaborate block signal system for its pier facilities, including perhaps the most densely signaled trackage in the world with 145 signals in 3.87 miles of track. All motorized cars as well as control trailers were equipped with tripper arms which, if brought in contact with a semaphore-like arm in a "stop" position, would immediately bring the train to a halt. All Sacramento Northern cars operating over the Key Pier were required to be equipped with these devices, and, if operating in Key territory, were required to adhere to Key System train rules. So effective were these regulations that more than 3,500,000 trains passed over the Pier before the first train accident occurred, on December 4, 1924—an accident which cost the lives of eight passengers, two trainmen, and injuries to thirty-six passengers.

At 7:54 A.M., westbound Key Train #729 was in a stop position, in compliance with signals. Cars 655, 656, 664, and 665 made up the consist. Traveling between 35 and 40 miles per hour was Sacramento Short Line (later to become part of the Sacramento Northern) Train #15 with a single

Shattuck and University Avenue was to be for thirty years the terminus of eastbound trains of the Key System's F Line. Here a three-car interurban train loads passengers alongside a streetcar of the Oakland Traction Co. (Key System). (Stephen D. Maguire Collection)

The intersection of Shattuck and University Avenues was to a trolley fan what Hollywood and Vine was to a movie fan, for here could be found not only the interurbans of the Key System and Southern Pacific, but an abundance of streetcars. In this 1908 view, a Key Route interurban train lays over before continuing to the Key Pier and the ferries. Streetcar No. 314 of the Telegraph Avenue line is heading toward the University of California campus while No. 197 of the Euclid Avenue line is making an eastbound appearance. No. 197 had been rebuilt in the Key Route's shops from a double deck car of the Highland Park Line. (Alameda-Contra Costa Transit District)

motor, No. 1014, as its consist. This train slammed into the rear of Key System No. 665 and telescoped it some eighteen and one-half feet. Later, a thorough investigation by the Interstate Commerce Commission laid heavy blame on the failure of the S.S.L. motorman to observe safe speed regulations.

The second disaster to strike the Key Pier occurred on February 17, 1928, when mishandling of the ballast controls on the Key's ferryboat *Peralta* caused her bow to dip into the water, washing some thirty passengers overboard. All but five were saved from drowning.

The year 1933 was ill-starred for the Key Pier. On January 21, some one hundred feet of ties on the westbound track caught fire and disrupted service for three days. On the evening of May 6, a second fire broke out, only this time with severe consequences. The fire erupted in the Pier Terminal and killed the power in the overhead wire, thus preventing any fire fighting equipment from reaching the blaze. Before the fire could be extinguished, the Key System suffered the total loss of the *Peralta*, the Key Terminal, and thirteen interurbans for an estimated damage loss of eleven million dollars. The cars lost were Nos. 513, 527, 555, 556, 559, 565, 567, 573, 585, 587, 661, 672, and 679. Until restoration of the Pier and ferry-interurban service, passengers were routed via Greyhound buses to the Oakland Mole and then to San Francisco aboard the Southern Pacific's ferries.

After cessation of the Key's ferry service, the fill land was used for yards for the bridge operations, and today that area is an integral part of the Bay Bridge's east portal. The terminal was demolished in 1942.

With construction of the Bay Bridge, a new era in East Bay transportation had begun. The ferryboat operations were ended, and provisions were made for rails across the bridge to accommodate the interurbans of the Key System, Interurban Electric Railway, and Sacramento Northern. To facilitate this, many of the older cars were dismantled and parts salvaged for use on a new type of car. Built at the Bethlehem Steel Company's plant in Wilmington, Deleware, these articulated (articulated: two carbodies sharing a common center wheel truck and operating as a single unit*) units came to symbolize the Key System's last years.

---

*Such an arrangement was adopted by a number of street railways and interurbans in North America because it allowed greater seating capacity, a car could thus negotiate sharp turns on narrow city streets, and it gave the operating company a chance to have, in effect, two cars in use with only three men (motorman, conductor, collector), rather than four (two motormen, two conductors), if the cars were to operate separately.

All cars destined for use on the bridge were equipped with automatic train control systems (see Chapter 2 for description of these controls), as well as the shoes for the aforementioned third rail. The third rail was necessary since the Key ran on 600 volts while the I.E.R. and the S.N. ran on 1200 volts.

With the opening of transbay service over the bridge (at a rate of two and one-half cents per passenger), riders from the East Bay had, for the first time, direct rail service to downtown San Francisco. The Municipal Railway of San Francisco and the Market Street Railway immediately undertook to reroute some of their streetcar lines to the newly built Transbay Terminal in order to accommodate commuters. San Francisco's famed Ferry Building began its long decline as a hub of commuter activity.

All three interurbans using the bridge deeded some of their rolling stock to the California State Toll Bridge Authority as collateral for installation of the automatic train control equipment and rails. Therefore, while these cars carried the heralds of their operators, they were in effect state property. When the Sacramento Northern bowed out of passenger operations, five of their cars which were owned by the state became surplus. The state junked them to Hyman Michaels Company. Badly needing more equipment due to the shortages of World War II, the Key System acquired them for the unbelievably low price of $800 on February 4, 1942, and sent them to their Emeryville Shops for conversion to Key System use. These five always ran together, and became such a fixture on the F Line-Berkeley

This 1907 postcard view shows three Key Route trains on the old Key Pier. The Key Route's interurbans and ferryboats were a direct assault on the Southern Pacific's transbay monopoly. Indicative of the massive capitalization needed for such a venture are the Key Route's bankruptcy of "Borax" Smith and the financing today of the Key's all-bus successor by S.P. taxes. (Alameda-Contra Costa Transit District)

Five Key Route platform men and one "super" in front of a train headed by No. 501 at the old Key Pier. The man at extreme left appears to be the motorman since he is wearing gloves and holding a controller handle. (Stephen D. Maguire Collection)

that they became collectively known by F Line riders as the *City of Berkeley*.

World War II took an enormous toll on the Key System's cars. With replacement parts and equipment unavailable, the equipment, which was under heavy strain due to gasoline shortages for private autos, began to show signs of premature old age. By war's end, the system was worn down. However, much is to be said for the carbuilders at Bethlehem Steel, for after final abandonment in 1958, with six exceptions, the bridge units were sold to Ferrocarril Nacional General Urquiza, in

No. 588 was built in St. Louis, Missouri for "Borax" Smith and was intended to carry Key Route passengers to San Jose. The rails never materialized and No. 588 and her sisters served quite well on the Key until scrapping in 1938. (Charles A. Smallwood)

Buenos Aires, Argentina, and ran well into the 1970s. The six exceptions were donated as follows: No. 167 to Orange Empire Trolley Museum, No. 169 to Oregon Electric Railway Historical Society, No. 175 to Nevada Heritage Foundation, No. 182 to Key Route Association, No. 186 to the Bay Area Electric Railroad Association, and No. 187 to the Railway and Locomotive Historical Society. Nos. 182 and 186 are now at the B.A.E.R.A.'s museum at Rio Vista Junction while No. 187 remains in storage. Nos. 169 and 175 were scrapped during 1977. Additionally the B.A.E.R.A. received streetcars 271 and 987. All other streetcars were scrapped.

During the latter years of World War II, the Key System was preparing on its drawing boards plans for more advanced articulated units, using three sections rather than two. Other modernizations of the Key's railway system, such as using more modern streetcars, were being proposed. However, planning ceased with the sale of the Key System.

In 1946, the Key System was sold again—this time to National City Lines. National City Lines was a holding company of American City Lines which had been purchasing transit systems across the country in such cities as Baltimore, Chicago, and St. Louis. In California, National City Lines took over the street railway systems in Sacramento and Los Angeles, among others. If there were ever any doubt that National City Lines was intent on converting the Key System's rail lines to motor buses, it was dispelled by an article in the Baltimore *Sun*, circa 1945, which said in part: "In a statement filed... National City Lines said it owned seventy-five percent of the common stock of American City Lines... the remaining twenty-

The skylights of the old Key Pier lend a ghostlike appearance to No. 504 and others as the trains of the S.F.O. & S.J. Ry. await the arrival of another ferryboat from San Francisco. The waiting room to the left was furnished with benches and the potted palms so typical of the age. In 1933 the entire structure would be lost in a fire. (Alameda-Contra Costa Transit District)

The Key Route was always up to the occasion when special trains were demanded. Two doughboys attend a special train to carry World War I hero Marshal Joseph Joffre of France to the Claremont Hotel in 1920. (Alameda-Contra Costa Transit District)

five percent of the common stock...held by General Motors Corp., General American Aerocoach, Phillips Petroleum and Firestone Tire & Rubber Company. These four companies also owned all of the 9,375 non-voting shares of American City Lines...." Strange bedfellows for an electrically powered rail transit system, and small wonder that they converted their rail lines to buses wherever they could, including their California properties.

Yet as late as July, 1948, trolley authority Steve Maguire still retained enough optimism about the Key's future as an interurban to predict in *Railroad Magazine* that the Key would "continue, in spite of City Lines operators." Was Maguire being overly optimistic or was he expressing a foresight which few could appreciate? The Key System *did* continue for almost ten more years "in spite of City Lines operators." Yet rail service, after a period of excellent bus service by another agency, *is* being restored.°

The Key System, beset with declining patronage and ever-rising costs (particularly for manpower), had begun converting its local streetcar service to bus operations in 1935. This cutback in rail service was eventually followed by the conversion of interurban service to San Francisco to bus—using the Bay Bridge's highway lanes rather than the rail right-of-way. The last of the Key System's train service came to a halt on April 20, 1958. Buses provided the Key's sole motor power until finally, beset with monumental problems of labor-management strife, worn out equipment, lack of revenue, and declining public affiliation

°In the same issue of *Railroad Magazine*, San Francisco Mayor Elmer Robinson was quoted as saying that San Francisco's downtown traffic problem would not be solved until a subway was constructed under Market Street. This subway will be completed as part of the Bay Area Rapid Transit (BART) project.

On May 6, 1933, a fire erupted on the Key Pier which not only destroyed the complex but thirteen interurban cars and the ferryboat *Peralta* as well. Afterwards, *Peralta*'s steel superstructure was so warped from the heat that she was sold for scrap. Towed to Puget Sound, Washington, she was given a new superstructure and rechristened the *Kalakala*.
Left: *Peralta* was secured in the slips when the fire broke out and was enveloped in flames before she could be removed to saftey. (Charles A. Smallwood Collection)
Above right: No. 679 is already a total loss and the Pier is a mass of flaming wreckage. (Vernon J. Sappers Collection)

With the new San Francisco-Oakland Bay Bridge and its railway system looming overhead, the Key Pier, built to replace the one lost in the fire of 1933, has only a few days left of operation insofar as the transbay ferries were concerned. The X Line, taking passengers to the ferries bound for the World's Fair on Treasure Island, will continue to use the Key Pier for a few more months before the Key System's trains cease ferryboat connections forever. Taken in January 1939, this photo shows the tower bearing the "tripper arms" which could shut down the power on the system if unauthorized contact were made with the tripper arms on a Key System or Sacramento Northern train. (Wilbur C. Whittaker)

Three trains inside the new Key Pier. Designed and built for projected service over the San Francisco-Oakland Bay Bridge, they appear content to allow transbay travelers their final rides on the Key's ferries. In this photo, the end doors do not have windows; they were added later. (Wilbur C. Whittaker)

In May of 1937, the bridge railway was not quite ready to have the interurbans of the Key System relieve the ferryboats of their delightful duties. Two Key System trains are in the sheds after crossing the maze of trackage and the multitude of signals. (Wilbur C. Whittaker)

The interiors of the Key System's bridge units were utilitarian but hardly spartan. The windows provided plenty of natural reading light and the leather seats were comfortable. With the conductor posted with his fare box at the center entrances, the units were able to absorb a large number of passengers in minimum time. This photo, taken on October 20, 1952, shows almost no change from the original appearance. (Stephen D. Maguire Collection)

The new bridge units are ready, but the bridge railway is not, and so another trainload of Key System passengers has just disembarked and is about to sample yet another ride across San Francisco Bay on a Key System ferry. The well-dressed ladies appear headed for a day of shopping and lunch in downtown San Francisco, with perhaps a matinee at one of the city's many theaters. The sign above their heads will tell them where to catch their trains upon return to the East Bay. (Wilbur C. Whittaker)

With a well-trained hand, this Key system motorman takes his passengers from San Francisco to various points in the East Bay. Above the motorman's hand is the series of signal lights which will indicate the permissive speeds while operating in the territory of the Bay Bridge. (State of California Toll Bridge Administration)

On September 24, 1938, Governor Frank F. Merriam of California guides a special Key System train across the newly constructed bridge railway for state officials. Units 187 and 179 are coupled together to make this special. (State of California Toll Bridge Administration)

This was unusual—a Key System bridge unit using the pantograph on the Bay Bridge! The overhead wire was to be energized at 1200 volts for the I.E.R. and Sacramento Northern while the Key System was to have used the 600-volt outside third rail. For the occasion of the special train with Governor Merriam, however, the overhead was energized at 600 volts. Apparently this picture was posed, for otherwise the Governor would have been running his train backwards. (State of California Toll Bridge Administration)

January 6, 1939—in eight days this E Line-Claremont train will no longer meet the ferries at the Key Pier. Despite the profusion of construction material, the Bridge Railway Yards are virtually ready for the transbay passengers to travel directly to San Francisco aboard their local interurbans. (State of California Toll Bridge Administration)

Friday, January 17, 1939—while the Key System trains appear well settled in their newest western terminal, some passengers appear unsure whether they prefer the direct service to San Francisco to the old ferryboat ride with its various amenities. (State of California Toll Bridge Administration)

The front of the Transbay Terminal on Mission Street was as much a site of transit activity as the interior. Three streetcar tracks were necessary to provide secondary transit for transbay travelers. On August 28, 1947, two cars of the Municipal Railway of San Francisco are on the left while two cars once operated by the Market Street Railway and now owned by the Municipal Railway are on the track at right. In the concourse to the right, two buses of the Key System are picking up and discharging passengers while a bus of the Municipal Railway is on First Street in the background. Traffic on the streetcars was so heavy that a small control tower was installed in front of the terminal to oversee streetcar movements. While the interior is now given entirely to bus transportation the streetcars continue to serve the terminal. (San Francisco Municipal Railway)

In 1955, a B Line-Oakland train crosses Fremont Street on its way to the Transbay Terminal. In a few more years both the Key trains and the Hudson below will be memories. (Tom Gray)

Bridge Unit No. 175 in 1956 as she gracefully weaves her way through the track network to enter the Transbay Terminal. The I.E.R. and the Sacramento Northern interurbans are long gone from the bridge railway scene but the Key System continues to use the third rail on the bridge right up to the end of operations. (Tom Gray)

with the type of transit the National City Lines had to offer, the entire system was sold to a newly created district, the Alameda-Contra Costa Transit District.

The A/C, as the new system came to be known, is universally acknowledged as one of the best transit systems in the United States. Progressive, innovative, and aware of the public's needs, it has done more than its share of labor in the transit field, and continually increasing ridership stands as evidence that the public will support public transportation if a high caliber system is offered.

In 1961, the voters of San Francisco, Alameda, and Contra Costa Counties voted by the narrowest margin to restore the trunk of the Key System, Interurban Electric Railway, and the southern portion of the Sacramento Northern. In so doing, the Bay Area Rapid Transit District, or BART, was given the authority to restore interurban service between those counties.

Such was the desire to restore the San Francisco-East Bay electric railways that studies are underway to extend BART to Stockton and Sacramento, as well as down the San Francisco Peninsula to San Jose. Already BART operates its trains as far as Daly City, therefore serving—at least in part—territory once covered by no less than four interurban lines (Sacramento Northern, Key System, Interurban Electric Railway, and the Market Street Railway). Inclusion of the Sacramento-Stockton and San Francisco-San Jose corridor routes would add two more (Central California Traction and Peninsular Railway) to the list.

Key System Rolling Stock

100-104 Class
Articulated

This class was rebuilt from the 650 class cars for use on the Bay Bridge. Retaining their center entrances and electrical equipment, the 100-104 class had new automatic train equipment, modified air brakes, and new arch roofs.

Builder: Key System
Year: 1937-1938
Length: 110'5½"
Weight: 147,949 lbs.
Motors: Four G.E. 240A
Gear Ratio: 18:57
Trucks: Brill 27-2X ("A" end)
      St. Louis 23B ("B" end)
      St. Louis 23B (center)
Controller: C6J
Body: Steel

105-110 Class
Articulated

This class was built by Bethlehem as companion to the 100-104 class. Entirely new except for window sashes which were salvaged from the 650s.

Builder: Bethlehem Steel Company
Year: 1937-1938
Length: 110'5½"
Weight: 140,000 lbs.
Motors: Four G.E. 240A
Gear Ratio: 18:57
Trucks: Brill 27-2X ("A" end)
      St. Louis 23B ("B" end)
      St. Louis 23B (center)
Controller: C6J
Body: Steel

Page 2

War Measure

Street Car Regulations Are Enforced

The transportation problem in this city as well as in many others has been so serious of late, that many drastic measures had to be taken in order to keep vital transportation, such as moving of workers in essential industries, going regularly.

Technites who ride the street cars, busses, or trains will be especially affected by the new regulations. Mr. Howard O. Welty, principal, stated, "From now on, on account of the overcrowded traffic, students will be denied the use of their car tickets before 9 o'clock in the morning. All tickets must be stamped in the main office in order to be valid.

"Part time students, those who work part of the day, will be granted the privilege of using their tickets before 9 a. m., provided they have theirs approved by the main office, while all others will be void before nine and after 4:30 p. m.," concluded Mr. Welty.

So students who come or leave school by means of municipal vehicles must comply with these orders as acts contrary to those orders will mean trouble as well as hampering the transportation of vital workers.

The December 2, 1942 issue of the *Scribe News*, weekly paper of Oakland's Technical High School, carried this page 2 story to emphasize to students the importance of the Key System to the war effort. As vital as the big time railroads were to the war effort, the interurbans did their part also. (Jack Trotter Collection)

A single-unit train of the F Line-Berkeley is about to leave the Bridge and enter the Bridge Railway Yards in 1956. (Tom Gray)

Above, a two-unit train of the A Line-12th Street in 1954 as she approaches the Bay Bridge for the return trip to Oakland. The overhead wires for the I.E.R. and S.N. have long been removed but the spans remain. (E. R. Mohr photo/Tom Gray Collection)

Right, good photos of Key System trains on the Bay Bridge were hard to obtain because of prohibitions against pedestrians, the danger of the third rail, uneven light, and moving trains. This one was taken in October of 1952 from the front of a San Francisco-bound train. (Stephen D. Maguire Collection)

Left, in 1956, Key System bridge unit No. 128 leaving San Francisco for Oakland with the tower of the Ferry Building in the right background. The Ferry Building was left virtually obsolete as a transit terminal by Key System trains crossing the Bay Bridge. (Tom Gray)

Builders: Bethlehem Steel Company
   and St. Louis Car Company
Year: 1937-1938
Length: 110′5½″
Weight: 140,000 lbs.
Motors: Four G.E. 240A
Gear Ratio: 18:57
Trucks: Brill 27-2X ("A" end)
   St. Louis 23B ("B" end)
   St. Louis 23B (center)
Controller: C6J
Body: Steel

Builder: Bethlehem Steel Company
Year: 1937-1938
Length: 110′5½″
Weight: 138,000 lbs.
Motors: Four G.E. 240A
Gear Ratio: 18:57
Trucks: Brill 27-2X ("A" end)
   St. Louis 23B ("B" end)
   St. Louis 23B (center)
Controller: C6J
Body: Steel

Builder: Bethlehem Steel Company
Year: 1937-1938
Motors: Four G.E. 66B
Gear Ratio: 21:73
(All other data same as 125-133 class)

Builder: Bethlehem Steel Company
Year: 1937-1938
Motors: Four Westinghouse 302D
Gear Ratio: 18:60
Trucks: Nos. 154-160, St. Louis 23B (all sets);
   Nos. 161-163, 1948 Commonwealth ("A"
      and "B" ends) and St. Louis 23B (center)

Builder: Bethlehem Steel Company
Year: 1937-1938
Motors: Two Westinghouse 302 ("A" end), Two
   Westinghouse 322 ("B" end)
Trucks: 1948 Commonwealth (all sets)
(All other data same as 125 class)

111-124 Class
Articulated
   Utilizing the frames of the 650 class, Bethlehem built the "A" sections while St. Louis built the "B" sections. No. 117 was the first car to operate over the Bay Bridge in regular service.

125-133 Class
Articulated
   Introducing the slanted sides and wide windows, these cars later symbolized the Key System's bridge operation. The 125 class used electrical and brake equipment salvaged from the 500 series, but was equipped with new automatic train control equipment.

134-153 Class
Articulated
   These cars were a subclass of the 125s, the differences being in the motors, gear ratios, and the trucks on Nos. 152 and 153. Nos. 152 and 153 had St. Louis 23B trucks in all sets while the rest of this class corresponded with the 125-133 class.

154-163 Class
Articulated
   These cars were a subclass of the 125-133 class, the differences being in the motors and gear ratios as well as the types of trucks. No. 160 was later given Baldwin trucks from ex-Sacramento Northern cars. Nos. 161-163 were later given General all-steel cast trucks which had been purchased by National City Lines for proposed new units.

164 Class
Articulated
   Later given General all-steel cast trucks which had been purchased by National City Lines for proposed new units.

Above, 1955—this train, bound for Domingo Avenue on the E Line-Claremont, has just left the Bridge and is about to enter the yards. (Tom Gray)

Left, Bridge Unit No. 161 heads a train away from the Key Pier on the X Line for the World's Fair, No. 188 of the Key heads a train on the F Line-Berkeley, and a one-car train on the I.E.R. #6 Line is on the bridge approach. (Wilbur C. Whittaker)

Below, the engineer's plans for the new interurban distribution center, August 3, 1935. (State of California Toll Bridge Administration)

Builder: Bethlehem Steel Company
Year: 1937
Length: 110′5½″
Weight: 138,000 lbs.
Motors: Four G.E. 240
Gear Ratio: 18:59
Trucks: Commonwealth
Controller: C6J
Body: Steel

Builder: Bethlehem Steel Company
Year: 1937
Length: 110′5½″
Weight: 138,000 lbs.
Motors: Four Westinghouse 555CL
Gear Ratio: 16:72
Trucks: Commonwealth
Controller: C6J
Body: Steel

Builder: St. Louis Car Company
Year: 1901
Length: 49′2″
Weight: 61,000 lbs.
Motors: Two G.E. 66
Gear Ratio: 21:73
Trucks: St. Louis 23-A

165-179 Class
Articulated

Built by Bethlehem Steel at their Wilmington, Deleware plant (as were the other Bethlehem cars), they were completely new except for pantographs salvaged from the 500 and 650 series of cars. Unit 165 was the first delivered and placed on public display at the new Piedmont Station in January, 1937. Unit 179 was the first Key System unit to operate over the Bay Bridge in a test run. With the start of bridge operations, units 151-187 were turned over to the California State Toll Bridge Authority as collateral for installation of train controls and rights.

180-187 Class
Articulated

A subclass of the 165 class, these were the last numbered cars of those built by Bethlehem Steel. Units 182 and 186 are today owned and maintained in running condition at the Bay Area Electric Railroad Association's museum at Rio Vista Junction. No. 187 is owned by the Pacific Coast Chapter of the Railway & Locomotive Historical Society and is in storage pending permanent display.

488-499 Class

The history of these cars typifies the variables of the Key System itself. Purchased in 1904 from the Lehigh Valley Transit, they were originally numbered 250-267 and used as streetcars by the Oakland Traction Co. In 1906, twelve of these cars were assigned to the S.F.O. & S.J. Ry. In order to operate over the Key Route, they had to be equipped with pantographs, couplers, pilots, St. Louis trucks, whistles, and other equipment. Originally, Nos. 488-489 and 496-499 were motors and the remainder were trailers. In 1911, they were converted to articulated units by removing one set of controls from a motorized car and placing it in a trailer. In 1916, they were rebuilt into one-man streetcars and remained in local service until being scrapped in 1934. No. 498 was destroyed in a wreck in 1911.

Cars 495-499

This series was not a class, and should not be confused with the Lehigh cars of the same number. Cars 495-499 were ex-Sacramento Northern cars 1005, 1006, 1010, 1015, and 1018, respectively. Further information can be found on these cars in Chapter 8. Today, No. 495 (ex-S.N. 1005) is the property of the Bay Area Electric Railroad Association and resides at Rio Vista Junction in its Sacramento Northern livery. In January, 1948, No. 499 was de-motorized and used as a control trailer.

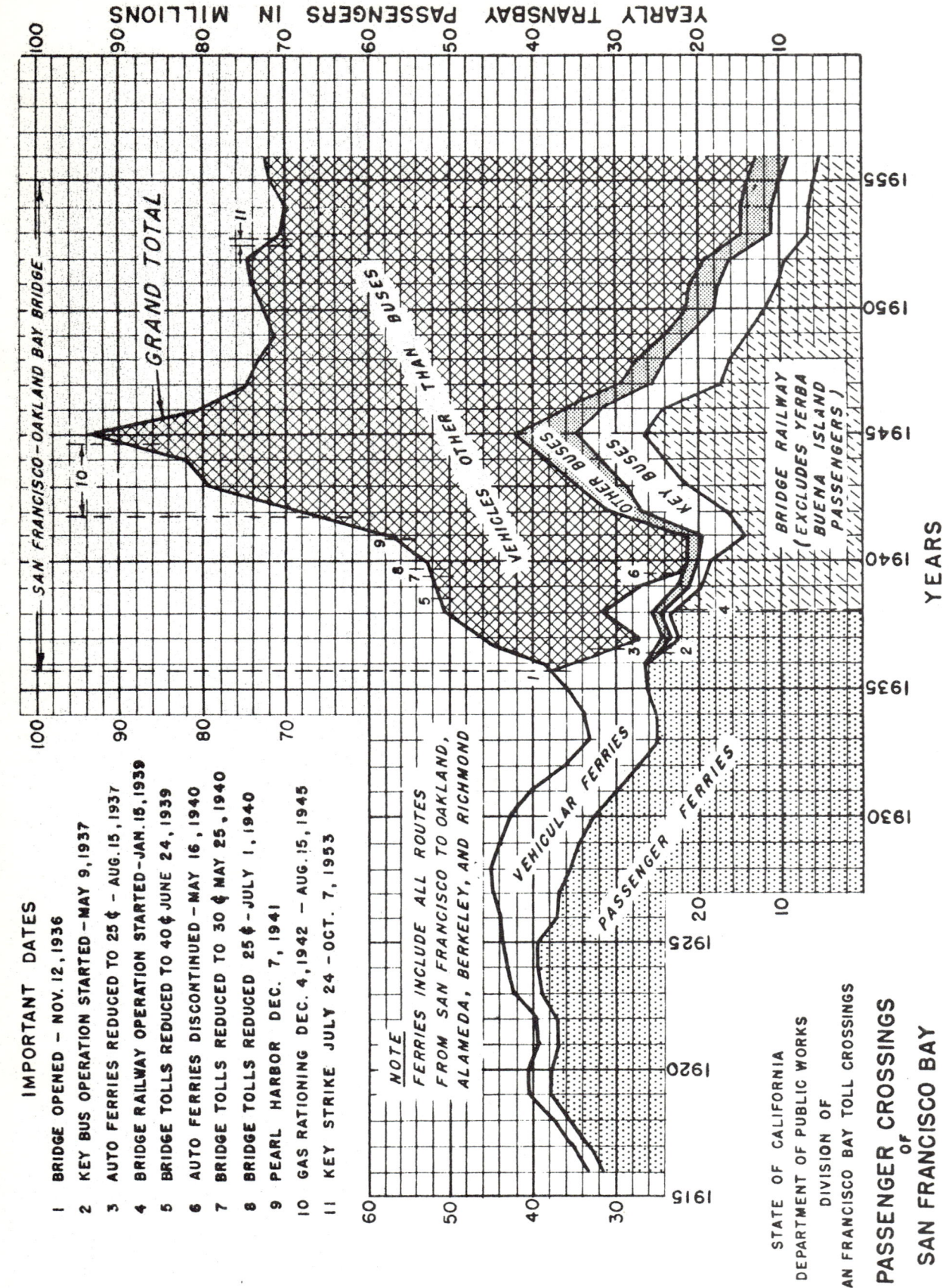

Builder: St. Louis Car Company
Year: 1903
Length: 54′7¼″
Weight: 71,640 lbs.
Motors: Two G.E. 66
Gear Ratio: 21:73
Trucks: St. Louis 23B
Controller: C6J
Body: Wood

Builder: St. Louis Car Company
Year: 1904
Length: 58′5″
Weight: 72,700 lbs.
Motors: Two G.E. 66
Gear Ratio: 21:73
Trucks: St. Louis 23B
Controller: C6J
Body: Wood

Builder: San Francisco, Oakland & San Jose Con. Railway
Year: 1909
(All other data same as 517 class)

Builder: S.F.O. & S.J. Con. Ry.
Year: 1909
Length: 69′3½″
Weight: 58,800 lbs.
Motors: None
Trucks: St. Louis 23-B
Body: Wood

Builder: S.F.O. & S.J. Con. Ry.
Year: 1909
Length: 69′3½″
Weight: 77,054 lbs.
Motors: Two G.E. 66
Gear Ratio: 21:73
Trucks: St. Louis 23-B
Controller: C6J
Body: Wood

501-516 Class

These were the original cars used for service to the Key Pier by the San Francisco, Oakland & San Jose Railway. This class was the first to use the newly perfected Brown diamond roller pan pantograph. A mainstay on the Key with their orange paint with gold lettering and trim, they were extremely handsome and served until 1937 and 1938 when they were dismantled in favor of newer equipment for operations over the Bay Bridge. No. 505 was at the head end of the maiden run, October 26, 1903.

517-548 Class

Of essentially the same style as the 501 class, these cars were built to meet the increased demands for equipment as the Key gained in popularity. Minor modifications from the 501 class included a longer platform and a separate entrance for passengers so they would not interfere with the motorman. Originally Nos. 517-520 were two-motored, Nos. 521, 537-540 were control trailers, and cars 522-536 were non-control trailers. Nos. 521-530 were rebuilt to two-motored cars in 1910. Nos. 531-535 were rebuilt to two-motored cars in 1919. Nos. 536-540 were later motorized. No. 517 was a medalist at the Louisiana Purchase Exposition in 1904 and bore a bronze plaque in commemoration thereafter. No. 533 was leased during World War I to San Francisco, Napa & Calistoga Railway. Dismantled in 1937-38.

549-550 Class

These two cars, built in the company's shops in accordance with the specifications of the St. Louis 517 class, were non-control trailers which were later motorized. Note: Nos. 541-548 were also built at the company's shops at the same time, but so closely followed the St. Louis plans that they were considered St. Louis cars.

551-560 Class

These non-control trailers were built in the company's shops in Emeryville in the same manner as Nos. 541-550. All were scrapped in 1937.

561-566 Class

Nicknamed by the personnel as the "long 500s," these cars were home-built to handle the increased traffic. Due to peak hour loads, they bore longer bodies.

In 1913, the traffic on 12th Street at Broadway in Oakland was already thick enough to drive an A Line motorman and his conductor up the wall. (Alameda-Contra Costa Transit District)

Left, No. 168 heads a westbound A Line train on Beck Street in 1948. This was territory once served by the Southern Pacific and I.E.R. (Tom Gray)

Above, a midmorning train on the A Line at the intersection of 12th and Alice Streets. (Alameda-Contra Costa Transit District)

Below, bridge unit No. 182 on the A Line in 1948. (Tom Gray)

Left, No. 177, bound for Havenscourt, pauses for a passenger stop on East 14th Street in 1949. (Tom Gray)

Builder: St. Louis Car Company
Year: 1911
Length: 69′3½″
Weight: 78,200 lbs.
Motors: Two G.E. 66
Gear Ratio: 21:73
Trucks: St. Louis 23-B
Controller: C6J
Body: Wood

Builder: American Car Company
Year: 1917
Length: 52′6″
Weight: 63,000 lbs.
Motors: Two G.E. 240
Gear Ratio: 18:57
Trucks: Brill 27-2X
Controller: C6J
Body: Steel

Builder: American Car Company
Year: 1917
Length: 52′6″
Weight: 66,120 lbs.
(Other data same as 650-655 class)

Builder: Key System Shops
Year: 1923
Length: 57′7″
Weight: 66,120 lbs.
Motors: Two G.E. 240A
Gear Ratio: 18:57
Trucks: Brill 27-2X
Controller: C6J
Body: Steel

Builder: Key System Shops
Year: 1923
(Other data same as 662 class)

567-591 Class

The last of the St. Louis cars built for "Borax" Smith in his final attempts to complete the interurban line to San Jose, they served until the advent of Bay Bridge operations. No. 574 was the last of the 500s to be dismantled and scrapped. All carried the Brown diamond pantograph, but Nos. 511-516, 658-659, and 662-688 carried a single-type US #6 trolley pole as well.

650-655 Class

An Oakland city ordinance for a number of years prohibited Key Route trains from running on Twelfth Street in downtown Oakland. This necessitated transfers for passengers. Therefore the San Francisco-Oakland Terminal Railways ordered these cars, which were streetcars to all outward appearances yet were heavy duty and equipped with the necessary features to enable them to carry passengers direct from the Key Pier into downtown Oakland. These twelve center entrance cars so proved their value that they were used on other lines as well. They were scrapped between 1936 and 1938 with parts being used for the new bridge units.

656-661 Class

Part of the same order as the 650-655 class with only minor variations.

662 Class

Except for a 5′1″ increase in length, these home-built cars strongly resembled the original cars of the Key Route. Nos. 662-688 were of this class, although 663-664 and 665-688 were subclasses. Used heavily on the Twelfth Street line, they were versatile enough to be used on other lines as well. No. 650 and No. 662 were rebuilt into an articulated unit in 1932, rebuilt into a bridge unit in 1937, and renumbered No. 100.

663-664 Class

What marked the difference between this class and car No. 662 was the roof. While No. 662 had a deck-type roof, this subclass had, as an experiment, a steam coach-type roof. The rebuilding of other roofs in this manner had been intended, but the plans never materialized.

Right, 1946—at the corner of 40th Street and San Pablo Avenue in Emeryville, four of the Key System's former Sacramento Northern's cars are running "deadhead," or out of revenue service. These cars were never strangers to the Key System's rails, for the S.N. shared trackage with the Key for many years, especially on 40th Street and the Key Pier. (Ken Kidder photo/Tom Gray Collection)

1956—westbound No. 167 has just emerged from the Northbrae tunnel on what was once I.E.R. trackage. (Tom Gray)

No. 186 at the Key's new Thousand Oaks Station in 1956 about dusk. (Tom Gray)

The C Line train at the end of a run from San Francisco on February 3, 1957. Both the Piedmont Station and No. 176 were built in 1937. (Stephen D. Maguire Collection)

Eastbound No. 187 passes westbound No. 167 at the Northbrae Tunnel in 1956. (Tom Gray)

With No. 498 on the point, these five former Sacramento Northern cars make up a train on the Key System's F Line, and are given the nickname *City of Berkeley* by that line's regular patrons because of their regular assignment to that line. In this 1946 photo they are running in North Berkeley. (Tom Gray Collection)

665-668 Class

Having a nine-foot width versus an 8'10" width on the others of this type, there was again little variance. These four cars were equipped with a deck roof. No. 685 was taken out of service in 1938 and put into the Key Yards for storage after her sisters had been scrapped. She went to the torch in 1946.

Builder: Key System Shops
Year: 1923-24
Length: 47'2"
Weight: 66,126 lbs.
Motors: Two G.E. 240A
Gear Ratio: 18:57
Trucks: Brill 27-2X
Controller: C6J
Body: Steel

501-580 Class

Not to be confused with other Key system cars of the same number, these cars were purchased by the United States Maritime Commission from the Interborough Rapid Transit Company of New York in 1942. They were then shipped out to Oakland to be used on former S.P. tracks to the Richmond Shipyards. Overhauled in the Key's Emeryville Shops, they were then painted in maritime grey and equipped with pantographs and pilots. In themselves they were of historical interest for in 1897 (after being pulled behind steam locomotives on the Second Avenue elevated line in New York) they were among the first cars to become fitted with electric motors and multiple unit control systems as designed by electric railway pioneer Frank J. Sprague. After the war, all except Nos. 561 and 563 (ex-I.R.T. 844 and 889) were scrapped. The two survivors were presented to the Railway and Locomotive Historical Society which, in 1965, presented them to the B.A.E.R.A., which now maintains them in I.R.T. colors at Rio Vista Junction. The pantographs for the ex-I.R.T. cars came from the old I.E.R. cars.

Builder: Wason Car Company
Year: 1888
Length: 46'5½"
Weight: 56,000 lbs.
Motors: Two G.E. 66
Gear Ratio: 21:73
Trucks: Baldwin
Controller: C6J
Body: Wood

Some of the Key's streetcars were outfitted with pantographs for use over interurban trackage in shuttle service. While they never crossed the Bay Bridge, they did use the Key's rights-of-way in the East Bay. Their value cannot be underestimated since they lengthened the interurbans' route mileage while freeing the interurbans themselves for trunk line duties. Herein are listed those streetcars used on interurban trackage as of May, 1941.

271 Class

Sold to S.F.O. & S.J. Ry. in 1904 from Lehigh Valley Transit Company. Originally No. 251 of the Oakland Traction Company. Rebuilt in 1933 as a one-man car. Retired September 29, 1946. Now at California Railway Museum, Rio Vista Junction.

Builder: St. Louis Car Company
Year: 1901
Length: 47'2"
Weight: 54,400 lbs.
Motors: Four G.E. 70
Gear Ratio: 19:67
Trucks: St. Louis 23-A
Controller: K28
Body: Steel and wood

Whereas San Francisco could boast of having four streetcar tracks on her main thoroughfare, Market Street, Berkeley's Adeline Street had not only four interurban tracks but two streetcar tracks as well. An eastbound train in the F Line, a westbound train on the I.E.R.'s #3 Line, and Key System streetcar No. 407 on the #3 Line complement each other at the intersection of Adeline Street and Alcatraz Avenue in 1940. (Roy Covert photo/Tom Gray Collection)

The Key System's *City of Berkeley* at Bancroft Way—one block away from the University of California—while running on Shattuck, heading for San Francisco. The F line was indispensable in handling large crowds going to see the Golden Bears of U.C. on football Saturdays. (Tom Gray)

Headed by No. 541, a four-car train of the Shipyard Railway is seen running northbound in Richmond during World War II. Service on the Shipyard Railway was to be the last hurrah for these 1888 vintage cars whose history saw them pulled by steam locomotives as well as by experimental electrical cars. (Stephen D. Maguire Collection)

No. 125 approaching the Domingo Avenue Station, eastern terminus of the E Line-Claremont.

World War II brought with it not only gasoline and tire rationing but an increased traffic demand as well. To furnish transportation to the shipyards in Richmond, the U.S. Maritime Commission contracted with the Key system to provide this service. The cars came from the New York City elevateds, the grey paint from the Maritime Commission, the pantographs from the I.E.R. cars, the overhead wire and rails from the Southern Pacific, and the crews from the Key System. Here, a six-car consist is running toward the southern terminus at 40th Street and San Pablo Avenue in Emeryville. (Ken Kidder photo/Tom Gray Collection)

955-956 Class

Builder: American Car Company
Year: 1926
Length: 45'6"
Weight: 41,980 lbs.
Motors: Four G.E. 247A
Gear Ratio: 15:58
Trucks: Brill 77E1
Controller: C169A
Body: Steel

Originally streetcars of the Key System's 900 series, they were rebuilt for shuttle service on the Westbrae line to Albany. In June of 1941 they were rebuilt for local service and reverted to streetcar status.

985-994 Class

Builder: American Car Company
Year: 1926
Length: 45'6"
Weight: 41,980 lbs.
Motors: Four G.E. 247A
Gear Ratio: 15:58
Trucks: Brill 77E1
Controller: C169A
Body: Steel

Equipped for multiple unit running, they were stripped of multiple unit apparatus in 1945. No. 987 was destroyed in a wreck on March 30, 1930, replaced by No. 899. Nos. 993-994 were equipped with pantograph for B Line shuttle service, but not used. They did serve the Westbrae line about a month prior to abandonment, as well as the C Line extension on off-peak hours from Piedmont Station.

Car No. 987 II

Builder: Key System Shops
Year: 1926
(All other data same as 985 class)

Ex-No. 899, renumbered to replace original No. 987, which was destroyed in a wreck.

In addition to the rosters of interurbans and streetcars, the Key System retained a vast variety of work and freight equipment which included fire cars, rail grinders, differential dump cars, flat cars, freight steeple cabs, line cars, sprinklers, crane cars, and even a 2-6-2 steam locomotive! Five of those cars are now residing at the B.A.E.R.A.'s California Railway Museum at Rio Vista Junction. They are:

Freight Motor No. 1001

Home-built at Emeryville Shops in 1910 to handle freight switching duties in the Oakland area and to transfer freight cars from the Sacramento Northern's 40th and Shafter yards to other roads, No. 1001 served well until the end of electrification in 1958. In 1912, No. 1001, bedecked with bunting and flags, pulled the special train of President William H. Taft into the city of Oakland.

Wrecker No. 1011

Built at Emeryville Shops by the Oakland Traction Company in 1906, No. 1011 carried a complete machine shop with tools to handle any kind of emergency.

Line Car No. 1201

This overhead line and tower car was outshopped by Carter Brothers in 1895 for the California Railway. It served as a coach pulled by steam locomotives, and later by electric cars. Later it was electrified and equipped with pantograph and trolley pole and used as a line car. It is still in active use by the B.A.E.R.A.

Shop Switcher No. 1215

This diminutive vehicle was used to move "dead" cars in the company's shops in Emeryville. Single-trucked and utilizing one trolley pole, she was home-built and in use until 1958.

Line Car No. 1218

Rebuilt from a railroad flat car in 1929 by the Key System, this car is still serviceable and is in active use by the California Railway Museum.

Key Route's No. 412 was acquired when the Key took over the old East Shore & Suburban in Richmond, and was one of several types of streetcars equipped with both a pantograph (shown raised) and trolley pole in order to be used on interurban extensions. By looking closely the reader can see how the car has been rebuilt from a California type to an all enclosed body. No. 412 is shown here at Sacramento Street and University Avenue, Berkeley. (W. E. Gardiner photo/Ray Hannah Collection)

From the appearance of this picture—a weed-choked roadbed, a lonely and worn passenger shelter, and houses some distance away—it is plain to see why the service did not warrant the use of the big interurban cars and why the smaller streetcars were adequate. (Tom Gray)

Steeple cab No. 1001 with motorman Bill O'Brien and conductor Carew on the Leona Heights line. When first built by the Key Route in 1910, she was equipped with a trolley pole and painted black. In 1912 she was fitted with a pantograph and later painted Key Route orange. The highlight of her career came in 1912 when she pulled the special train bearing President William H. Taft into the City of Oakland to lay the cornerstone for the new City Hall. No. 1001 was a frequent visitor to the S.N. yards at 40th Street and Shafter Avenue while performing freight transfer duties. (Bancroft Library)

Two streetcars coupled together to make a train in 1940 while serving on the K Line-Alcatraz Avenue. The train is turning off College Avenue onto Alcatraz Avenue. Note the use of trolley poles rather than pantographs. (Tom Gray)

Key System streetcar No. 993 is shuttling on the G-Line-Westbrae in 1937. (Tom Gray)

Chapter Four
The Big Subs

Market Street Railway

San Francisco's public transit development had, by 1890, progressed from plank toll roads to steam dummies to horsecars to cable cars. However, obvious limitations on these types of people-movers prevented any kind of single-car, single-fare ride out of the city and down the San Francisco Peninsula to San Mateo in competition with the Southern Pacific's local trains which went as far as San Jose.

In order to provide such service, a franchise was granted by San Francisco in 1890 to a group of backers who called themselves the San Francisco and San Mateo Railroad Company. Routed from Market and Steuart Streets along Steuart, Harrison, Fourteenth, Guerrero, Chenery Street and San Jose Road, the tracks came to a halt at the San Mateo County line. Thus, on July 29, 1891, San Francisco had the beginnings of an interurban service. Throughout several ownerships, route changes, and appearances of rolling stock, the line was to run until January 16, 1949—some fifty-seven and one-half years!

Failing to meet expenses, the bondholders forced a sale and on April 11, 1896, a group of new owners, calling themselves the San Francisco and San Mateo Electric Railway,* took over and immediately began steps to upgrade the cars, improve the road, and uphold the intent of their corporate name inasmuch as the previous ownership had never taken the line past Baden. Forty new cars were purchased to replace the conglomeration of single- and double-truck cars. The fifty-pound rail for downtown San Francisco was replaced with eighty-five-pound rail in 1897, and 1899 saw the county line relaid with sixty-pound rail. In May of 1900, the line finally was extended, a franchise having been granted to run to the city of San Mateo. Such enterprise fared well, for on May 18, 1901, a group of Baltimore capitalists, known locally as the "Baltimore Syndicate," bought the road for the sum of $1,200,000 to form the nucleus of what was to become the United Railroads of San Francisco. This new management completed the unfinished trackage to San Mateo and spoke of extension to San Jose and up the east side of the Bay to Oakland.

A year later, on March 20, 1902, the United Railroads of San Francisco was formed from the consolidation of the San Francisco and San Mateo Electric Railway (electric), Market Street Railway (horse, cable and electric), Sutter Street Railway (horse, cable and electric), and the Sutro Railroad (electric). The U.R.R. had an authorized capital stock of $40,000,000, divided into 200,000 shares of common at $100 each and 200,000 shares of preferred at $100 each. In 1907, the company provided an additional issue of 50,000 shares of seven percent cumulative first preferred stock at $100 each. On February 16, 1909, the company reduced its common stock from $20,000,000 to $18,000,000. At the time of the 1920 reorganization, $5,000,000 of first preferred, $20,000,000 of preferred, and $17,948,600 of common stock was outstanding, with all stock owned or controlled by the California Railway and Power Company.

The United Railroads designated the interurban route as the #40 Line, a designation which was to last until abandonment of service. Parenthetically, the Municipal Railway (latter day successor

---

*It was not uncommon for railroad corporations, in reorganizing, to change their names from rail*road* to rail*way*, and vice versa, occasionally spelling railroad as rail-road or rail road. Likewise with rail-way and rail way. Interurban companies were known to add or delete the word "electric" in their name changes.

51

It was most unusual for one of the #40 Line's cars to appear on Larkin Street rails—they were in totally different divisions. No. 1241 is probably assigned to a special run. San Francisco City Hall is in the background. (Stephen D. Maguire Collection)

Southbound near San Bruno, #40 Line tracks parallel those of the Southern Pacific. (Stephen D. Maguire Collection)

to the United Railroads) has chosen to revive the number for a commuter feeder line to the S.P. depot.

After a most rapid rate of construction, the line was opened to San Mateo on December 31, 1902, barely beating the deadline of January 1, 1903, in order to satisfy franchise demands. For the most part, the line was single track and the new cars had not yet arrived from the carbuilders in St. Louis, Missouri. To compensate, car No. 583 began shuttle service between Holy Cross Cemetery in what is now Colma to San Mateo on an hourly basis. Public acceptance was evident by no less than 900 passengers ringing in the New Year by riding the new trolley line. By 1904, *The Journal of Electricity, Power and Gas* was able to report:

"With the extension of the system of the United Railroads of San Francisco from Holy Cross Cemetery to San Mateo, the promoters of the original S.F. and S.M. Electric Railroad Company have witnessed the realization, albeit attained by others, of their conception of an all-electric line between the heart of San Francisco and the charming suburb of San Mateo...

"The ties are of redwood, six inches by six inches by eight feet. They are placed two feet six inches from center to center. The rail is a seventy-two-pound T-rail, on the private right of way. The joints are cast welded, with an expansion joint every 1,000 feet. Each cast-weld weighs 110 pounds. In the town of San Mateo a nine-inch girder rail is used. With the exception of a slight grade in San Mateo the interurban line is practically level... Except in San Mateo the entire interurban line is heavily ballasted with crushed rock. Track centers are thirteen feet and the gauge is standard.

Four carmen in front of No. 3 of the San Francisco & San Mateo Electric Railway about 1895 at 30th Street and San Jose Avenue. The man at far left wearing the bowler is probably an official of the company while John J. Crowley, Sr., is at the extreme right. This car is a single-truck job, and all cars of this class were scrapped before 1902. Despite the lettering on the car it never made it to San Mateo. (Charles A. Smallwood Collection)

"Wooden side-pole construction is used on the entire interurban section. The poles carrying high tension wires are seven inches by seven inches at the top, thirteen inches by thirteen inches at the base, and thirty-five feet long. The other poles are eight inches by eight inches at the top, twelve inches by twelve inches at base, and thirty-five feet long. They are all of redwood, and the portion which extends into the [ground] was coated with crude oil. They are painted a dark green, with a mixture of linseed oil, yellow ochre, and lamp black.

"The cross-arms are all made of Oregon pine, those carrying the high tension wires being four inches by six inches by five feet, and four inches by six inches by seven feet. The three high-tension wires are arranged on a triangle on one side of the pole, making it possible to add another set if so desired. One wire is carried on the upper cross-arm and two on the lower.

S.F. & S.M. Ry. Co. No. 20 in front of the company offices at San Jose Avenue and 30th Street about 1895. The man at the left is conductor John J. Crowley, Sr. This car was one of the original ones on the line, but at the time it had been slightly altered by the installation of windows on the ends; prior to that they were open. This car was a true California type, having open ends with a center enclosed section, very suitable for the state's mild climate. Car No. 20 strongly resembles the cable cars of the California Street (San Francisco) line—indeed, they were made by the same carbuilder. (John J. Crowley, Jr., Collection)

One of the first cars of the S.F. & S.M. Ry. Co, at the corner of San Jose and Sickles Avenues. Note the solid plank used for a fender and the single trolley pole. The crowd is possibly en route to Holy Cross Cemetery, as visiting cemeteries was a popular pastime in those days. (Randolph A. Brandt Collection)

The wire is No. 0 and is triple braded, waterproof. The Locke No. 100 brown porcelain, single petticoat, iron pin insulators are used. The cross-arms carrying the feeder wires are four inches by six inches. Steel pin porcelain insulators are used. There are at present five feeder wires from Millbrae substation, all being 500,000 circular mills. The trolley wire is No. 00 hard-drawn copper. The span wires are five sixteenths-inch galvanized iron strand wire. The ears are all soldered. The construction work on this follows the same high standards as that adopted on other parts of the system."

Ranging from erratic four-wheelers to slightly longer double-trucked cars to twenty-nine and one-half-foot city cars to suburban cars to bona fide interurban cars, the history of rolling stock on the #40 Line was a history of the development of electric traction itself, and fairly demonstrated the potential of electric competition with a class 1 steam road—in this case the Southern Pacific's Peninsula service.

Actually, not all classes of cars ever made the complete journey from San Francisco to San Mateo, and then some of them only briefly. Two classes stand out, however, and they were the 1225-1244 class of suburban cars and the 1-12 class of interurban cars, or the "Big Subs."

In 1903, the United Railroads of San Francisco purchased the 1225-1244 series from the Laclede Car Company° of St. Louis, Missouri. Seating forty passengers, they were to be the mainstay of the San Mateo run right up to the last day in 1949, despite being withdrawn for city service for awhile and despite several rebuildings. This class was PAYE, or pay-as-you-enter, type, double-end, and called for two-man operation (conductor on rear platform and motorman on front). Later this two-man operation was to become a bone of contention as the successor, Market Street Railway, attempted to stem the tide of financial losses by converting to one-man operation on all lines, including the #40 Line to San Mateo.

Attempts to do so in San Francisco were halted by the courts, but some of the cars which went as far as Daly City did use single-man operation. With the exception of No. 1227, the 1225-1244 class cars as well as the Big Subs were always two-man. No. 1227 was rebuilt for one-man use under Market Street Railway ownership, but was stored in the barn for a month and then returned to two-man condition without ever having been used. In line with one-man needs, No. 1227 was equipped with air-operated folding doors. These doors were kept when No. 1227 was returned to duty.

Another United Railroads stamp was placed on the line when the route was simplified to run from Fifth Street in San Francisco to Mission Street, thence out Mission Street to Daly City. In Daly City the cars picked up their own right-of-

°This carbuilder was bought out by the St. Louis Car Company in 1903.

The car on the right is of a class formerly assigned by the United Railroads to the San Mateo line, and after less than two years' service the cars were either sold, reassigned to city service, or rebuilt for other uses. Trolley companies frequently provided mail car service in the cities for the Post Office and the car shown here was one of two which were rebuilt for that use and designated Mail Cars D and E. Mail Car E has probably just picked up a load of mail from the East from one of the Southern Pacific's ferries. The date of this photo is 1906, and could not have been taken on or after April 18 since on that date both mail cars were lost in the Fire and Earthquake.

way past the cemeteries and on down the Peninsula to Burlingame Avenue in Burlingame. Once in Burlingame, the #40 Line ran on city streets as follows: California Drive, Baldwin Avenue, B Street, Third Avenue to the Southern Pacific depot in San Mateo. The return trip saw the cars run on Second Avenue, B Street, Baldwin Avenue, Ellsworth, Poplar Avenue, San Mateo Drive and California Drive back to the right-of-way.

Later, under ownership of the Municipal Railway of San Francisco, the cars were routed onto Valencia Street for a few blocks in order to avoid traffic congestion with the Mission Street streetcars during the rush hour.

April 18, 1906, saw San Francisco's public transportation systems in a state of utter collapse due to the Fire and Earthquake, but remarkable recovery was made in the restoration of the San Mateo interurban service, and by May 6, 1906, the cars were rolling again.

Nevertheless, San Francisco was faced with a distinctive problem due to the destruction from the 'Quake, and that was the extensive damage to the cable slots and trackage of the city's far-flung cable car system. For some number of years, the United Railroads had been in the process of converting as many cable car lines as possible to electric lines, and their plans included the five cable car lines on Market Street as well as the cable line on Sutter Street. At that time, however, there was a segment of San Francisco's populace which insisted that the U.R.R. place the electrical conduit underground (an arm would reach down into the underground shaft through a slot similar to the cable slot and pick up the electricity) to avoid unsightly overhead trolley wires on Market and Sutter Streets. This the U.R.R. refused to do. Blueprints were then drawn for special cable cars of extraordinary length to serve on Market and Sutter, but before concrete action could be taken, San Francisco was hit with its most famous earthquake and fire.

At this point, with the cable car tracks on Market and Sutter Streets a shambles, permission was granted by the city to operate electric streetcars, with overhead wire, over Market and Sutter

United Railroad's No. 1239 at the corner of 5th and Market Streets in 1905, ready to begin another trip to San Mateo. The windows are open, and the motorman and conductor are posing for the photographer. In a year San Francisco will be in ruins and the 1225 Class cars will be needed for city service while the Big Subs will occupy center stage on the interurban line to San Mateo.

Streets for a two-year period.* The U.R.R. wasted no time in electrifying the cable lines on Market and Sutter, but in the sudden rush to accomplish this there was a corresponding need for additional rolling stock. Such was the need that streetcars ready for shipment to Chicago were diverted to San Francisco to become known as the "Chicago Cars."

The search for new, or at least useable, streetcars took President Patrick Calhoun of the U.R.R. to the shops of the St. Louis Car Company. As the Fates would have had it, the St. Louis people had just filled job order No. 580, which called for the construction of twenty-two cars of the classic interurban mold. Six of those cars were consigned to the Erie Railroad, while the remaining sixteen had been ordered by the Philadelphia & Western Railway and the Fates chose almost that precise moment for the P. & W. to experience severe financial difficulties and leave the St. Louis Car Company holding sixteen unsold passenger interurbans. Calhoun wasted no time in securing twelve of the P. & W. cars for the U.R.R.'s San Mateo line. The remaining four were picked up by the fledgling Northern Electric Railway of Chico which was only too happy to be able to secure additional interurban equipment in mint condition without having to wait for the comple-

*Needless to say, the U.R.R. never did restore the cables to either Market or Sutter Streets, and thus provided some of the background which later contributed to the civic scandals which resulted in the arrest and conviction of several city officials and the political ascent of Hiram Johnson.

This is the domain of the motorman aboard U.R.R. No. 1235. The handle to the left is the controller which regulates the speed of the car. The middle handle operates the air brake while the large handle connects to the emergency brake. The small stool propped against the bulkhead can be positioned in the hole in the floor in back of the controller box for the relative ease and comfort of the platform men. Photographed by the company photographer on October 18, 1912, No. 1235 will be remodeled about eight years later and the platform will be much enlarged. Years later this car will make the Last Run. (United Railroads photo/Charles A. Smallwood Collection)

tion of a job order which might take as long as six months to fill.

While the four cars which went to the N.E. were to undergo renamings, renumberings, and rebuildings, the twelve which were sent to San Francisco were numbered 1-12 and retained those numbers until their untimely demise.

What proud cars they were as they roared down Mission Street and seemingly raced the Southern Pacific steam trains down the Peninsula! While the 1903 cars from Laclede had been of suburban styling, the new 1906 cars of the St. Louis Car Company were of the true interurban design, and gave San Francisco its first and only orthodox interurban cars. Being entirely closed, with flush platforms and a railroad-type roof, the "Big Subs," as they came to be known by San Franciscans, seated fifty-six riders. "Big Subs"

Sister to Nos. 106-109 of the Northern Electric Railway, Big Sub No. 4 waits on the tracks in front of Geneva Barn for her next assignment. Perhaps she has just come in from a run since her eclipse fender is down and her rear trolley pole is up. While some may dispute whether or not the #40 Line was a true interurban line, there is no question that No. 4 and the other Big Subs (short for Big Suburbans) were representative of interurban equipment.

By August 30, 1920, the Big Subs reluctantly are running out their last years of service. In their bays at the Geneva Barn, they dwarf No. 1230 at left. The absence of a headlight is no accident, for arc lamps were used and when the cars ran during the daytime or were out of service the lamps were taken to the electrical department for servicing. When needed, they were hung on the brackets in the center panel of the dash. (United Railroads photo/Charles A. Smallwood Collection)

The advent of electric railways often brought forth increased real estate development, and the #40 Line was no exception. The Burlingame Railway Co. was the brainchild of promoters in Burlingame, and their single car made connections with the United Railroads' interurban line. The car was powered by a battery which accounts for the lack of any kind of current collection system. The Bay Area's only battery-powered streetcar didn't last long, but the interurban line and Peninsula real estate values did. (Charles A. Smallwood Collection)

Artist Albert Tolf has delighted thousands with his cartoons of San Francisco, both past and present. This one, which originally appeared in the San Francisco News, portrays Big Sub No. 7 in her heyday. (From In Old San Francisco by Albert Tolf. Used by permission)

was no idle sobriquet, as the monsters weighed in at no less than 75,640 pounds. In looking at photographs of the Big Subs, one may note that often the headlamps do not appear. This was because they used arc lights, and during the daylight hours the lamps were left at the shops for servicing and then hung on special hangers on the dashes for evening and night trips.

As originally outshopped by the St. Louis Car Company, the Big Subs were equipped with wooden pilots, or what is known outside of railroad circles as cowcatchers; the name was apt since they were originally designed to shove unwary animals off the tracks of steam locomotives. Large wooden or metal pilots were characteristic of large interurban vehicles, whether or not they had an abundance of trackage along city streets. Later the Big Subs' pilots were removed in favor of the folding eclipse fenders which were standard equipment on San Francisco's streetcars until after World War II. The function of the eclipse fenders remained, however, to push a person or animal up and over the fender, rather than see him crushed by a railway car.

Rambling toward San Mateo is Market Street Railway's No. 1229 as the 1225 Class appeared after the 1920s renovation program. The platform has been lengthened and sliding doors have replaced the gates. Painted green, the car bears the patented White Front of the M.S. Ry. The two lamps on the dash illuminate the White Front at night. No. 1229 must be scheduled to run past dark since her headlamp is in place.

Southbound toward San Mateo, M.S. Ry. No. 1241 passes the waiting shelter at the Duck Ranch. (Stephen D. Maguire Collection)

Market Street Railway's No. 1227 was the only one of the 1225 Class cars to have been fitted out for one-man operation. Never used as such, she soon returned to service as a two-man car although she retained her automatic folding doors up to the end. In this photo No. 1227 is going directly to Tanforan Racetrack in San Bruno. The open countryside pictured here is to be the setting for one suburban housing tract after another following the Korean War. (Stephen D. Maguire Collection)

A footnote remains to be told about these eclipse fenders. When a car was in operation, the rear fender was folded up and held in place by a hook and chain, and young lads, seeking a free ride, would climb up on the rear of the car and sit on the folded fenders. Needless to say, this was a dangerous practice and more than one platform man was relieved when the eclipse fenders were replaced.

The Big Subs fulfilled their intended purpose of freeing the previously used 1225-1244 class cars for city use and for the cemeteries runs. Occasionally, they were seen on the Daly City trips. Claiming the #40 Line all to themselves, the Big Subs' powerful seventy-five horsepower motors meant meeting timetables presented no problem as they easily took the few hills and grades on their route. Their massive size and strength, however, proved to be their own undoing.

Built originally to be run in trains of two or more cars, the Big Subs became much too cumbersome on downtown Mission Street as the number of local streetcars—which shared the same tracks—increased. Then too, the 1-12 class cars used copious amounts of electrical power, which was badly needed for the local cars. Most reluctantly, the agonizing decision was made to suspend use of the Big Subs and restore the #40 Line to all 1225-1244 class service.

Unwilling to totally discard the Big Subs, the U.R.R. management, in the fall of 1923, merely placed them in storage at the old Third Street carbarn, hoping for the day to arrive when they could be restored to their former glory. That day never came, and in 1933, cars 2, 3, 6, 7, 9, and 11 were towed out to Elkton Yards and burned for scrap. Two years later, the fateful "last trip" to Elkton was made by 1, 4, 5, 8, 10, and 12 to face the torch. On March 25, 1935, Market Street Railway Car No. 10 was cremated, ending San Francisco's all too brief flirtation with true interurbans.

The 1225-1244 cars had, however, never entirely disappeared from the San Mateo line. Having been used for the abbreviated runs to the cemeteries, they were ready to take up the slack, and as they were rebuilt they began to supplement the 1-12 class. Rebuilt in the 1920s, they

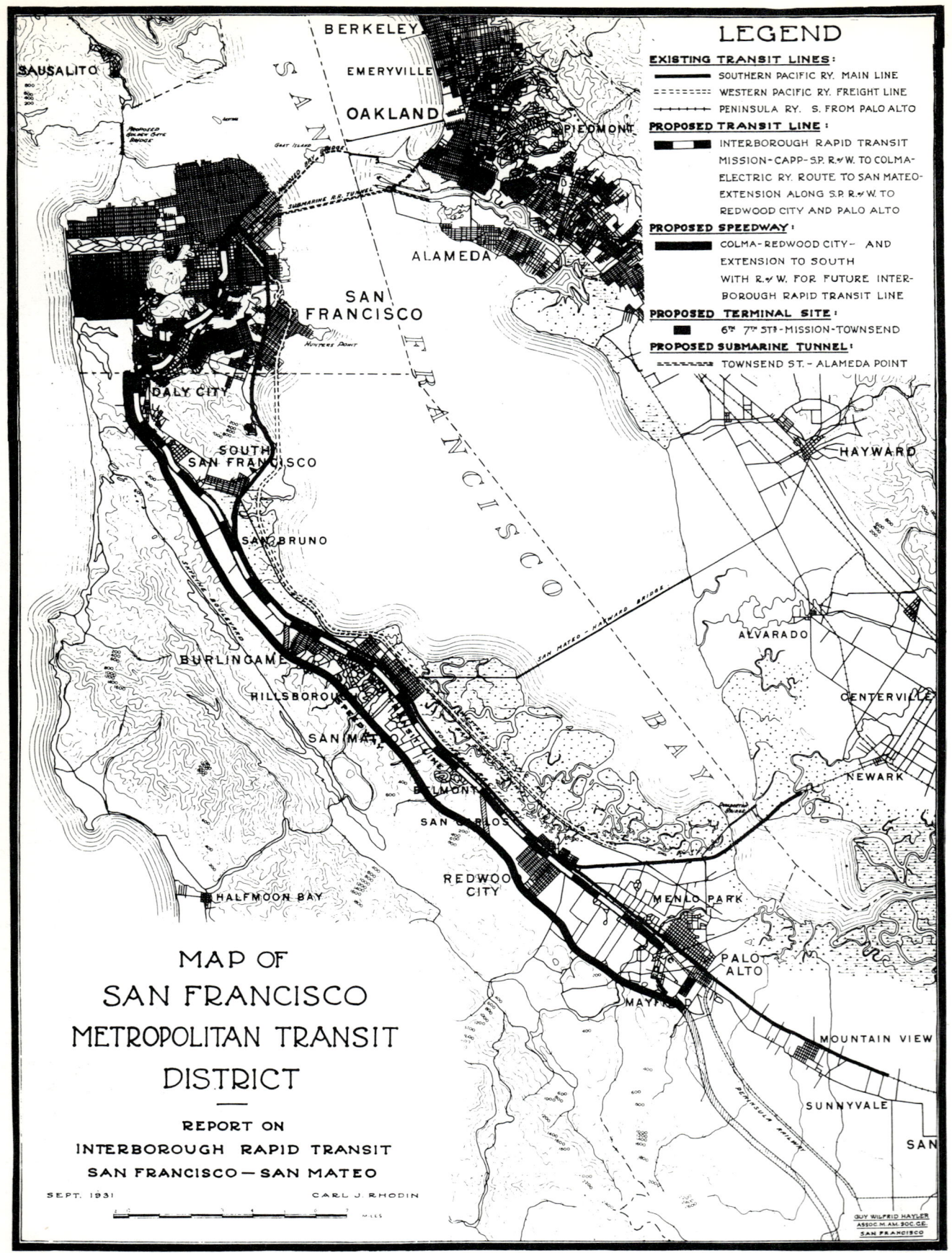

In 1932, the prestigious Commonwealth Club of California made an extensive study of Bay Area transit needs. With remarkable foresight, it was predicted that an electrified railroad from San Francisco to San Jose was needed, and called for a transit tube under the Bay. Much of this has been incorporated by the Bay Area Rapid Transit District (BART). (Courtesy of Commonwealth Club of California)

No. 1237 appears in her Market Street Railway livery of green, White Front, and red Byllesby shield on the side while a string of trippers, or special cars, awaits the crowds returning home after a day at Tanforan Racetrack in 1946. At the lower left corner of 1237's dash is a brass plate indicating that the White Front paint job is a Byllesby patent. The interurbans are gone and the racetrack is now the site of a suburban shopping center. (Tom Gray)

emerged as PAYE cars with lengthened and enclosed platforms, electric heaters, cushioned leather seats (which replaced the old cane-covered seats) and partitions which made them three-compartment cars. The old K-14 controllers were altered to the K-28B type. Despite the notoriety of the Big Subs, the 1225 class cars became symbolic and the best remembered of the cars on the San Mateo interurban.

Unable to meet the demands of the bondholders (a total of $35,577,000 was still outstanding from the various railways involved in the earlier consolidations), the United Railroads filed for reorganization under the California Railroad Commission in 1920. A decision rendered on December 22, 1920 provided for the takeover (which was effected in March of the following year) by a group of prominent San Franciscans headed by Frank B. Anderson, William H. Crocker, Herbert Fleishacker (who served for thirty years as president of Central California Traction), John D. McKee, and E. S. Heller. The new company issued $11,750,000 of prior preference, $5,000,000 of preferred, $4,700,000 of second preferred, and $10,700,000 of common stock, totaling $32,150,000. The name United Railroads then became part of San Francisco's history while the name Market Street Railway was revived. For the next twenty-three years the name Market Street Railway would be proudly borne by the San Mateo interurbans as well as by San Francisco's famed cable cars and other transit equipment.

In November of 1925, control of the Market Street Railway was acquired by the Standard Power & Light Corporation, a subsidiary of the Standard Gas & Electric Company. Management of the Market Street Railway was given to the Byllesby Engineering & Management Corporation.

In 1903, when the 1225 class cars were delivered from the Laclede Car Company, they sported the red paint of the United Railroads. When the Market Street Railway took over on February 16, 1921, the cars received a dark green color. Then in 1926 the Byllesby group experimented with a novel idea in car painting. The cars were painted green but with a pure white front which was illuminated at night by two lamps. So successful was this as a safety feature that all M.S.Ry.'s cars, including the 1225 class, were given the white front paint job. The only exceptions were the Big Subs which were still in storage. In 1927, a patent

By 1947 it was questionable how long the #40 Line would continue. No. 1233 is on the private right-of-way in Milbrae wearing the colors of her last owner, the Municipal Railway. (Tom Gray)

Although the body of No. 1233 is still in good condition in 1947, her eclipse fender shows signs of wear and tear as she rolls through San Bruno toward San Mateo under the Southern Pacific overpass which is under construction. (Tom Gray)

Rounding the curve from San Mateo Drive into Baldwin Avenue in Burlingame in 1947, No. 1241 makes clear who is king of the road! (Tom Gray)

Right, a set of trippers awaits the throng of teenagers about to go home from Burlingame High School in 1947. No. 1241 is in the Muni's blue and gold paint job while the next car behind her sports the Muni's latest style: green and cream with the "wings" painted on the sides. The third car still has the White Front paint minus the dash lamps and the Byllesby shield. (Tom Gray)

Left, after the takeover of the Market Street Railway by the Municipal Railway, several different paint schemes were tried. The most unusual of all was the one given to No. 1232, seen here as she pauses with streetcar No. 939—another ex-M.S. Ry. car—at Holy Cross Cemetery. The dash on No. 1232 is painted gold with a blue point under the center window. The picture was taken in 1948 and while the design didn't last long, the former White Front Cars weren't to last much longer either. (Tom Gray)

On November 29, 1948, No. 1242 rolls southbound in her fifth and final paint scheme—the Muni "wings." Until 1939 Leipsic Junction was the connection for the South San Francisco Line. (San Francisco Municipal Railway)

On November 29, 1948, No. 1233 defiantly passes a bus of the Municipal Railway. Her insolence, however, is to be short-lived, for the buses will replace all electric rail service on Mission Street in less than two months. (San Francisco Municipal Railway)

was granted to Byllesby for the white front scheme, and as long as the Market Street Railway operated, a plaque denoting this appeared on the cars' dashes. The Byllesby colors lasted until the final takeover by the Municipal Railway of San Francisco in 1944. From then until 1949 the cars wore the Muni livery of blue with gold trim and later their final colors of Muni green with cream fronts; the Muni management chose not to purchase rights for use of the white front. Actually, it was city policy at the time not to pay royalties of any kind, and this led to the development of a specific streetcar for the Municipal Railway.

In 1930, beset with increasing operating costs and a need for new cars, a conference of the heads of street railways was held in Chicago. Hence emerged the authorization and funding to develop a new streetcar featuring maximum safety, a quiet, comfortable ride, and adaptable for one- or two-man operation. The result was the P.C.C. (for President's Conference Committee) car which was adopted by many street railways across North America. The conference owned the patent rights, using royalties to finance future developments. Since San Francisco would not pay royalties, a so-called "Magic Carpet" car was built which had the fundamental design features of a P.C.C. car as well as the mechanical ones. By having the builder pay any royalties out of the money received from the city and by not using the P.C.C. name, the Muni Railway was able to avoid the royalty issue. The Magic Carpet cars are all out of service today, and with rare exceptions, the P.C.C. car is the only kind of streetcar left in North America.

The Market Street Railway had toyed with the prospect of using P.C.C.-type cars, but the two-man restriction, as well as financial restrictions stemming from franchise expiration requirements, precluded fulfillment of such dreams.

Under the Municipal Railway ownership came the #40 Line's only experiment with modern, post 1-12 class equipment. Hoping to modernize, the Muni ran one of its Magic Carpet cars down to San Mateo in order to see how a P.C.C. car would fare on that run. Unfortunately, these cars were unsuited to interurban use, and the experiment was not repeated.

The 1225-1244 class cars resumed their monopoly of the #40 Line until they were scrapped by the Muni. No. 1244 was the first victim of the Muni wreckers, in 1947, with 1225 being scrapped the following year. By the end of 1949, the remainder were only a memory.

Two other groups of cars which serviced the #40 Line deserve mention. In 1918, the United Railroads of San Francisco converted three city streetcars for use on the interurban line, Nos. 1715, 1716, and 1722. They served adequately until the completion of the rebuilding of the 1225 class, whereupon they were returned to local service. No. 1722 was involved in a wreck with Big Sub No. 12, however, and was prematurely removed from the line for extensive rebuilding. No. 1722 never did return to the San Mateo run.

For a brief period during World War II, the Market Street Railway experimented with city cars of the 944-994 class, which had been built for one-man operation, on the Daly City to San Mateo segment, but they were never constructed for interurban use and as such proved to be impractical.

Electric power for the San Mateo interurbans was originally supplied from the North Beach power plant to the Millbrae substation (some 85,000 feet) at 13,200 volts. At Millbrae the current was stepped down to 440 volts and then converted to 550 volts d.c. All machinery was of the General Electric type. In the latter years of United Railroad ownership, the railway company ceased generating its own power and thereafter purchased all its electricity from the Pacific Gas & Electric Company, closing down the North Beach powerhouse.

Before we pass from the #40 Line, mention must be made of the cemetery service. The U.R.R. maintained special cars which transported both mourners and the deceased to the cemeteries which were located on the Peninsula in what is now Colma, and for many years the business was so successful that many of the #40 Line cars only went as far as Colma. With the coming of paved roads and automobile hearses, business fell off, and the funeral cars were converted to other uses. The San Francisco-to-cemeteries cars continued, however.

In 1900, San Francisco adopted a new City Charter which contained provisions for eventual municipal ownership of all public utilities. Thus the Municipal Railway, purchasing the Geary Street cable car line and converting it to an electric railway, opened for business in 1912. Later, other franchises were acquired by the Muni until there were only two privately owned systems left—Market Street Railway and the California Street Cable R.R. Co.—and they were both past their financial prime. By 1944, the M.S.Ry. was broke, and the opposition to the bond issues needed to purchase the outfit made a strong case for future bond issues in order to revitalize the entire system. The casandras proved correct, for the postwar years saw the Muni trying to maintain service by substituting motor buses for the former Market Street Railway's dilapidated streetcar network.

By the end of 1948, the avowed policy of San

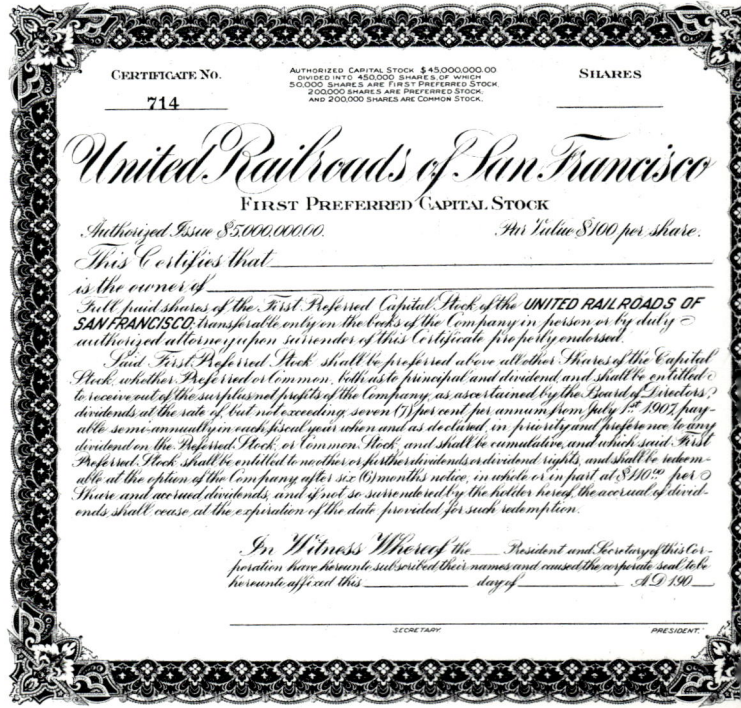

Francisco's city fathers was to convert as many streetcar and cable car lines as possible to bus operation. The #40 Line was doomed: its tracks into San Francisco operated on crowded Mission Street, and plans existed to eliminate the rails on Mission Street altogether. Had the #40 Line had a right-of-way in San Francisco, it may have been retained for its ample ridership. On January 16, 1949, No. 1235, with railfan-motorman Lorin Silleman at the controller, made the last run, putting the finish to the only interurban line ever to operate on the streets of San Francisco.

#40 Line Rolling Stock

In 1891, when electric railways were introduced to the streets of San Francisco by the San Francisco and San Mateo Electric Railroad Company, trolley cars were still very much in their infancy. Carbody design, independent of past performance with horses and cable cars, was still to come into its own. As a consequence, San Francico's first "interurbans" resembled—and actually were shorter than—the cable cars of the California Street line in San Francisco, having an open section on each end with longitudinal seats facing outward and a closed center section with longitudinal seats facing inward. Running parallel to the open sections were running board steps.

These early trolleys did not last long, for in 1900 the S.F. & S.M. E. Ry. ordered new cars from the Hammond Car Company of San Francisco and the St. Louis Car Company. Number 41-50 and 51-70, respectively, they were renumbered when the line was absorbed into the United Railroads of San Francisco. Whereas the first classes of cars on this line never went to San Mateo, the 41-50 class cars were on hand for the inauguration of service between the namesake cities. By no stretch of the imagination, however, can they be classified as true interurban or suburban cars, yet they pioneered interurban service in the San Francisco Bay Area and shall be listed. It should be noted, however, that with the arrival of the suburban-type cars from the Laclede Car Company in 1903 they were relegated to city service.

Today, samples of these early carbodies are extremely rare, and in each case their existence is due more to a curious sequence of events than to any intention to preserve specimens of electric railway history.

Number 0304 is the only original car of the pre-1903 group remaining, and only because between 1905 and 1906 she was converted to a line car by the United Railroads, becoming No. 0304. And after much rebuilding over the years, she is now Municipal Railway No. 0304, still in service, and may be seen on San Francisco's streets from time to time, maintaining the overhead wire for the city's streetcar lines.

Two other cars, while not members of the pre-1903 roster, are representative of the carbodies of the period. One, ex-Presidio & Ferries No. 20, ex-Municipal Railway No. 317, ex-Market Street Railway No. 755, is a single-truck California type, built by Hammond Car Company in 1895. Presently at the California Railway Museum in Rio Vista Junction, California, it is badly in need of restoration.

The last example was on the roster of the Municipal Railway as No. 578. Converted from a passenger carrier to a sand car by the Market Street Railway, it bore the number 0601. A single-truck California type built in 1895, it was restored to its original condition by the Municipal Railway in 1956, and today is preserved at the California Railway Museum.

San Francisco & San Mateo Electric Railway Company Cars

1-14 Class

Builder: Hammond
Year: 1891
Length: 26'
Motors: Two 15 h.p.; S.R.G.
Controllers: Rheostat
Trucks: McGuire, single
Body: California type, wood

Cars scrapped prior to 1902.

Builder: Hammond
Year: 1891
Length: 28'
Motors: Two Walker W.P. 50, 25 h.p.
Controllers: K 2
Trucks: McGuire, double
Body: California type, wood

Builder: Hammond
Year: September, 1894
Motors: Two G.E. 800; 25 h.p.
Controllers: K
Trucks: Brill 21-E, single
Body: California type, wood

Builder: Hammond
Year: 1898
Motors: Two G.E. 52, 27½ h.p.
Controllers: K 10
Trucks: Brill 21-A, single
Body: California type

Builder: Hammond
Year: March, 1900
Length: 29'6"
Weight: 32,720 lbs.
Motors: Two G.E. 58, 37½ h.p. (8 cars); four G.E. 58, 37½ h.p. (2 cars)
Controller: K 10; H 19
Trucks: McGuire 39, double
Body: California type, wood, railroad-type roof

Builder: St. Louis Car Company
Year: 1901
Length: 44'8"
Motors: Four G.E. 58; 37 ½ h.p.
Controllers: B 19
Trucks: McGuire 39, double
Body: California type, wood

Motors: Two S.R.G.; 15 h.p.
Controllers: Rheostat
Trucks: McGuire, single

Builder: S.F. & S.M. E. Ry. Shops
Year: 1900
Motors: Two W.P. 50; 25 h.p.
Controller: K 2
Trucks: McGuire, single

15-27 Class
Some were sold to other companies: Reno Traction Co., 2; Humboldt Transit Co., Eureka, 6; East Shore & Suburban Railway, 1; San Jose-Los Gatos Interurban Railway, 2; rest were scrapped in 1905.

28-33 Class
Renumbered by U.R.R. into 601-637 group. Sold to San Jose in 1905.

34-37 Class
Renumbered by U.R.R. into 601-637 group. Sold to San Jose in 1905.

41-50 Class
Seated 30. Renumbered by U.R.R. to 671-680 in 1902. One car was sold to Mt. Olivet Cemetery Association, No. 2 in 1906. One car was sold to Reno Traction Co., No. 3 in 1906. One car was sold to South San Francisco Railway & Power Company, No. 45. Two cars were rebuilt to U.R.R. mail cars "D" and "E" and were lost in 1906 fire. Four cars were rebuilt by U.R.R. in 1918 and renumbered 727-730; scrapped in 1927. The last car was rebuilt to Line Car No. 0304 and today is on the roster of Municipal Railway as No. 0304.

51-70 Class
Fifty seats. Renumbered 681-698 by U.R.R. No. 67 was rebuilt in 1902 to U.R.R. Funeral Car No. 2; rebuilt to U.R.R. Private Party Car *Sierra* in 1908. U.R.R. No. 696 was rebuilt in 1907 to Wrecker No. 0507; retired by Municipal Railway June 15, 1956. No. 698 was renumbered 696 in 1915 when the class underwent rebuilding. Cars scrapped in 1926-1927.

Freight Car

Sprinkler

Trucks: Arch bar, double

Funeral Car
Named *Cypress Lawn*. Originally a trailer, it had to be towed by a work car until motorized by U.R.R. in 1901 and renumber Funeral Car No. 1. Out of service by 1908.

United Railroads Cars

1-12 Class

Builder: St. Louis Car Company
Year: 1906
Length: 52'11"
Weight: 75,640 lbs.
Motors: Four G.E. 73; 75 h.p.
Gear Ratio: 21:54
Controller: C6K
Trucks: 61A, St. Louis; 34" wheels
Body: Double end, wood, railroad roof

Known as "Big Subs." Seated 56. Sisters to Sacramento Northern's 106-109. All cars in storage in 1923. Nos. 2, 3, 6, 7, 9, and 11 were destroyed in 1933. Remainder destroyed in 1935. These cars never received the patented white front paint scheme.

1225-1244 Class

Builder: Laclede Car Company
Year: 1903
Length: 48'1"
Weight: 56,138 lbs.
Motors: Four G.E. 57; 50 h.p.
Gear Ratio: 22:63
Controller: K 14
Trucks: Brill 27E; 33" wheels
Body: Double end, steel, deck roof

Seated 40. Rebuilt in 1920s to enclosed and longer platforms, three sections, electric heaters, original wicker seats replaced with leather, and K 28 controllers. When outshopped, the cars had ribbed sides; rebuilt to straight steel sides in 1930s. No. 1225 was scrapped by Muni Ry. in 1948. No. 1226 was scrapped in 1944 by M.S.Ry. after a wreck at Tanforan. Nos. 1227-1238, 1241-1243 were scrapped by Muni Ry. in 1949. No. 1239 was destroyed in a wreck at Holy Cross Cemetery prior to World War II. No. 1240 was destroyed in a wreck at the corner of New Montgomery and Mission Streets, San Francisco, when she collided with a truckload of marble before World War II.

Market Street Railway Cars

944-994 Class

Builder: Market Street Railway
Year: 1931-1933
Length 47'0"
Weight: 45,840 lbs; 47,860 lbs.
Motors: Four G.E. 90; 50 h.p.
Gear Ratio: 19:67
Trucks: Brill 27 G.E.2
Controllers: K 28
Body: Double end, wood and steel, arch roof

These were city cars which had been converted to one-man operation. They ran only during 1943 and 1944 and at that only between Daly City and San Mateo. They were unsuited for interurban-type running and were returned to other lines.

1715, 1716, 1722 Class

Builder: United Railroads of San Francisco
Year: 1818
Length: 46′6″
Motors: Four G.E. 57; 50 h.p.
Gear Ratio: 22:63
Controllers: K28-B
Trucks: McGuire 10-A
Body: California type, arch roof, double end

Originally members of 1550-1749 class of the U.R.R., they were outshopped by the St. Louis Car Co. in 1906-1907. Between 1915 and 1918, three cars of this class, Nos. 1690, 1722, and 1745, were involved in bad wrecks and had to undergo extensive rebuilding. In 1918, they emerged from Elkton Shops of U.R.R. as Nos. 1715 (ex-1690), 1716 (ex-1745), and 1722. They were assigned to the #40 Line, where they remained until completion of a rebuilding program on the 1225 class. No. 1722 was damaged in a wreck with Big Sub No. 12 on March 31, 1918, necessitating another rebuilding. It was then returned to city lines. No. 1715 was scrapped by Muni Ry. in 1948; Nos. 1716, 1722 scrapped by Muni Ry. in 1949. Seated 44. On rare occasions, other cars of the 1550-1749 class would be seen on the #40 Line, but usually only as far as the cemeteries.

Municipal Railway of San Francisco Cars

1001-1005 Class

Builder: St. Louis Car Company
Year: 1939
Length: 50′5″
Weight: 35,600 lbs.
Motors: Westinghouse 306 CA
Controllers: 1001, 1002, and 1004 had G.E. controls while the rest had Westinghouse controls.
Body: double end, steel, arch roof, P.C.C. style

These so-called "Magic Carpet" cars of the Municipal Railway were only used on the #40 Line once, and that was on an experimental basis; the experiment was a failure, and the 1001-1005 class cannot be considered a good representative of an interurban car. Seated 60 passengers. No. 1003 is at the California Railway Museum at Rio Vista Junction, California.

Chapter Five
The Four Rail Tracks

The Northwestern Pacific

The very name of the Northwestern Pacific conjures up diverse recollections—the narrow gauge steam trains to the Russian River, those million-dollar manifests of lumber which roll down the Northern California coast, the magnificent ferryboat *Eureka*, the name train *Redwood*, and those ever-efficient high speed electric interurbans which carried commuters over southern Marin County for thirty-eight years. Beloved, cherished, and missed, but not patronized enough at the last to satisfy parent Southern Pacific, the interurbans form the basis of this chapter.

The N.W.P. was in itself a creation for the convenience of the Santa Fe and the Southern Pacific. Their joint ownership meant the end of the haggling and the acquisition of smaller roads in their breakneck competition to provide train service to the northern coastal regions of California. Service was begun on January 8, 1907, as the final merger of the Petaluma & Haystack R.R., North Pacific Coast, North Shore R.R., San Francisco & North Pacific R.R., California Northwestern Railway, Eel River & Eureka, Eureka & Klamath River, Oregon & Eureka, San Rafael & San Quentin, Sonoma Valley Prismoidal Railway, and the Sonoma Valley Railroad.

In 1902, predecessor North Pacific Coast Railway was one of the most accident-prone railroads in the history of California railroading. Washouts, ferryboat sinkings, faulty track, train wrecks, and the short end of damage suits kept this narrow gauge steam road in a seemingly continuous state of corporate reorganization. At about the same time that the North Pacific Coast directors were to become the latest in a long line of ownerships to toss in the towel, the phenomenon of electrically powered railways was proving to be more than simply the vision of geniuses such as Thomas A. Edison and Frank J. Sprague.

Thus it was not hard for one John Martin to conceive of the electrification of the N.P.C.R.R. Martin was already well known for his work in the construction of high voltage transmission lines over long distances—an absolute essential for an electrified railroad. Martin, be it noted, was traveling in expensive company and this group paid a healthy price for the road, a price accepted with the utmost alacrity by a group of owners who couldn't wait to unload what they considered a financial turkey. Martin's associates included R. R. Colgate, the soap tycoon, William M. Preison, R. M. Hotaling, C. A. Grow, and Eugene J. deSalba, a magnate of the Bay Counties Power Company. John Martin himself had headed the latter.

The first order of business for Martin and associates was to change the railroad's name from North Pacific Coast Railroad to North Shore Railroad. The second was to select a new board of directors and executives. Those chosen were: William M. Rank, general manager; E. L. Braswell, superintendent; O. E. Griffin, auditor; S. F. Alden, general freight and passenger agent; A. H. Babcock, electrical engineer; B. H. Fisher, engineer of ways and structures; F. A. Stevens, master mechanic; W. W. Mason, Jr., carhouse foreman; and George E. Heintz, freight and passenger agent. John Martin headed the company as president while Eugene J. deSalba became vice-president. The new executives of the North Shore Railroad did not come without impressive credentials. Alden was a highly recommended eastern traffic agent, Griffin was a member of the accounting department of the Southern Pacific, Fisher had served with the Oakland streetcar lines, and Mason had come from the Boston Elevated Railway Company.

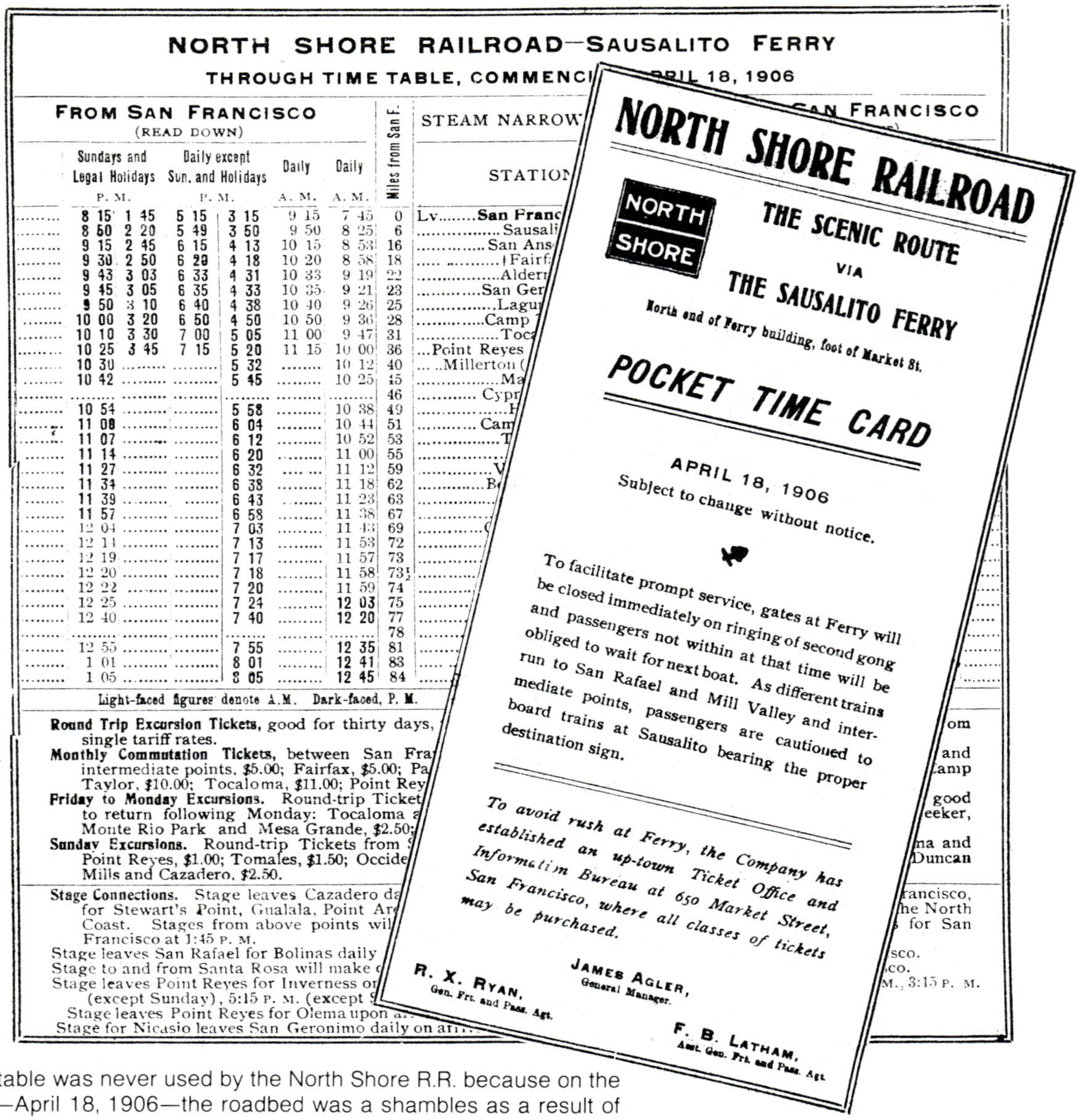

NORTH SHORE RAILROAD—SAUSALITO FERRY

THROUGH TIME TABLE, COMMENC[...] APRIL 18, 1906

FROM SAN FRANCISCO (READ DOWN)

	Sundays and Legal Holidays P. M.		Daily except Sun. and Holidays P. M.		Daily A. M.	Daily A. M.	Miles from San F.	STEAM NARROW[...] STATION[...]
....	8 15	1 45	5 15	3 15	9 15	7 45	0	Lv........San Franc[...]
....	8 50	2 20	5 49	3 50	9 50	8 25	6	................Sausali[...]
....	9 15	2 45	6 15	4 13	10 15	8 53	16	..............San Ans[...]
....	9 30	2 50	6 20	4 18	10 20	8 58	18	....†Fairf[...]
....	9 43	3 03	6 33	4 31	10 33	9 19	22	................Alderr[...]
....	9 45	3 05	6 35	4 33	10 35	9 21	23	.............San Ger[...]
....	9 50	3 10	6 40	4 38	10 40	9 26	25	...............Lagu[...]
....	10 00	3 20	6 50	4 50	10 50	9 36	28	..............Camp [...]
....	10 10	3 30	7 00	5 05	11 00	9 47	31	..................Toca[...]
....	10 25	3 45	7 15	5 20	11 15	10 00	36	...Point Reyes [...]
....	10 30	....	....	5 32	....	10 12	40	... ..Millerton ([...]
....	10 42	....	....	5 45	....	10 25	45	..................Ma[...]
....	....	....	....	....	....	....	46	.... Cypr[...]
....	10 54	....	....	5 58	....	10 38	49	..................H[...]
....	11 08	....	....	6 04	....	10 44	51	.... Cam[...]
....	11 07	....	....	6 12	....	10 52	53	..................T[...]
....	11 14	....	....	6 20	....	11 00	55	....
....	11 27	....	....	6 32	....	11 12	59	...............V[...]
....	11 34	....	....	6 38	....	11 18	62	..............B[...]
....	11 39	....	....	6 43	....	11 23	63	....
....	11 57	....	....	6 58	....	11 38	67	....
....	12 04	....	....	7 03	....	11 43	69	..............C[...]
....	12 14	....	....	7 13	....	11 53	72	....
....	12 19	....	....	7 17	....	11 57	73	....
....	12 20	....	....	7 18	....	11 58	73½	....
....	12 22	....	....	7 20	....	11 59	74	....
....	12 25	....	....	7 24	....	12 03	75	....
....	12 40	....	....	7 40	....	12 20	77	....
....	....	....	....	....	....	....	78	....
....	12 55	....	....	7 55	....	12 35	81	....
....	1 01	....	....	8 01	....	12 41	83	....
....	1 05	....	....	8 05	....	12 45	84	....

Light-faced figures denote A.M. Dark-faced, P. M.

Round Trip Excursion Tickets, good for thirty days, [...] single tariff rates.
Monthly Commutation Tickets, between San Fra[...] intermediate points, $5.00; Fairfax, $5.00; Pa[...] Taylor, $10.00; Tocaloma, $11.00; Point Rey[...]
Friday to Monday Excursions. Round-trip Ticket[...] to return following Monday: Tocaloma a[...] Monte Rio Park and Mesa Grande, $2.50;[...]
Sunday Excursions. Round-trip Tickets from S[...] Point Reyes, $1.00; Tomales, $1.50; Occide[...] Mills and Cazadero, $2.50.

Stage Connections. Stage leaves Cazadero da[...] for Stewart's Point, Gualala, Point Ar[...] Coast. Stages from above points wil[...] Francisco at 1:45 P. M.
Stage leaves San Rafael for Bolinas daily [...]
Stage to and from Santa Rosa will make c[...]
Stage leaves Point Reyes for Inverness or[...] (except Sunday), 5:15 P. M. (except S[...]
Stage leaves Point Reyes for Olema upon a[...]
Stage for Nicasio leaves San Geronimo daily on arr[...]

[...]AN FRANCISCO

[...]om [...] and [...]amp [...] good [...]eeker, [...]na and [...]Duncan [...]rancisco, [...]he North [...] for San [...]sco. [...]sco. [...]M., 3:15 P. M.

NORTH SHORE RAILROAD

NORTH SHORE

THE SCENIC ROUTE

VIA

THE SAUSALITO FERRY

North end of Ferry building, foot of Market St.

POCKET TIME CARD

APRIL 18, 1906

Subject to change without notice.

To facilitate prompt service, gates at Ferry will be closed immediately on ringing of second gong and passengers not within at that time will be obliged to wait for next boat. As different trains run to San Rafael and Mill Valley and intermediate points, passengers are cautioned to board trains at Sausalito bearing the proper destination sign.

To avoid rush at Ferry, the Company has established an up-town Ticket Office and Information Bureau at 650 Market Street, San Francisco, where all classes of tickets may be purchased.

R. X. RYAN, Gen. Frt. and Pass. Agt.

JAMES AGLER, General Manager.

F. B. LATHAM, Asst. Gen. Frt. and Pass. Agt.

This rare timetable was never used by the North Shore R.R. because on the date of issue—April 18, 1906—the roadbed was a shambles as a result of California's most famous earthquake. (Fred P. Codoni Collection)

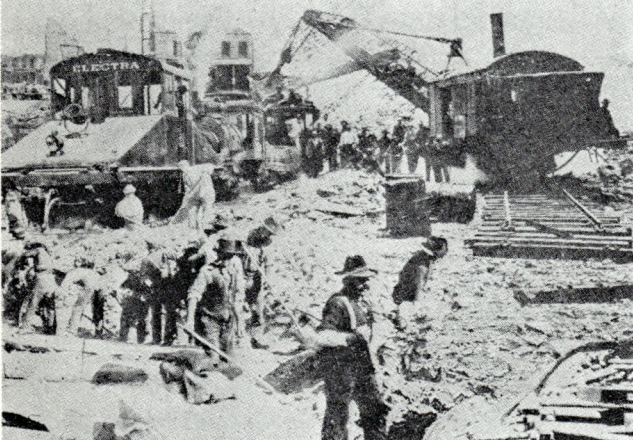

This 1906 vintage postcard shows North Shore R.R. steeple cab *Electra* busy at work in San Francisco cleaning up the wreckage of the Fire and 'Quake.

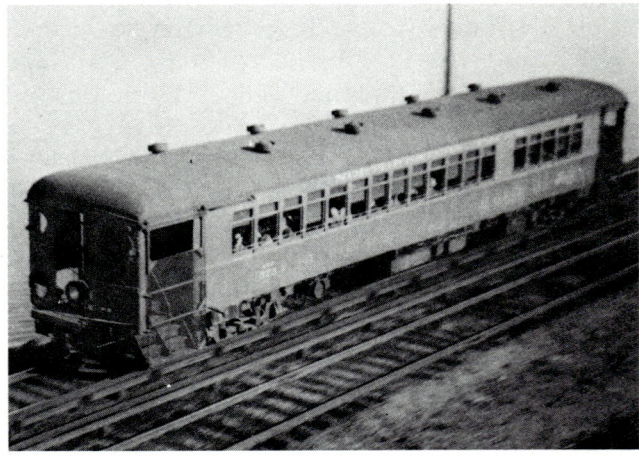

Speeding along the shoreline of Richardson Bay, N.W.P. No. 375 is serving as a one-car train. (Stephen D. Maguire Collection)

A three-car consist which included a baggage-express motor was not unusual for the N.W.P. The tracks to the right are for steam operations. (Stephen D. Maguire Collection)

Long on talent and enthusiasm, the new group of owners set about on the third and fourth orders of business, namely to raise cash and modernize the road. On May Day of 1902 the cash was raised from the Mercantile Trust Company of San Francisco in the form of a $6,000,000 loan, repayable at six percent interest in forty years. Two and one-half million was earmarked for improvements.

In order to electrify, several factors had to be considered. The major one was that all trackage and rolling stock were narrow gauge while a decision had been rendered to convert to standard gauge, double track. Initially, to accomplish this, two additional rails were added to each track. One rail (an original narrow gauge rail) became the electrified, or "third rail," which would carry the current. Then another rail was laid to accommodate the standard gauge trains. Therefore, for some time to come, it was not uncommon to see standard gauge locomotives pulling narrow gauge cars over the same tracks which were also shared by the third rail interurbans. The narrow gauge was finally abandoned on August 21, 1929.

This railroad, which became the first third rail electric railway in California, was built with sixty-pound rail and mounted on eight-foot by six-inch by eight-inch redwood ties, spaced two feet center to center. For the contact rail, more than one-half was sixty-pound rail with the remainder being the fifty-six-pound rail which had been used for the narrow gauge. On most of the road

This five-car train is probably a school tripper serving Tamalpais High School in Mill Valley. (Stephen D. Maguire Collection)

the contact rail was mounted on wooden insulators, and every precaution was taken to prevent accidental electrocution arising from contact with it by the use of wooden covers, cattle guards, and signs. In spite of these precautions, accidents did occur. At San Rafael, one lad accepted a dare from his playmates to step on the rail and was nearly killed.

Newspapers in San Francisco and Marin County reported from time to time that animals were being electrocuted by the third rail. Perhaps the most noteworthy was the incident which appeared in the Marin County *Journal* on May 11, 1905, which read:

"A bull wandered away from some ranch and began hunting trouble. He knocked out the fence in jig time

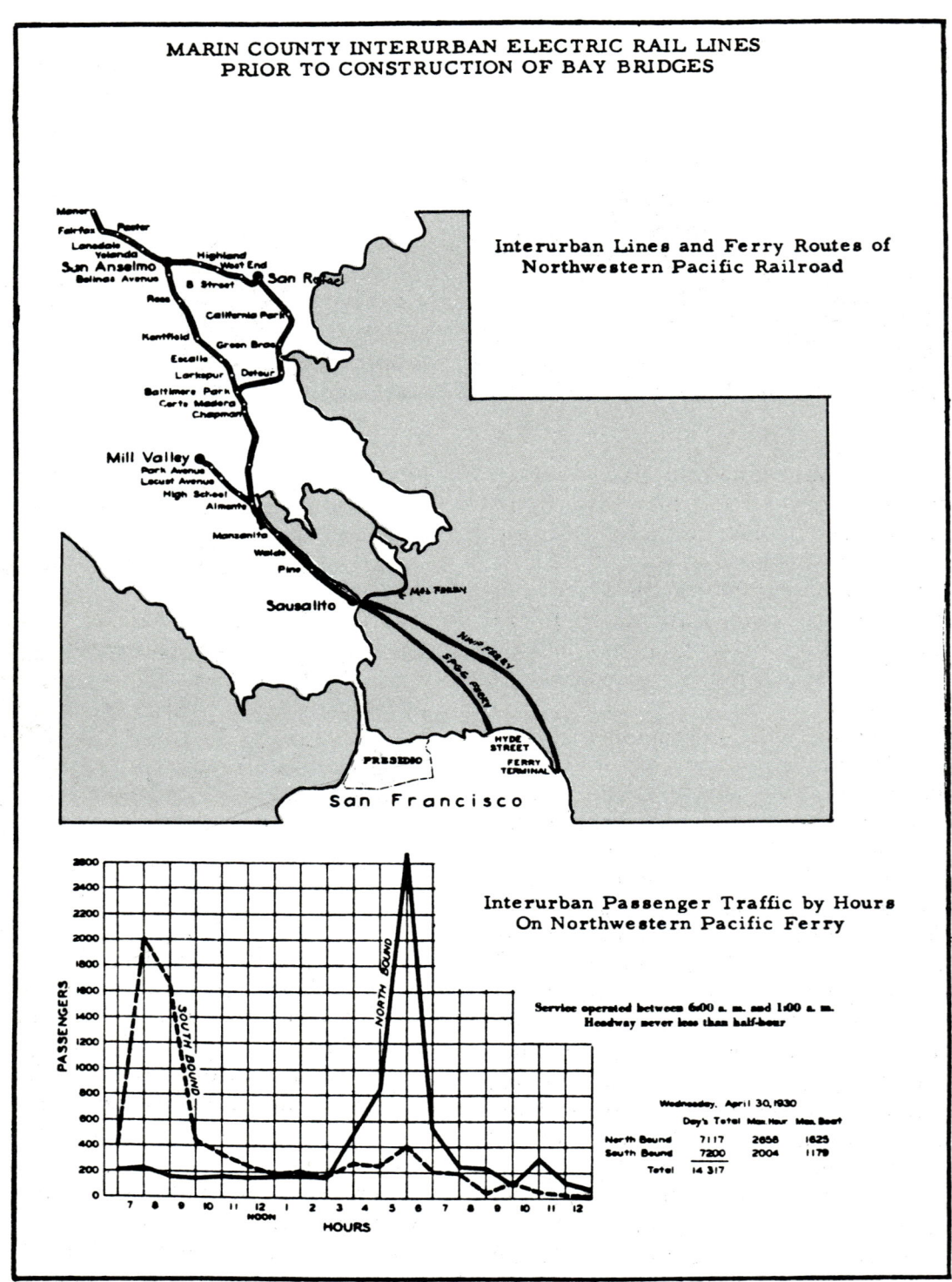

This chart demonstrates the ridership of the N.W.P.'s interurban service in 1930. (Courtesy of the Golden Gate Bridge, Highway and Transportation District)

and found himself on the railroad track. Here the third rail loomed up before him. He lowered his head and charged. A cloud of hair and smoke rose into the air and mister bull went down for the count.

"He took his time about getting up. When he did he rushed again. Once more he hit the gravel. These tactics were repeated about four times, when the rail succeeded in killing and almost incinerating the animal. This act took place about a quarter mile from West End Station [sic]."

The electric interurbans began service with an inaugural run in the evening of August 19, 1903. The first revenue trip began on the Sausalito-Mill Valley run on August 21, 1903, to be followed by the Sausalito-San Rafael run two months later on October 17.

It had been anticipated that the San Rafael-San Quentin trackage would be electrified, but instead the run was discontinued on November 1, 1903, later to be revived using steam trains.

The Alto powerhouse, located approximately midway between Sausalito and San Anselmo, was the main source of power to run the railroad, with substations at San Anselmo and San Rafael. The N.W.P. received three phase current at 50,000 volts from the Bay Counties Transmission Company, transformed it down to 4,500 volts, and converted it to 550 volts d.c. for interurban usage. As both a reserve and an auxiliary, a steam engine was installed at Alto to drive the generators. Further, at Alto there was a storage battery consisting of 288 type G-15 chloride cells with a discharge capacity of 560 amperes per hour, and a capacity for fluctuating work fifty percent greater. At San Rafael the substation was set up with a 225-kw., 550-volt General Electric direct current generator. Originally a storage battery house, the San Anselmo substation was remodeled in 1908 and the batteries were removed and the building enlarged. Two 550-kw. generators were installed in place of the batteries. In January of 1912, another 500-kw. generator was placed in operation at San Anselmo.

In April of 1904, Edward H. Harriman of the Southern Pacific purchased the North Shore Railroad, taking all 60,000 shares of stock for an estimated $800,000, much to the relief of Martin and associates who had poured thousands of dollars into the railroad, only to see their money disappear as water on the sands of the desert.*
In spite of the 1902 loan, a ten percent assessment had to be levied against the stockholders in order to continue operations. Harriman's motives must have been tied in with his purchase of the long-time rival to the North Shore (and predecessor North Pacific Coast Railroad), the California Northwestern Railway. The San Francisco and North Pacific Railroad had always been standard gauge and when A. W. Foster and associates took control on March 23, 1893, it was reorganized into the California Northwestern Railway. In 1903, Foster sold the C.N.W. to Harriman, but stayed on as president.

During the week of August 11, 1904, A. W. Foster was made president of the North Shore, thus giving him managerial control of not only the N.S.R.R., but the C.N.W. as well. On June 8, 1905, James Agler was named general manager of both railroads, virtually uniting the two. The Atcheson, Topeka & Santa Fe had at one time

*The $800,000 figure is Wald Sievers'; see *N.W.P. Narrow Gauge* in bibliography. Gilbert H. Kneiss in *Redwood Railways* gave a figure of $100,000. Considering the precarious financial picture of the N.S.R.R. at any given time, it is probable that Kneiss's estimate is more reliable.

This four-car train is running from Manor to Sausalito on November 14, 1937, with what by now is pretty old equipment. (Stephen D. Maguire Collection)

Above, passenger-baggage combo No. 504 heads a train at the old West End Station at "G" Street in San Rafael. (Randolph Brandt Collection)

been interested in purchasing the North Shore, and even held an option for its purchase, which it had allowed to lapse in hopes of extending its trackage southward from Eureka instead.

On November 24, 1906, the Santa Fe and the Espee conferred and a jointly owned holding company emerged, which was to affect consolidation of all Santa Fe and Espee trackage on California's north coast. The holding company was known as the Northwestern Pacific Railroad, with Captain A. H. Payson from the Santa Fe as President and James Agler from the Southern Pacific as General Manager, later succeeded by Warren S. Palmer, general superintendent of the S.P.

In 1929 the Santa Fe sold its interest in the Northwestern Pacific to the Southern Pacific, and today the N.W.P. remains not only a subsidiary of the parent road, but a mainstay of freight service from Eureka to the N.W.P.-S.P. interchange at Schellville, albeit minus the electric interurbans.*

*At the same time, full control of the N.W.P. by the S.P. initiated a successful application with the Interstate Commerce Commission to abandon the narrow gauge section.

In 1907, the Northwestern Pacific's tracks had four rails: the outside rail for carrying electric power for the interurbans, rails for the standard gauge steam and electric trains and an inside rail for the narrow gauge steam train. (Marin County Historical Society)

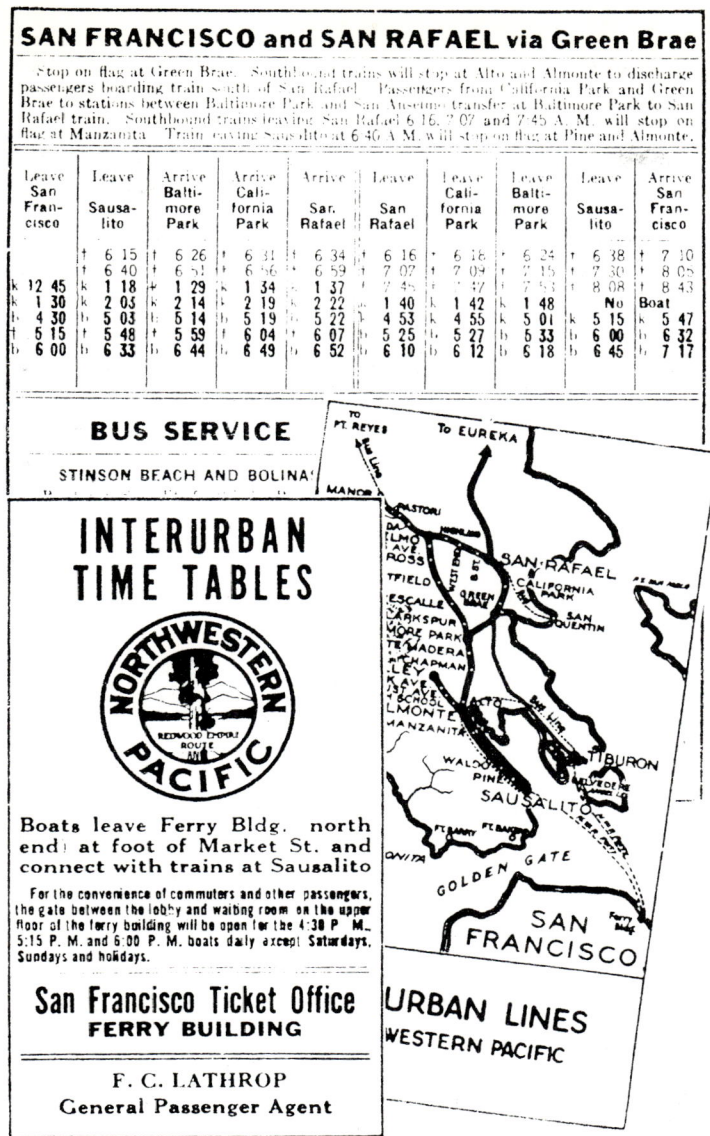

Lines, and ex-No. 254, together with her Bay Area sisters, bore Metropolitan Coach Lines on her signboards. On Sunday, April 9, 1961, ex-No. 254 had the dubious honor of making the last run (Los Angeles to Long Beach), signifying the end of the Big Red Cars in Southern California and of all interurbans in the Golden State.

The Northwestern Pacific's wooden cars never combined runs with the big steel and aluminum cars, largely due to differences in motors and controllers, and, interestingly, the Northwestern Pacific never used the electrics for freight duties, other than baggage, R.P.O. mail, and express. Freight came under the purview of N.W.P. steam operations.

Note should be made of the title of ownership of the N.W.P.'s cars. While the railway owned the old wooden cars, the latter day steel and aluminum cars from St. Louis belonged to the parent railroad, Southern Pacific, as part of that road's roster of trust equipment which was shifted from subsidiary railroad to subsidiary railroad as needs arose.

In addition to the commute runs, for many years the N.W.P. provided rail connections with the Mt. Tamalpais and Muir Woods Scenic Railway, known to its riders as the "Crookedest Railroad in the World." The reference was not to its reputation but rather to the circuitous wind-

Full control by the Espee brought about a general upgrading of equipment, highlighted by the purchase of the seventeen steel cars from St. Louis. Built to the same proportions as the Southern Pacific (later Interurban Electric Railway) cars in Alameda County, these 111,200-pound leviathans released many older cars for retirement. The massive size of these cars was such that when they were transferred to the Pacific Electric Railway (another S.P. subsidiary) in Los Angeles after cessation of interurban operations in Marin County, they quickly earned the nickname "The Blimps." Northwestern Pacific trailer No. 254 was one of those Blimps, and was renumbered Pacific Electric 4516, later P.E. 303. On October 1, 1953, the Pacific Electric's passenger operations were sold to Metropolitan Coach

This is the only time any rolling stock from Marin County's interurban service was seen with a trolley pole while under North Shore or Northwestern Pacific ownership. In need of motive power for debris clearance after the Fire and Earthquake, the *Electra* was fitted out with the pole and set to work in San Francisco. Here *Electra* is assisted by Western Meat Co. steam loco No. 1. Shortly afterward, this 500 H.P. steeple cab will find herself in Los Angeles as Pacific Electric Ry. No. 1544. Today she is on display in Griffith Park, Los Angeles.

The old Mill Valley Station of the N.W.P. about 1910. (Charles A. Smallwood Collection)

The new Mill Valley Station, with No. 377 waiting for a return trip, survived the interurbans and Greyhound's suburban lines and now serves patrons of the Golden Gate Bridge, Highway, and Transportation District's buses. Behind No. 377 is where the rails of the Mt. Tamalpais & Muir Woods Railway once were. (Charles A Smallwood)

During the 1920s the N.W.P. modernized all of its suburban stations, and the new West End Station in San Rafael is a far cry from the wooden shed shown earlier. (Charles A. Smallwood)

ings of its track, as it traveled a roller coaster-type course up to the summit of Mt. Tamalpais where a breathtaking view of San Francisco Bay was afforded the visitor, accompanied by a fashionable restaurant for refreshment.

The death knell for the combined railroad-ferryboat operations came in 1937 with the opening of the Golden Gate Bridge, linking San Francisco with Marin County. The ferryboat business was the hardest hit, for now San Franciscans, as well as Marin County commuters, had direct access to the two counties without waiting in long lines for the ferries in Sausalito which met the interurbans. Of added significance, the new bridge also rendered the automobile-carrying ferries unnecessary.

Disenchanted with breakdowns on older equipment as well as an earnest policy of the parent road to eliminate the money-losing commuter lines, the public flocked to its automobiles in such increasing numbers that the California Railroad Commission issued Decision No. 33103 on May 21, 1940. Simply stated, this decision permitted abandonment of the interurban-ferryboat services, and on February 28, 1941, the gallant electrics which had served southern Marin County for so many years were abandoned, and the southern terminal of Northwestern Pacific passenger operations was shifted from Sausalito to San Rafael.

In 1972, the Northwestern Pacific Railroad ended all train service between Sausalito and San Rafael and today that unused section of right-of-way (which is adjacent to Highway 101) is being sought as a right-of-way for commuter bus operations.

The combination interurban and ferry services were replaced by Greyhound buses over the Golden Gate Bridge, and today much of the same service in southern Marin is provided by the Golden Gate Bridge, Highway, and Transportation District, but Marin residents long for the days of the fast, pollution-free, and efficient trains which sped them from Sausalito to Mill Valley in ten minutes (as an example) while the bus today makes the same run in twenty-three minutes. Some call this "progress."

Northwestern Pacific Rolling Stock

There were but two basic groups of rolling stock on the Marin County interurbans: The old wooden cars and the massive steel and aluminum cars which were delivered in 1929-30. The wooden cars themselves could be divided into two sub-groups: First, the ancient narrow gauge coaches which dated as far back as 1885 and were converted to standard gauge electrics by the North Shore R.R., and the second generation of wooden cars ordered from the carbuilders between 1902 and 1908 during the period of modernization and electrification. To outward appearances, however, both subgroups were the same and only minor modifications distinguished them. Since their fundamental design was that of a railroad passenger car, their appearance prompts a non-railfan to ask where the locomotive was. Indeed, a lineup at Sausalito of both steam and juice trains showed little variation between the consists.

The reader is asked to note that carbuilding is generally influenced by the architecture of the age. For example, railroad cars of the Victorian era were ornate, with colored glass in the celestory windows, and endowed with gilt and wood-carving inside. Contemporary rapid transit vehicles tend toward sweeping, graceful lines, wide windows, and maximum use of aluminum and glass. Hardware and interior fixtures are no exception.

All the wooden cars had railroad-type roofs, and enclosed vestibules were found only in the combos and the express, baggage, and mail

As passengers disembarked from the ferryboats in Sausalito, they walked over to the trains which would take them to points north, either by interurban or by steam. (Marin County Historical Society)

Passenger-baggage combo No. 356 was one of a number of wooden cars which were retired from active service in 1932. (Charles A. Smallwood)

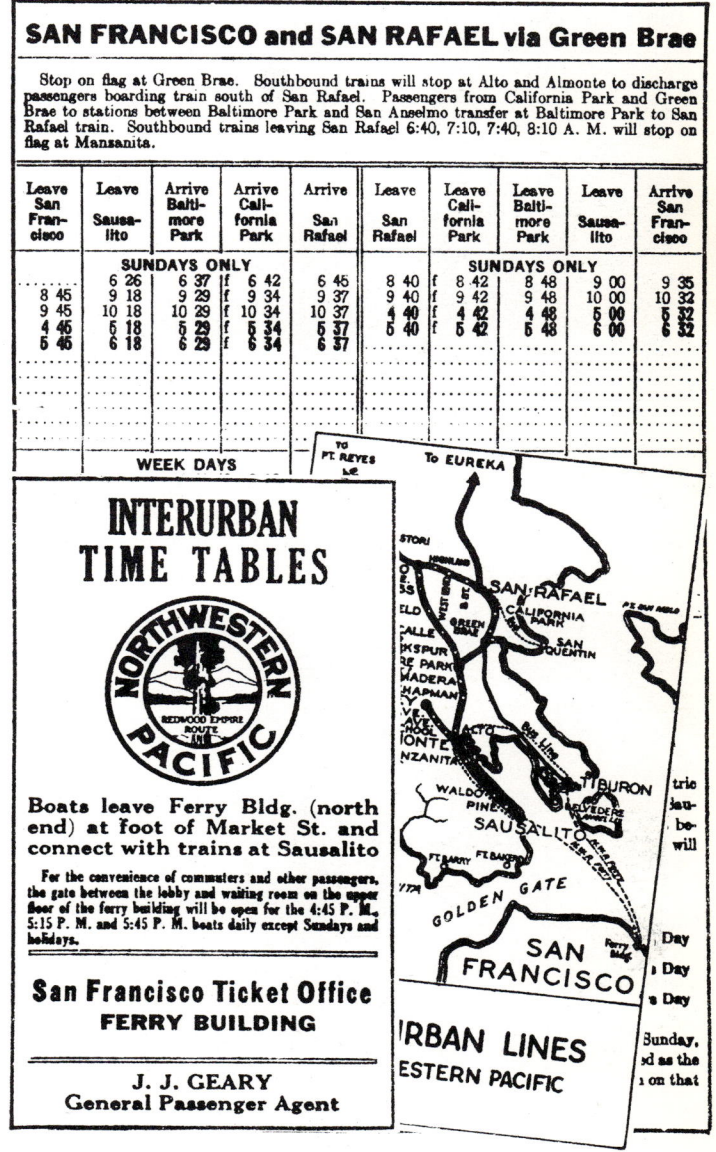

Possessing none of the stately configurations of her wooden predecessors, this N.W.P. coach is nonetheless a striking figure as she rolls into San Anselmo on November 13, 1939. While the roof design of the wooden cars was known as "railroad" roof, the steel and aluminum cars had "turtle," or "arch," roofs. (Charles A. Smallwood)

A string of venerable wooden coaches heading for San Anselmo and Manor passes through Baltimore Park on November 13, 1939. Located between Corte Madera and Larkspur, Baltimore Park served as the junction for the branch to San Rafael via Greenbrae. (Charles A. Smallwood)

A single-car train entering San Anselmo upon its return from Manor. Ability to operate in either single or multiple units gave the interurbans a versatility which steam locomotive-powered trains did not possess on short runs. (Charles A. Smallwood)

When the Southern Pacific abandoned its interurban service in Portland, Oregon, some of the cars found their way to the Northwestern Pacific roster. They were not, however, to be used in interurban service, but as trailers for the gas-electric cars on the mainline. Later they were used in the steam service. They were all returned to the Espee's roster on November 1, 1936. (Charles A. Smallwood)

Below, baggage-express combo No. 370 is at the point of a three-car train rolling over the Greenbrae Trestle and about to enter the Greenbrae Tunnel to emerge in San Rafael. The trestle and tunnel remain to this day, though rarely used by the N.W.P. (Charles A. Smallwood)

In 1939 Kentfield had not changed much from the days when the N.W.P. offered a wooden station and four-rail tracks. The automobile and the Golden Gate Bridge would soon put an end to the interurbans. (Roy Graves photo/Marin County Historical Society Collection)

motor; the passenger motors and trailers had short outside platforms. The wooden cars were powered by two General Electric 66 motors, each having 125 horsepower. The motors were mounted on Hedley trucks with four and one-half-inch journals and thirty-five-inch wheels. Each car had a rolling truck with four-inch by seven-inch journals and thirty-three-inch wheels, except for passenger motors 330, 333, 334, and 335 which used Baldwin trucks. All motorized cars with the exception of the 1929-30 cars used either one or two General Electric C6K controllers, depending upon whether or not the car was single- or double-ended.

In 1930, the N.W.P. inherited nine steel interurban cars from the Southern Pacific's abandoned interurban operations in Oregon. These Pullman-built cars seated sixty passengers and were given Northwestern Pacific numbers 210-218. Dubbed the "Kitten Cars" by N.W.P. trainmen because of the configurations of the end bulkheads, they were assigned to the steam-powered segments of the railroad. While retaining their S.P. interurban characteristics, they nonetheless did not appear on the N.W.P.'s electric roster.

Passenger Motors

301-302 Class

Builder: St. Louis Car Company
Year: 1902
Length: 50'3"
Weight: 65,200 lbs.
Body: Single end, wood

No. 301 had 64 seats; to M. W. on March 16, 1936. No. 302 had 70 seats; retired March 1, 1941.

303-308 Class

Builder: North Shore RR Shops
Year: 1902
Length: 50'3"
Weight: 65,200 lbs.
Body: Single end, wood; No. 305 double end, wood

No. 303 had 70 seats; to M.W. on January 17, 1942. No. 304 had 70 seats; retired March 1, 1941. No. 305 had 68 seats; to M.W. 269. No. 306 had 64 seats; to M.W. 244 January 11, 1936. No. 307 had 70 seats; retired March 1, 1941. No. 308 had 64 seats; destroyed in fire on August 6, 1913.

309 Class

Builder: Pullman
Year: 1897
Length: 50'3"
Weight: 58,320 lbs.
Body: Single end, wood

A former narrow gauge coach, this fifty-seater was rebuilt into trailer No. 227 on April 20, 1911.

310-311 Class

Builder: St. Louis Car Company
Year: 1908
Length: 50'3"
Weight: 70,600 lbs.
Body: Single end, wood

Both cars seated 70 and both were retired on March 1, 1941.

312-319 Class

Builder: St. Louis Car Company
Year: 1908
Length: 50'3"
Weight: 75,100 lbs.
Body: Double end, wood

All cars seated 68. No. 313 went to M.W. 262 on March 28, 1941. All others were retired on March 1, 1941.

Against a background of Mt. Tamalpais and Richardson Bay is this interurban car on April 14, 1938. (Stephen D. Maguire Collection)

Grade crossings on the N.W.P. force the cars to coast to the next section of third rail. (Charles A. Smallwood)

No. 316 has been on the head end of this three-car train from Sausalito to San Rafael's main station at 4th Street and Tamalpais Avenue but will be on the rear as the train reverses direction for the return trip.

How could an unpracticed observer differentiate between the big cars of the N.W.P. and the Big Red Cars of the S.P./I.E.R.? For one thing, the headlamps on the N.W.P. swung open to the right when facing the car while the opposite was true of the S.P. cars. This is No. 383 at San Rafael. (Charles A. Smallwood)

No. 252 with at least one car in tow moves along Sausalito's northern shoreline. Ironically, the big steel and aluminum-type cars shown here will serve on the Pacific Electric longer than they will serve Marin County. (Charles A. Smallwood)

Until World War II turned Sausalito into a frenzy of shipyard activity, the town was railroad with suburban living thrown in. Near the end of the electric era, many ancient wooden coaches were taken off their wheels and used as offices or sheds. (Charles A. Smallwood)

A big steel and aluminum car races along the tracks between San Anselmo and San Rafael on November 13, 1939. The sign on the left is a warning of the 600-volt third rail. While no humans were electrocuted by this high voltage rail, many animals were less fortunate, and the list of victims ranged from snakes to a bull. (Charles A. Smallwood)

Builder: St. Louis Car Company
Year: 1902
Length: 50′3″
Weight: 65,500 lbs.
Body: Double end, wood

Builder: Pullman
Year: 1902
Weight: 75,000 lbs.
Body: Double end, wood

Builder: Pullman
Year: 1902
Weight: 75,000 lbs.
Body: Single end, wood

Builder: St. Louis Car Company
Year: 1929
Length: 70′½″
Weight: 111,200 lbs.
Trucks: St. Louis CM 84
Controller: Two Westinghouse XM 28
Body: Double end, steel, enclosed vestibule

Builder: St. Louis Car Company
Year: 1930
All other data same as 375-379 Class.

Builder: St. Louis Car Company
Year: 1902
Length: 40′5″
Weight: 65,200 lbs.
Body: Single end, wood, enclosed vestibule

Builder: Pullman
Year: 1897
Length: 39′
Weight: 57,600 lbs.
Body: Single end, wood, enclosed vestibule

320-328 Class
All cars seated 68. No. 320 to M.W. 245 on February 5, 1936. No. 323 to M.W. 250 on May 14, 1937. Nos. 324, 328 were retired March 31, 1939. The remainder were retired March 31, 1941.

329-330 Class
Both cars seated 67. No. 330 had Baldwin trucks. No. 329 to M.W. 263 on September 12, 1941. No. 330 to M.W. 264 on September 24, 1941.

331-335 Class
No. 332 seated 74, the rest seated 70. No. 333 to M.W. 265 on August 23, 1941. No. 335 to M.W. 266 on September 22, 1941. Nos. 331, 332, and 334 were retired March 1, 1941.

375-379 Class
These motors seated 98. Built to same proportions as S.P./I.E.R. cars. Owned by Southern Pacific and leased to N.W.P. After cessation of N.W.P. interurban service they were transferred to Pacific Electric where they were renumbered P.E. 4500-4504.

380-386 Class
This group was not actually a class, but rather the second shipment of large and extremely serviceable interurban cars. Cars 375-386 had the typical "owl" look of portholes on end bulkheads. The arrival of these cars put many older wooden cars into retirement. Later P.E. 4505-4511.

Passenger-Baggage Combo Motors

350-358 Class
No. 354 to M.W. on March 28, 1941, the remainder were retired on May 31, 1932. Nos. 351, 353 seated 56, and the remainder had 36 seats.

359 Class
The 359 Class included North Shore No. 201, which was destroyed in a wreck on August 6, 1913 and did not participate in 1913-1914 renumbering. No. 359 was formerly N.S.R.R. No. 202. Both cars were converted from narrow gauge, seated 32, and were motorized in 1904. No. 359 to main line combo No. 185 on June 11, 1920.

This big car is near San Rafael's B Street Station. (Charles A. Smallwood)

Except for the missing interurban trains, the small town of Ross retains the same quiet, tree-shrouded atmosphere today as it had in 1939. This two-car interurban train is about to leave Ross. Next stop on the way to Sausalito will be Kentfield. (Charles A. Smallwood)

The towerman appears to be taking a breath of fresh air as a single-car train passes Tower 2 on its way to Sausalito from Mill Valley. (Stephen D. Maguire Collection)

Manor was as far as the N.W.P.'s electrics went, and on November 13, 1939, No. 384's magnitude humbles the waiting station. She is the only former N.W.P. passenger car from electric days to be preserved. Today she resides at the Orange Empire Railroad Museum in Perris, California. (Charles A. Smallwood)

Pine Station. The hills of Marin County remain, as do the waters of Richardson Bay. The roadbed, long ago single-tracked, is no longer in use by the Northwestern Pacific, and the interurban cars were reduced to scrap by 1962. (Charles A. Smallwood)

This full broadside view of No. 379 serves to indicate just how long those steel and aluminum cars really were. (Charles A. Smallwood)

Builder: St. Louis Car Company
Year: 1908
Length: 40'5"
Weight: 73,900 lbs.
Body: Single end, wood, enclosed vestibule

360-361 Class
Both cars seated 32. No. 360 was retired on May 31, 1932. No. 361 was destroyed in a fire on February 24, 1921.

Express, Baggage and Mail Motor

370 Class
This unique vehicle was the only one of its kind on the N.W.P. roster and the only car built by Barney & Smith to be used on Bay Area interurbans. No. 370 was retired on March 1, 1941. Carried no passengers.

Builder: Barney & Smith
Year: 1903
Length: 53'10"
Weight: 56,300 lbs.
Body: Double end, wood, enclosed vestibule

Passenger Trailers

201-212 Class
All cars of this class seated 66. Nos. 201-203 were retired December 19, 1930. Others were converted to motors as follows: No. 204 to 327 March 20, 1915; No. 205 to 328 on March 20, 1915; No. 206 to 321 on March 27, 1914; No. 207 to 322 on March 24, 1914; No. 208 to 323 on February 20, 1914; No. 209 to 324 on March 31, 1914; No. 210 to 325 on April 14, 1914; No. 211 to 326 on March 3, 1914; No. 212 to 320 on November 11, 1913.

Builder: St. Louis Car Company
Year: 1902
Length: 50'3"
Weight: 46,440 lbs.
Body: Double end, wood

213-220 Class
All cars of this class seated 66. All cars of this class motorized as follows: No. 213 to 319 on September 1, 1913; No. 214 to 317 on May 28, 1912; No. 215 to 318 on May 28, 1912; No. 216 to 316 on September 30, 1911; No. 217 to 314 on April 10, 1911; No. 218 to 315 on April 10, 1911; No. 219 to 312 on May 11, 1910; No. 220 to 313 on May 11, 1910.

Builder: St. Louis Car Company
Year: 1908
Length: 50'3"
Weight: 56,000 lbs.
Body: Double end, wood

221-224 Class
Seated 66 passengers. These cars were originally narrow gauge coaches. No. 221 was retired on October 1, 1924. No. 222 was retired on October 21, 1924. Nos. 223 and 224 were retired on September 1, 1924.

Builder: Pullman
Year: 1897
Length: 58'10"
Weight: 43,600 lbs.
Body: Double end, wood

225-226 Class
Seated 58 passengers. Both cars were originally narrow gauge coaches Nos. 725 and 726, respectively. Both retired September 1, 1924.

Builder: Pullman
Year: 1897
Length: 52'4"
Weights: No. 225, 43,000 lbs; No. 226, 42,640 lbs.
Body: Double end, wood

Builder: Pullman
Year: 1897
Length: 48′1½″
Weight: 42,600 lbs.
Body: Double end, wood

Builder: Carter Brothers
Year: 1889
Length: 46′4″
Weight: 39,400 lbs.
Body: Double end, wood

Builder: Wason
Year: 1885
Length: 47′9″
Weight: 40,500 lbs.
Body: Double end, wood

Builder: Pullman
Year: 1902
Length: 53′10″
Weight: 56,500 lbs.
Body: Double end, wood

Builder: St. Louis Car Company
Year: 1929
Length: 70′½″
Weight: 79,000 lbs.
Trucks: St. Louis CM 72
Controller: Two Westinghouse XM 28
Body: Double end, steel, enclosed vestibules

No. 227
Seated 50. Originally a narrow gauge coach. Converted to caboose No. 6202 on July 10, 1924.

230-233 Class
No 230 was destroyed in a fire on December 19, 1930. Remainder retired December 31, 1930. All cars had 62 seats.

234-239 Class
All cars seated 62. No. 239 was destroyed in a fire on February 24, 1921. Remainder were retired on December 31, 1930.

240-244 Class
All cars had 66 seats. Converted to motors as follows: No. 240 to 329 on May 31, 1923; No. 241 to 330 on July 1, 1923; No. 242 to 333 on November 1, 1924; No. 243 to 334 on November 1, 1924; No. 244 to 335 on November 1, 1924.

250-256 Class
Companion pieces to motors 375-386. All cars seated 103 and were control trailers. These cars went to P.E. with Nos. 375-386; P.E. Nos. 4512-4518. No. 254 made final interurban run in California under colors of Metropolitan Transit on April 9, 1961, from Los Angeles to Long Beach.

Note: Cars 230-239, 332, 370 came to North Shore R.R. from San Francisco & North Pacific R.R. roster. Cars 329-331, 333-335 came to North Shore from California Northwestern Railway roster.

In addition, one electric steeple cab was on the N.W.P. roster. This B-B locomotive was built at the North Shore's shops in 1902, and christened *Electra*. *Electra* weighed 100,000 lbs. and was rated at 500 horsepower. Since electrification was only a minor portion of N.S.R.R. trackage, not to mention that the rate of consumption of electricity actually slowed down the other trains on the line, *Electra* was soon deemed expendable from the roster, and was leased in 1906 to the San Francisco Debris Commission to aid in cleaning up the damage and rubble accumulating from the Fire and Earthquake. Subsequent ownership included the United Railroads of San Francisco, Southern Pacific (Central Pacific No. 201), and in 1917 the Pacific Electric (P.E. No. 1544), before eventual retirement to Traveltown in Los Angeles where *Electra* remains on permanent display.

Chapter Six
The Blossom Line

Peninsular Railway Company

As one drives over the freeways which connect Cupertino, Los Gatos, Santa Clara, San Jose, and other communities in Santa Clara County, one is apt to forget that before World War II the economy was almost totally agricultural and the population dispersed. At the turn of the century, San Jose was, for San Franciscans, a distant place only two generations removed from initial attempts to be linked by a steam railroad which would come to be one of the nuclei of the mighty Southern Pacific.

Boasting its fine climate and soil, Santa Clara County developed a region reknown for its fine fruit crops. Then, too, the county was home to two fledgling universities: Stanford in Palo Alto and the University of Santa Clara. Clearly, the area would be further developed if people had some kind of transportation other than horse-and-wagon through adobe, a clay which was hard in summer and in winter turned to virtually impassable muck. Since the years between the Spanish-American and the First World Wars were the heyday of interurban construction, there was no apparent reason why Santa Clara County should not employ this progressive means of public transit. Remember that Francis M. Smith was still working on his ambitious plans to connect San Jose with Oakland via interurban. And it was not inconceivable that the United Railroads of San Francisco would extend their #40 Line from San Mateo to San Jose. Moreover, the groundwork for the Peninsular Railway had been in existence since as early as 1891 in the form of the San Jose & Alum Rock Park Railway, the San Jose & Santa Clara Railway, and the San Jose Street Railway. Later these roads were to be merged into the San Jose Railroads. These railways not only demonstrated the practicality of the high iron on short hauls but also the advantages of electric motive power.

Since the interurban was essentially a diminutive train, it often traveled on a right-of-way. Its road was mounted steel, and as such was unhindered by mucky roads and the like. The large trolley cars could, and most often did, have room near the motorman (or engineer) to carry light freight such as newspapers and express packages. Later, many interurban lines enlarged the express compartments so much that as little as one-third of the original passenger space was left for its intended purpose. The interurban, then, was in a position to compete with the steam railroads for short hauls and less-than-carload (l.c.l. in railroad terminology) freight as well as short passenger runs.

This kind of supplement to the service offered by the Southern Pacific greatly appealed to such solid citizens as James Rea, an associate of the Electric Improvement Company of San Jose and a promoter as well as a politician. Rea, in turn, interested others such as O. A. Hale, the department store tycoon, and W. S. Granger. Granger and Rea then set about to have an interurban line constructed which would run from San Jose to Los Gatos—some eighteen miles. However, railroad building has always been expensive and it wasn't until funds came through from the Germania Trust Company of St. Louis, Missouri that actual construction could begin. Later, out of gratitude to the St. Louis financiers, a car would be christened *Germania* in their honor.

Utilizing car No. 101 to head a work train, the road to Los Gatos was completed by February of 1904. The San Jose-Los Gatos Interurban Railway—as it was then called—followed this route: From the S.P. depot at Market and Bassett Streets in San Jose to San Carlos Street, to Stevens Creek

When San Jose was a small community it was thought that a powerful arc lamp atop a tall tower would be sufficient to light the town at night. The structure was built but short-lived. In this colored postcard, a streetcar of the San Jose Railroads runs along Santa Clara Street under the tower while a single-engine biplane passes overhead.

Road, Saratoga Road to Saratoga, and then southeasterly to Los Gatos through the foothills.

On this run, hourly trips were soon established and success was so apparent that Rea soon built another route to Los Gatos, this time going via Bird, Coe, and Lincoln Avenues, Willow Street, Meridian Road, Hamilton Avenue, San Jose-Los Gatos Road, and on to Campbell. South of Campbell, track was shared with the Southern Pacific on that road's new Almaden Branch as far as the San Jose-Los Gatos Road. This called for an elaborate, but safe, signal and train orders system. Following the aforementioned construction was the building of another line connecting Saratoga with Congress Springs.

Coinciding with the rapid expansion of trackage, carbarns and shops were built at the southeast corner of Sunol and San Carlos Streets in San Jose. These ample carbarns were of wood and corrugated iron construction and the carbarn alone covered an area of two hundred by eighty feet. Separate buildings housed the machine shops, storehouse and armature house. Six tracks entered the carbarn itself, which had a repair pit under the four inside tracks which measured one hundred by forty-five feet. Quite adequate for the new red cars.

Success breeds success, so they say, and it wasn't long before older, yet shorter, railways began to assume the air of interurbans and in short order the electrics were connecting Palo Alto, Stanford University, Monte Vista, Cupertino, and Alum Rock Park. However, this was not unusual in the early days of electric railroading, nor was it unusual for these shorter lines to merge into a single network such as the Key System in the East Bay or the Pacific Electric in Los Angeles.

In 1909, the San Jose-Los Gatos Interurban Railway, together with the Santa Clara Interurban and the Peninsular Railroad Company, which had been incorporated in 1904 and 1905, respectively, came under the control of the Southern Pacific, and the signboards were repainted to reflect the interurbans' new name: Peninsular Railway. In November of 1910, the Southern Pacific acquired the San Jose Railroads for $4,000,000. Thereafter, all San Jose street railway operations would come under the aegis of the

Los Gatos was another community served by the Peninsular Railway, and this photo shows three types of transportation: horse and wagon, horseless carriage, and interurban car of the 50-59 Class. (Randolph Brandt Collection)

San Jose Railroads, while the Peninsular Railway would handle the intercity runs as well as the local streetcar service in Palo Alto and the Alum Rock Park run. The Peninsular Railway would operate as a separate and independent railway except for a minor stretch of track from Mayfield to Vasona Junction, some 16.75 miles.

In 1911, the Peninsular Railway built 2.35 miles of track in Oakland as part of the Southern Pacific's electrification program in the East Bay. With construction finished, the Peninsular Railway sold that trackage to its parent road in 1915. Interestingly enough, that was the only connection, however tenuous, that the interurbans of the East Bay and the South Bay would ever have.

Just as when the Espee assumed control of the Northwestern Pacific the electric line was upgraded, the same took place with Santa Clara County's interurbans. Newer cars were purchased and given the traditional paint color of S.P. electrics: red with gold trim. Trackage was increased to the point where by the eve of World War I the cars of the Peninsular Railway were rolling over almost one hundred miles of steel.

Blessed with an almost flat topography, the system had only one trestle, and even that was later amended into a low level embankment. For this reason and that of its right-of-way, the traction system was able to adhere to some fairly quick timecards. For example, Saratoga to San Jose took fifteen minutes, nonstop. This combination of grade and carding led to a share of grade-crossing accidents involving Santa Clara County residents who were under the illusion that the big interurbans were on the order of Fontaine Fox's famed Toonerville Trolleys, or

No. 57 passes the Stephens Creek area en route to Cupertino and Los Altos from San Jose. Today the same area is given to shopping centers, light industry, and single-family housing. (Wilbur C. Whittaker Collection)

at best, city streetcars.° Indeed, some runs kept such fast timecards that they were nicknamed "flyers."

Together with their scheduled runs, the Peninsular Railway ran numerous picnic specials and excursion trips to such places as Alum Rock Park and Congress Springs. The best known of these was the sixty-five mile Blossom Valley Trip which carried sightseers around the western side of Santa Clara Valley to view the unforgettable display of blossoms when the fruit orchards were in flower. Hence the traction company's slogan, "The Blossom Line."

The original roadbed of the Blossom Line was of first class construction. Rails were either sixty

°A large share of railroad accidents is due in part to the misconception that railway equipment enables the train to make a sudden stop at high speeds.

The Peninsular's rails liked to stay on *terra firma,* and as early as 1912 work crews were busy replacing the Bonnie Brae Trestle with a bypass. (Charles A. Smallwood Collection)

PENINSULAR RAILWAY COMPANY TIME TABLES
EFFECTIVE MAY 18, 1920. SUBJECT TO CHANGE WITHOUT NOTICE
LOS GATOS—NIPPON MURA—SARATOGA—CONGRESS SPRINGS—AZULE—MONTA VISTA—LOS ALTOS—MAYFIELD—PALO ALTO—SAN FRANCISCO
SEE OPPOSITE PAGE FOR SCHEDULE BETWEEN SAN JOSE AND PALO ALTO

‡Denotes Sunday... noon is shown by LIGHT faced figures and time from 12:01 noon to 12:00 midnight by DARK faced figures.

	Leave Daily	Leave Sund. Only	Leave Daily	Leave Sund. Only	Leave Daily	Leave Daily Except Sund.	Leave Daily	Leave Daily	Leave Daily	Leave Daily	Leave Daily	Leave Daily	Leave Daily	Leave Daily
	10 35	11 10	11 30		1 05	2 15		3 38		5 19			10 10	
	10 42	11 15	11 34		1 09	2 19		3 42		5 23			10 14	
	10 49	11 18	11 39		1 15	2 24		3 48		5 29			10 19	
Lv	10 48	11 05	‡11 05	12 10	1 10	2 20	From San Jose	3 40	From San Jose	5 20	From San Jose	7 05		From San Jose
	10 54	11 22	11 43	12 18	1 19	2 28		3 51		5 31	5 32	7 13	10 22	
Lv	10 57	11 26	11 49					3 56				7 18	10 27	
Lv	10 58	11 27		12 22	1 23	2 33		3 56		5 36	5 36			
	11 03	11 30		12 26	1 25	2 37		3 59		5 39	5 39			
	11 04	11 31		12 27	1 26	2 39		4 00		5 40	5 40			
Lv Su		11 32		12 28	1 27	2 40		4 01		5 41	5 41			
Ar M		11 33		12 29	1 29	2 42		4 02		5 44	5 44			
Lv Cu			11 49									7 18	10 27	
Lv Sorc			11 51									7 20	10 29	
Lv Mor			11 54									7 23	10 33	
Lv Meri			12 01		1 20	2 31	2 31	3 53	4 52		5 34	6 32	7 35	10 40	11 40
Lv Cupe			12 08		1 26	2 39	2 39	4 01	5 00		5 41	6 40	7 41	10 46	11 46
Ar Monta			12 11			2 43	2 43	4 05				6 43			
Lv Monta			12 11		1 29	2 43	2 43	4 05	5 03	5 44	5 45	6 45	7 44	10 49	11 49
Lv Simla			12 12		1 30	2 44	2 44	4 06	5 04	5 45	5 46	6 46	7 45	10 50	11 50
Lv Grant			12 13		1 31	2 45	2 45	4 07	5 05	5 46	5 47	6 47	7 46	10 51	11 51
Lv Loyola			12 15		1 33	2 48	2 48	4 09	5 07	5 48	5 49	6 50	7 48	10 53	11 53
Lv Springer			12 16		1 34	2 49	2 49	4 10	5 08	5 49	5 50	6 51	7 49	10 54	11 54
Lv Los Alto			12 20		1 37	2 53	2 53	4 14	5 11	5 53	5 53	6 55	7 52	10 57	11 57
Lv Alta Mes			12 22		1 39	2 55	2 55	4 16	5 13	5 55	5 55	6 57	7 54	10 59	11 59
Lv Mayfield			12 28		1 45	3 00	3 00	4 25	5 19	6 00	6 01	7 05	8 00	11 05	12 05
Ar Palo Alto			12 33		1 50	3 05	3 05	4 30	5 24	6 04	6 05	7 10	8 05	11 10	12 10

VIA SOUTHERN PACIFIC

Peninsular Railway Company
PALO ALTO DIVISION
TIME TABLES
EFFECTIVE MAY 18, 1920

LOS GATOS
NIPPON MURA, BONNIE BRAE

SARATOGA
CONGRESS SPRINGS
AZULE, FREMONT, SUNNY BRAE, SIMLA

MONTA VISTA
SIMLA, GRANT ROAD, LOYOLA

LOS ALTOS
ALTA MESA

MAYFIELD
PALO ALTO

Street car connections every 10 minutes to and from
LELAND STANFORD, JR. UNIVERSITY.

IMPORTANT:—Schedule applying between San Jose, Campbell, Los Gatos, Saratoga and Congress Springs is shown in separate Time Table issued by this Company.

F. E. CHAPIN, GENERAL MANAGER
SAN JOSE, CAL.

This California-type streetcar was one of several which the Peninsular operated in Palo Alto. Here, No. 32 meets with a Peninsular Ry. car in the left background at the Southern Pacific Station and will shortly begin her trip to Stanford University.

---

or seventy pounds per yard, mounted on redwood ties,** set two feet between centers, and ballasted with ample creek gravel. The cars were fed power from a simple span overhead of 00 hard drawn copper wire carrying 550 volts. Feeder cables were of stranded aluminum.

**The reader will note the predominant use of redwood for ties. Readily available in Northern California, it is impervious to rot and insects. The author has personally done woodwork on abandoned railroad ties from the North Pacific Coast R.R. which were said to be at least 50 to 60 years old and the wood was as good as the day it came from the sawmills.

Despite the popularity of the Peninsular Railway in the early years, the line was hard hit by the perfection and large scale production of the family automobile. With the autos came the demand for roads. Paved roads. Roads which could handle the ever increasing speed of autos. Wider roads with passing lanes. And when the roads had to be widened, the Peninsular Railway was told to move its tracks to make room. But the people who were demanding better roads were no longer paying customers of the Peninsular. Moreover, the Wall Street Crash of 1929 had, by

Today, Peninsular Railway No. 52 is treated with tender loving care at the California Railway Museum at Rio Vista Junction. In the 1920s she was a mainstay of the fleet as she waited for passengers at the Southern Pacific depot in San Jose. (Charles A. Smallwood Collection)

sprinkler car and the sand motor. In the days before asphalt and cement were universally used for street pavements, it was necessary for streets to be sprinkled with water in order to keep dust levels at a minimum. In order to secure franchise rights from a local government to use city streets, the railways often agreed to operate sprinkling equipment from their rails in the center of the street. These cars often resembled a gigantic barrel mounted on a short flatcar with a trolley pole affixed to the top of the barrel. A platform for the motorman and controls completed the structure.

A sand motor was used to transfer sand to the different carbarns. The sand was used by the cars in moist weather; a bit of sand dropped on the tracks helped provide friction for the car's wheels.

the early Thirties, done its share of dirty work and the decline of the interurban was in full scale nationally, as well as locally in San Jose. To be sure, some roads such as the Key System in Oakland, Pacific Electric in Los Angeles, and the North Shore Line in Chicago were able to hold on, but these roads served large population centers and did so only with heavy damage to corporate ledgers. Further, the Peninsular Railway was regarded as a poor relation by parent Southern Pacific, which kept the bulk of the freight business for itself and on its own books. In 1932, the short line to Campbell fell victim to Highway 17. A year later, the Peninsular Railway was a memory. So are the leisurely Sunday rides among the ubiquitous fruit orchards of Santa Clara County.

Peninsular Railway Rolling Stock

The rolling stock of the Blossom Line had the usual interurban collection of original, second-hand, and rebuilt cars. This conglomeration included cars from the Southern Pacific's pool of interurban equipment, short (thirty-two feet) cars posing as interurbans, and cars which saw service on both the San Jose Railroads and the Peninsular. Except for their imposing presence, some could easily have passed for city streetcars. Yet fundamentally, they were all similar in one respect: for years they were the last word in rapid transit.

The reader is apt to be curious about certain pieces of nonrevenue rolling stock such as the

No. 104 moves along a stretch of single track in Campbell. Another P. Ry. car follows. (Wilbur C. Whittaker Collection)

This car has just completed a journey from San Jose to Palo Alto via Cupertino and Los Altos. The future site of Stanford University's football stadium is to the right of this photo. (Wilbur C. Whittaker Collection)

We Now Print This Time Table	J. & T. COUSINS SHOES FOR WOMEN
¶ "The best advertisement for the Nace Printing Company is the Service they render." —A Customer	 18 to 26 East Santa Clara St. San Jose
NACE PRINTING CO., W. Santa Clara St.	KORRECT SHAPE SHOES FOR MEN

PENINSULAR RAILWAY (ELECTRIC)—THE BLOSSOM LINE
WELLS, FARGO & CO. EXPRESS

SAN JOSE TO PALO ALTO & SAN FRANCISCO VIA MERIDIAN, MONTA VISTA, LOS ALTOS & MAYFIELD

Miles	STATIONS	Daily	Daily	Daily	Daily	Sat. and Sun.	Daily	Sat. and Sun.	Daily	Sat. and Sun.	Daily	Daily	Daily	Daily	Daily	Daily	Daily	Daily
0.0	Lv San Jose—S.P. Depot	5 50	6 50	8 06	9 00	10 00	11 00	12 00	1 00	2 00	3 00	4 00	4 40	5 30	6 15	8 00	10 15	11 15
0.6	Lv Post Office	5 54	6 54	8 10	9 04	10 04	11 04	12 04	1 04	2 04	3 04	4 04	4 44	5 35	6 19	8 04	10 19	11 19
2.4	Lv Sanitarium	6 02	7 01	8 17	9 11	10 11	11 11	12 11	1 11	2 11	3 11	4 11	4 51	5 43	6 26	8 11	10 26	11 26
3.7	Lv Evergreen	6 05	7 06	8 21	9 14	10 14	11 14	12 14	1 14	2 14	3 14	4 14	4 54	5 46	6 29	8 14	10 29	11 29
4.4	Lv Winchester	6 07	7 08	8 22	9 17	10 17	11 17	12 17	1 17	2 17	3 17	4 17	4 57	5 49	6 32	8 17	10 32	11 32
	Lv Cypress Avenue	6 08	7 09	8 23	9 18	10 18	11 18	12 18	1 18	2 18	3 18	4 18	4 58	5 50	6 33	8 18	10 33	11 33
5.6	Lv Meridian	6 10	7 10	8 24	9 20	10 20	11 20	12 20	1 20	2 20	3 20	4 20	5 00	5 53	6 35	8 20	10 36	11 36
9.0	Lv Cupertino	6 18	7 18	8 32	9 23	10 28	11 28	12 28	1 28	2 28	3 28	4 28	5 08	6 01	6 43	8 28	10 44	11 44
10.2	Lv Monta Vista	6 21	7 22	8 36	9 32	10 32	11 32	12 32	1 32	2 32	3 32	4 32	5 12	6 05	6 47	8 32	10 48	11 48
11.6	Lv Simla	6 22	7 23	8 38	9 34	10 34	11 34	12 34	1 34	2 34	3 34	4 34	5 14	6 07	6 49	8 34	10 50	11 50
12.3	Lv Grant Road	6 23	7 24	8 39	9 35	10 35	11 35	12 35	1 35	2 35	3 35	4 35	5 15	6 08	6 50	8 35	10 51	11 51
13.1	Lv Loyola	6 24	7 27	8 41	9 37	10 37	11 37	12 37	1 37	2 37	3 37	4 37	5 18	6 10	6 52	8 37	10 53	11 53
13.8	Lv Springer Road	6 25	7 28	8 42	9 38	10 38	11 38	12 38	1 38	2 38	3 38	4 38	5 19	6 11	6 53	8 38	10 54	11 54
15.5	Lv Los Altos	6 29	7 32	8 46	9 42	10 42	11 42	12 42	1 42	2 42	3 42	4 42	5 23	6 15	6 57	8 42	10 58	11 58
17.2	Lv Alta Mesa	6 31	7 34	8 48	9 44	10 44	11 44	12 44	1 44	2 44	3 44	4 44	5 25	6 17	6 59	8 44	11 00	12 00
19.3	Lv Mayfield	6 35	7 38	8 51	9 47	10 47	11 47	12 47	1 47	2 47	3 47	4 47	5 28	6 20	7 03	8 47	11 03	12 03
20.6	Lv University Junction	6 40	7 41	8 55	9 51	10 51	11 51	12 51	1 51	2 51	3 51	4 51	5 32	6 23	7 06	8 51	11 07	12 07
20.9	Ar Palo Alto—S.P. Depot	6 41	7 42	8 56	9 52	10 52	11 52	12 52	1 52	2 52	3 52	4 52	5 33	6 24	7 07	8 52	11 08	12 08
0.0	Lv Palo Alto—Sou. Pac.	†6 53	†8 01	9 13			12 17		2 19	*3 31				6 16				
34.0	Ar San Francisco	†8 00	†9 00	10 10			1 25		3 25	*4 00				7 20				

SAN FRANCISCO & PALO ALTO TO SAN JOSE VIA MAYFIELD, LOS ALTOS, MONTA VISTA & MERIDIAN

Miles	STATIONS	Daily	Daily	Daily	Daily	Sat. and Sun.	Daily	Sat. and Sun.	Daily	Daily	Daily	Daily	Daily	Daily	Daily	Daily
0.0	Lv San Francisco	5 45		9 00		10 40	*11 40		3 00		4 20	*5 25	5 40	8 10		10 05	
34.0	Ar Palo Alto—Sou. Pac.	6 51		9 54		11 50	*12 43		3 58		5 18	*6 28	6 46	9 12		11 06	
0.0	Lv Palo Alto—S.P. Depot	*6 51	*7 50	9 00	10 00	11 00	12 00	1 00	2 00	3 00	4 00	5 00	5 40*	6 33	7 15	9 20	10 15	11 10
0.3	Lv University Junction	6 52	7 51	9 01	10 01	11 01	12 01	1 01	2 01	3 01	4 01	5 01	5 41	6 34	7 16	9 21	10 16	11 11
1.6	Lv Mayfield	6 55	7 55	9 05	10 05	11 05	12 05	1 05	2 05	3 05	4 05	5 05	5 45	6 38	7 20	9 25	10 22	11 15
3.7	Lv Alta Mesa	7 01	8 00	9 10	10 10	11 10	12 10	1 10	2 10	3 10	4 10	5 10	5 50	6 43	7 25	9 30	10 22	11 20
5.4	Lv Los Altos	7 04	8 04	9 14	10 14	11 14	12 14	1 14	2 14	3 14	4 14	5 14	5 54	6 47	7 29	9 34		11 24
7.1	Lv Springer Road	7 06	8 07	9 17	10 17	11 17	12 17	1 17	2 17	3 17	4 17	5 17	5 57	6 50	7 32	9 37		11 27
7.8	Lv Loyola	7 09	8 09	9 19	10 19	11 19	12 19	1 19	2 19	3 19	4 19	5 18	5 59	6 52	7 34	9 39		11 29
8.6	Lv Grant Road	7 10	8 10	9 20	10 20	11 20	12 20	1 20	2 20	3 20	4 20	5 19	6 00	6 53	7 37	9 40		11 30
9.3	Lv Simla	7 12	8 12	9 22	10 22	11 22	12 22	1 22	2 22	3 22	4 22	5 21	6 02	6 55	7 37	9 42		11 31
10.7	Lv Monta Vista	7 15	8 15	9 25	10 25	11 25	12 25	1 25	2 25	3 25	4 25	5 23	6 05	6 57	7 40	9 45		11 34
11.9	Lv Cupertino	7 17	8 17	9 28	10 28	11 28	12 28	1 28	2 28	3 28	4 28	5 27	6 07	7 00	7 42	9 47		11 36
15.3	Lv Meridian	7 24	8 24	9 34	10 34	11 34	12 34	1 34	2 34	3 34	4 34	5 36	6 15	7 08	7 49	9 52		11 44
	Lv Cypress Avenue	7 25	8 25	9 35	10 35	11 35	12 35	1 35	2 35	3 35	4 35	5 37	6 16	7 09	7 50	9 53		11 45
16.5	Lv Winchester	7 27	8 27	9 36	10 36	11 36	12 36	1 36	2 36	3 36	4 36	5 38	6 17	7 09	7 51	9 54		11 46
17.1	Lv Evergreen	7 28	8 28	9 37	10 37	11 37	12 37	1 37	2 37	3 37	4 37	5 39	6 18	7 12	7 52	9 55		11 47
18.5	Lv Sanitarium	7 31	8 33	9 40	10 40	11 40	12 40	1 40	2 40	3 40	4 40	5 42	6 22	7 13	7 55	9 58		11 52
20.3	Lv Post Office	7 37	8 41	9 49	10 49	11 49	12 49	1 49	2 49	3 49	4 49	5 50	6 30	7 22	8 04	10 07		12 01
20.9	Ar San Jose—S.P. Depot	7 42	8 46	9 54	10 54	11 54	12 54	1 54	2 54	3 54	4 54	5 55	6 35	7 27	8 09	10 12		12 06

Providing S. P. trains due at Palo Alto at 6.51 A. M., 3.58 P. M. and 9.12 P. M. are late, interurban cars scheduled to leave at 6.51 A. M., 4.00 P. M. and 9.20 P. M. will leave at 6.56 A. M., 4.05 P. M. and 9.30 P. M.

A special car will leave Palo Alto on arrival of Southern Pacific Theatre Train No. 60. This car will make all local stops between Palo Alto and car barns Sunol and San Carlos Streets. Upon request at San Jose office this car will be run into San Jose.

Light face figures A. M. Dark face figures P. M. *Daily. †Daily, except Sunday, to and from San Francisco connect at Palo Alto. ‡Sunday only.

Below, No. 107 of the Peninsular served for twenty-four years on the Santa Clara County interurban before being sent to the Pacific Electric Railway in Los Angeles. The big wooden car was finally scrapped by the P.E. in 1950. (Charles A. Smallwood)

Builder: American Car Company
Year: 1903
Length: 45'
Weight: 55,000 lbs.
Motors: Westinghouse 38B
Trucks: Brill 27 MCB 1
Controllers: K14
Body: Double end, wood

Builder: Peninsular Railway Shops
Year: 1930
Body: Double end, wood, one-man

Builder: Jewett Car Company
Year: 1913
Body: Double end, wood

Builder: Jewett Car Company
Year: 1912
Length: 42'8"
Motors: Two G.E. 210D
Trucks: 72 G.E. 1
Body: Double end, wood

Builder: St. Louis Car Company
Year: 1909
Length: 43'½"
Weight: 59,600 lbs.
Motors: Four W 306 A, 50 h.p.
Trucks: A2sB, St. Louis
Controller: W 264 D2, Multiple-unit

Builder: Jewett Car Company
Year: 1913
Length: 52'4¼"
Motors: Four Westinghouse 3382, 100 h.p.
Trucks: Brill 27 MCB 3 X
Controllers: Westinghouse 272 E
Body: Double end, wood

Interurbans

50-59 Class

Seated 52. Under San Jose-Los Gatos Interurban Railway ownership, they were numbered 2-10, 12, respectively. S.J.-L.G.I.Ry. Nos. 2, 4, 6, 8, 10 and 12 were named *Rea, Granger, Edith, Florence, Los Gatos,* and *Germania*, respectively, and were originally motors. The rest were originally trailers but were motorized by S.J.-L.G.I. Ry. Nos. 50-51 were rebuilt and renumbered 60-61 in 1930. Remainder rebuilt to one-man cars in 1920s. No. 52 is now at California Railway Museum.

60-61 Class

Rebuilt from Nos. 50-51 for one-man operation. Retired in 1934. No. 61 is now owned by Charles Smallwood and is being restored at California Railway Museum.

70-73 Class

Seated 40. Came to P.Ry. from San Jose Railroads where they were numbered 127-130, respectively, in 1927. Rebuilt to one-man cars in 1928. Sold back to San Jose Railroads in 1933 and ran as streetcars until scrapping in 1938.

74-77 Class

Seated 40. Rebuilt to one-man cars in 1928. Came to P.Ry. in 1927 from Fresno Traction where they were numbered 41-44, respectively. Sold to San Jose Railroads in 1933 and scrapped in 1938.

100-104 Class

No. 100 to Pacific Electric, renumbered P.E. 468, retired in 1934, No. 101 to Pacific Electric, renumbered 469, retired in 1934, No. 104 to Pacific Electric, renumbered 470, retired in 1934, all sales to P.E. in 1921. Nos. 102-103 to Fresno Traction in 1915 on lease, then sold to Pacific Electric in 1918 to be renumbered P.E. No. 466 and No. 467. All cars seated 48.

105-112 Class

Seated 60. Sold to Pacific Electric in 1933, kept in storage by P.E. until 1937. Renumbered P.E. 1050-1057, respectively. Retired by P.E. as follows: 1050, 1947; 1051, 1055 and 1057 in 1949; 1052-1054, 1056 in 1950.

CONGRESS SPRINGS FREE TO CAR PASSENGERS

PENINSULAR RAILWAY COMPANY TIME TABLE
Effective October 1st, 1925 — Subject to change without notice

SAN JOSE, MERIDIAN, SOROSIS, SARATOGA, CONGRESS SPRINGS, GLEN UNA, NIPPON MURA,
LOOP TROLLEY TRIPS—SAN JOSE TO LOS GATOS VIA SARATOGA, RETURNING VIA CAMPBELL

AMERICAN RAILWAY EXPRESS

Additional Cars From San Jose to Los Gatos via Campbell (see reverse side) Leave San Jose. ♦6.10, 7.00, 8.20, 9.00, 10.00, 11.00 a. m., 12.05, 1.10, 2.20, 3.30, 4.00, 5.10, 6.08, 7.50, 9.30, and 11.10 p. m.

	VIA SOUTHERN PACIFIC																											
	Lv San Francisco			6 00						11 00		12 15	1 15					3 00				4 20						
	Ar San Jose			7 50						12 40		1 40	2 40					4 00				5 50						
Miles	STATIONS VIA PENINSULAR RAILWAY CO.	♦																										
0.0	Lv San Jose (S. P. Depot)	5 45		6 40	7 21	8 00	9 05	9 25	10 05	10 25	11 05	11 25	12 01	12 25	1 00	1 25	2 05	2 45	3 25	4 25	5 05	5 40	6 05	6 25	7 20	9 20	11 15
0.6	" San Jose (Postoffice)	5 49		6 44	7 25	8 04	9 09	9 29	10 09	10 29	11 09	11 29	12 05	12 29	1 04	1 29	2 09	2 49	3 29	4 29	5 09	5 44	6 09	6 29	7 24	9 24	11 19
2.4	" Sanitarium	5 56		6 51	7 31	8 10	9 16	9 36	10 16	10 36	11 16	11 36	12 11	12 36	1 11	1 36	2 16	2 56	3 36	4 36	5 17	5 51	6 16	6 37	7 30	9 30	11 26
3.7	" Evergreen	6 00		6 55	7 35	8 14	9 20	9 40	10 20	10 40	11 20	11 40	12 15	12 40	1 15	1 40	2 20	3 00	3 40	4 40	5 21	5 55	6 20	6 42	7 34	9 34	11 30
4.4	" Winchester	6 02		6 57	7 38	8 17	9 22	9 43	10 23	10 43	11 23	11 43	12 17	12 43	1 17	1 43	2 23	3 03	3 43	4 43	5 23	5 57	6 23	6 44	7 36	9 36	11 32
5.6	" Meridian	6 05		7 00	7 41	8 20	9 25	9 46	10 26	10 46	11 26	11 46	12 20	12 46	1 20	1 46	2 26	3 06	3 45	4 46	5 26	6 01	6 26	6 47	7 40	9 40	11 36
6.5	" McDonald	Via Monta Vista		Via Monta Vista	7 45	Via Monta Vista		9 50		10 50		11 50		12 50		1 51		3 10		4 10		5 31		6 05	Via Monta Vista	6 52		9 44	11 40
7.4	" Moreland				7 47			9 52		10 52		11 52		12 52		1 53		3 12		4 11		5 34		6 07		6 54		9 47	11 43
8.8	" Sorosis				7 51			9 55		10 55		11 55		12 55		1 56		3 15		4 15		5 37		6 10		6 58		9 50	11 46
9.6	" Congress Junction	6 27		7 28	7 55	8 01	9 45	9 58		10 58		11 58	12 58		1 58	2 00	3 18		4 18		5 40	6 03	6 14	6 55	7 02		9 53	11 51
11.2	Ar Saratoga	6 32		7 33	8 00		9 50	10 04		11 04		12 04		1 04		2 04		3 23		4 23		5 45	6 08	6 19	7 00	7 09		9 58	11 55
12.6	Ar Congress Springs						9 56						12 12			12 55		*2 12		*3 15			*5 35		(6 0)				
	Lv Congress Springs						9 57																						
11.2	Lv Saratoga			6 33	7 34	8 01		10 05		11 05		12 05		1 05				3 24				5 46		6 20	7 00		9 59	11 56
12.5	" Glen Una			6 38	7 39	8 06		10 10		11 10		12 10		1 10				3 29				5 51		6 25	7 05		10 04	12 01
13.9	" Nippon Mura			6 42	7 41	8 09		10 12		11 12		12 12		1 12				3 31				5 53		6 27	7 07		10 06	12 03
15.6	Ar Los Gatos				7 47	8 15		10 18		11 18		12 18		1 18				3 37				6 00		6 34	7 13		10 12	12 09
	VIA SOUTHERN PACIFIC																											
	Lv Los Gatos			9 50				11 06									♦				5 35							
	Ar Santa Cruz			11 10				12 30													6 55							

Additional Cars From Los Gatos to San Jose via Campbell (see reverse side) Leave Los Gatos 7.10, 7.50, 9.10, 10.20, 11.20, a. m., 12.20, 1.20, 2.10, 3.50, 4.20, 6.10, 7.15, 10.20 p. m.

	STATIONS VIA SOUTHERN PACIFIC			♦																							
	Lv Santa Cruz			7 00										1 30							6 00	6 10					
	Ar Los Gatos			8 19										3 03							7 20	7 30					
Miles	VIA PENINSULAR RAILWAY CO.	♦	♦	†																							
	Lv Los Gatos	5 45	6 40	7 09	7 55	8 20		9 50		10 50		11 50	12 50					4 50		6 05	6 45		8 30	10 15			
	" Nippon Mura		6 45	7 13	8 01	8 25		9 55		10 55		11 55						4 55		6 09	6 50		8 35	10 20			
	" Glen Una			7 17		8 28		9 59		10 59										6 14	6 55		8 40	10 25			
	Ar Saratoga				8 10	8 32		10 04												6 19	6 59		8 45	10 30			
	Ar Congress Springs																										
	Lv C...																										

Southern California traction fans may think that Peninsular Railway No. 4 closely resembled Pacific Electric's No. 1618—they are right, for after only nine years on the Peninsular she went to southern California and was renumbered P.E. No. 1618. (Wilbur C. Whittaker Collection)

Saratoga Station is host to P. Ry. Nos. 111 and 57, sometime prior to 1930. Wilbur C. Whittaker)

Streetcars

Builder: Sacramento Electric, Gas & Railway Company
Year: 1906
Motors: Two G.E. 54
Trucks: Archbar
Controllers: Westinghouse K 10
Body: California type, wood, rebuilt as one-man, single end

Builder: Holman
Year: 1905
Length: 32′
Body: Double end, steel and wood

Builder: American Car Company
Year: 1907
Body: California type, deck roof

Builder: Sacramento Electric, Gas & Railway Company
Year: 1905
Motors: Two G.E. 54
Trucks: Brill 27 G
Controllers: Westinghouse K 10
Body: California type, deck roof

Builder: American Car Company
Year: 1919
Body: Steel, arch roof, fully enclosed, one-man cars

Builder: Sacramento Electric, Gas & Railway Company
Year: 1906
Motors: Two G.E. 54
Trucks: Brill 27 G
Controller: Westinghouse K 10
Body: California type, wood, deck roof; same dimensions as Nos. 21-26

No. 14
Known as the line's "dinky" car since the open sections were cut off when rebuilt for one-man operation in 1923.

15-16 Class
Seated 32. Off the roster by 1933.

17-20 Class
Later enclosed and converted to one-man operation. Nos. 17-19 were retired in 1930, No. 20 was retired in 1926.

21-26 Class
Ex-Santa Clara Interurban cars, Nos. 1-6, respectively. Nos. 23-24 were scrapped in 1926, Nos. 22, 25-26 were scrapped in 1930. No. 21 was in a wreck and scrapped in 1906.

27-31 Class
These cars were Birney Safety Cars and were originally intended for use in Palo Alto, but were used instead in San Jose. Transferred to San Jose Railroads in 1934, scrapped in 1938.

No. 32
First used on Naglee Park Line in San Jose, then transferred to service in Palo Alto in 1922. Returned to San Jose Railroads in 1930. Rebuilt to one-man operation for use in Palo Alto.

The lady is boarding a Peninsular Railway car on the Los Gatos line. The flowers may as well be a funeral wreath since this is the last day of operation on that run. (Randolph Brandt)

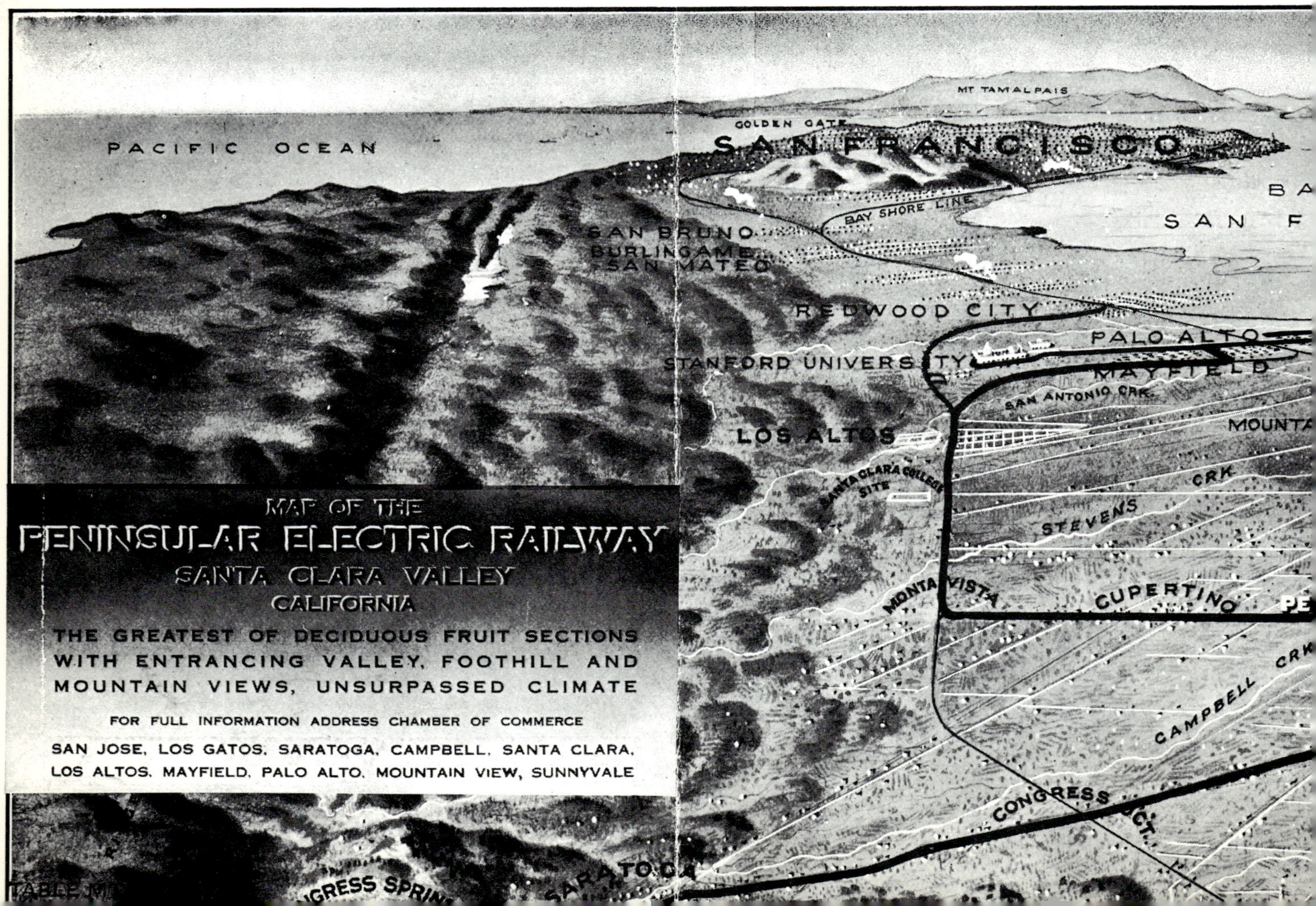

Freight and Work Equipment

Number	Type	Builder	Year	Body	Disposition
1	Freight motor	American	1903	Steel	Retired December 1926
2	Express motor			Steel	Sold to S.J.R.R. in 1934, scrapped in 1938
4	Freight locomotive	Westinghouse	1913	Steel	To P.E. No. 1618, scrapped in 1955
5	Wrecker	(Ex-steam coach from Alum Rock Line)		Wood	Retired 1930
9	Work motor	Peninsular Railway Shops	1912	Steel	Scrapped 1934
12	Sprinkler	Peninsular Railway Shops	1906	Steel	
14	Line car	Holman	1904	Steel	To S.J.R.R. in 1934, scrapped in 1938
112	Sand motor			Wood	
200	Work motor	Holman	1906	Steel	Rebuilt 1915, scrapped in 1934
201	Wrecker	Holman	1905	Steel	Ex-work motor; sold to S.J.R.R. in 1934; scrapped in 1939
300-307	Flat cars	Peninsular Railway Shops	1917-1918	Wood	304-307 scrapped 1930; 300-303 scrapped in 1934
308	Flat car	Peninsular Railway Shops	1920	Steel	Scrapped 1930

This artist's conception of Peninsular Railway trackage was inside a brochure extolling the virtues of not only living in the Santa Clara Valley, but riding the trolley cars as well. Circa 1910. (David L. Mitchell Collection)

Steeple cab No. 4 was used for a number of duties. Here she assists in paving work being done on Santa Clara Avenue in east San Jose. (Charles A. Smallwood)

This may have been a company photo since motor No. 2 of the Peninsular is posed with a drag of stock cars from parent Southern Pacific. The lead car is from the Texas & New Orleans, another Espee property. (Charles A. Smallwood Collection)

Chapter Seven
The Big White Cars

Petaluma & Santa Rosa Railroad

By the turn of the century, the town of Santa Rosa had experienced much of the same transportation problems as had larger cities. The town had outgrown its horsecars, and by 1903 was prepared to resort to electric-powered vehicles to take people beyond town limits. The residents of Sonoma County—of which Santa Rosa is the seat—and Marin County had long hoped that the steam railroads would one day connect them with the larger population centers. After all, this was farm country; crops had to be brought to market, and the major market was in San Francisco. Construction of steam roads in the North Bay regions had been sporadic at best, with track being laid by the various railroads mainly because of competitive pressures and threats of bondholders' lawsuits. The logical response, then, to this gap in active steam railroading was the formation of the Petaluma & Santa Rosa Electric Railway on June 20, 1903, with John A. McNear of Petaluma as president, Burke Corbett as treasurer, Frank A. Brush, W. A. Cattwell, and sugar magnate Rudolph Spreckels as members of the Board of Directors. Authorized capital stock was established at $1,000,000.

The line which was to feature the big white cars was initially the unification of franchises given to operate street railways in Santa Rosa. This was not unusual in interurban development, as we have already noted in the study of several lines in the Bay Area. Therefore, the Santa Rosa Street Railway, the South Side Street Railway, the Union Street Railway, the Central Street Railway, and the Santa Rosa Street Railways, all of Santa Rosa, and the Petaluma Street Railroad surrendered their franchise rights to the Petaluma & Santa Rosa Electric Railway.

The line reached from Petaluma to Santa Rosa via Liberty, Stony Point, Roblar, Quarry, Orchard, Cunningham, Alten, Sebastopol, and Leddy, with extensions to Forestville via Graton, and to Two Rock via Cherry from Liberty. The system's trackage was a fraction better than thirty-seven miles long, and the use of steamboats to connect directly with San Francisco widened the range considerably.

The steamer *Gold* was the fledgling company's first acquisition of transportation equipment. This vessel had been operating daily between Petaluma and San Francisco for a number of years before becoming part of the P. & S.R., and upon purchase was immediately placed in service to aid in construction.

The building of the P. & S.R. was highlighted by a violent and vicious battle between the building crews and the railroaders on the California Northwestern, recently purchased and reorganized by A. W. Foster (see Chapter Five). Again one must remember that the freight business from this new road would originate largely from the farms and ranches of Sonoma County, and Foster must have realized that ill feeling from days past would catch up with his C.N.W. and a large share of the business would go to the new road. Mr. A. W. Foster, however, was not about to be pushed around by some upstart "juice" line.

Track laying commenced in Petaluma in April of 1904, proceeded on schedule, and by October the first service was running to Sebastopol. On December 1, 1904, there was regular service between Petaluma and the C.N.W. tracks on the outskirts of Santa Rosa, and here the stage was set. One of the reasons for the success enjoyed by electric interurbans during their heyday was their ability to travel over city streets in the manner of streetcars and then over rights-of-way in the manner of steam trains, thus affording them the best

"Last to leave, first to arrive" was the slogan of the P. & S.R.

(John Muzio Collection)

Tuesday, April 5, 1904, near the steamer landing at the foot of Copeland Street in Petaluma. The activity is centered around the driving of the first spike on the Petaluma & Santa Rosa Electric R.R. The witness in the center with the watch chain is Art Newburgh of the Petaluma *Argus Courier*.

of two worlds as they deposited passengers at regular stops throughout the city or town en route to a central terminal. And to get to the proposed central terminal in Santa Rosa, the tracks of the Petaluma & Santa Rosa Electric Railway would have to cross those of the California Northwestern twice. Foster said that if the "juice" line wanted to cross his tracks, they could build either an underpass or an overpass. A grade crossing, in Foster's opinion, constituted a menace to public safety.

No less than ninety-two Santa Rosa merchants then signed a petition to A. W. Foster. The meaning was clear: either the Petaluma & Santa Rosa crossed the California Northwestern tracks at grade or their entire freight business would be given to McNear, Spreckels, and Company. Foster complained that old friends were turning on him, but he remained undaunted in his firm resolve to keep the new road from crossing his tracks. His reply was a slashing of fares (Sebastopol fares were reduced from thirty to ten cents, five cents below the interurban's fare, as well as other reductions.) and an order for C.N.W. locomotives 12 and 13 to be equipped with steam nozzles capable of shooting steam in all directions and kept ready in the Santa Rosa yards.

Petaluma & Santa Rosa construction workers then brought their tracks right up to and on the other side of the rails of the C.N.W. During the night the trolley wire was extended across the C.N.W. tracks. (The next morning the C.N.W.'s shop foreman gave the wire a sour look, slung his steel tape measure over the wire to do a little measuring, formed a short circuit, and was given an instant lesson in the science of electricity until the tape managed to extricate itself from the wires—aided, no doubt, by the foreman's physical gyrations.)

On January 3, 1905, General Manager Alfred Bowen of the new interurban line had his men take a ready-built crossover, load it on a flatcar, and shove it right up to the proposed point of intersection. The plan called for the construction men to hacksaw the C.N.W. tracks, shove the crossover into place, and continue with the business of laying rails for the new road. At this point, C.N.W. Nos. 12 and 13, converging from

In the opening of the Battle of Santa Rosa, California Northwestern No. 12 vents her steam nozzles on the P. & S.R. track crew. (Charles A. Smallwood Collection)

Flanked by locomotive No. 12 and her steam nozzles, C.N.W. workmen hurry to fill the P. & S.R.'s excavations. (Charles A. Smallwood Collection)

Shovelfuls of dirt fly as C.N.W. men fill in the P. & S.R. excavation while electric men guard the crossover track and materials (left). (Charles A. Smallwood Collection)

opposite directions to the intersection, employed their newly equipped steam nozzles in such a manner as to scald the P. & S.R. crews as they were about to apply their hacksaws to the C.N.W.'s rails. The gandy dancers saw what was coming and quickly got out of the way, and the only victim of Foster's steam bath was a bystanding nickelodeon ticket taker who was badly scalded. By this time hundreds of townspeople were on hand to watch the event.

The P. & S.R. construction team then withdrew, rather than face another scalding from the two locomotives. To demonstrate their persistance, however, they took their crossover with them. Foster's two locos took advantage of the respite to "re-arm" with fuel and water.

The next move belonged to the Petaluma & Santa Rosa. The trolley car *Woodworth* ran down to the stub end of the track, arousing no suspicions since the cars had been making it a practice to run from that point to Sebastopol until completion of construction would let them travel all the way to the new station. But when the *Woodworth* came to a halt, out poured not only passengers but the P. & S.R. gandy dancers, in the manner of the Trojan Horse. Seizing a stack of ties which were waiting, they hurriedly placed them over the track, brought out the hidden mules and horses, and physically dragged the 38,815-pound interurban over the C.N.W. rails to her own steel on the other side!

So far, so good. But there was yet another barrier of C.N.W. rail in the way (a spur to a winery) and before it could be negotiated the courts granted an injunction against the interurban to the steam road, and *Woodworth* was marooned. Any plans of Bowen's to use the stranded car for shuttle service (with passengers

A crowd estimated at 3,000 watches the steam and electric men brawl outside the gates of the Grapevine Winery. (Charles A. Smallwood Collection)

Chief Severson and the Santa Rosa Police attempt to restore order. (Charles A. Smallwood Collection)

As peace is restored, bystanders view the remnants of P. & S.R. wagons which were used to carry sand in a vain attempt to stop C.N.W. steam locomotives. (Charles A. Smallwood Collection)

transferring by foot) were now useless unless he could get the injunction dissolved.

Meanwhile, the merchants of Santa Rosa were proving their support of the interurban by providing, at their own expense, an omnibus service between the stub-end track and the intended depot. Two months later, Judge Seawell of the Superior Court dissolved his injunction and on the first of March the fray began anew.

On that morning, the P. & S.R. men again returned to the scene of action with their crossover, together with workmen who were well supplied with picks and shovels, with Superintendent Fairchild in charge. The crew of the C.N.W., as might be expected, were ready for action, and so were nozzle-fitted locomotives 12 and 13. The C.N.W. men were armed with picks, shovels, and cars loaded with earth and gravel. No sooner did the electric crew begin to progress with an excavation than the steam men dumped their load of earth and filled the hole. As the trolley men tried to contest, the C.N.W. "steam artillery" would return and scatter the crew. When Nos. 12 and 13 would close their steam valves, the trolley men

Generations of growing boys have wanted to be ship captains, airplane pilots, baseball heroes, firemen, and generals when they grew up. The list definitely should include trolley car motormen, perhaps like Bill Parks of the P. & S.R., shown here with his skipper, or conductor, Chris Christensen. (Randolph Brandt Collection)

A proud motorman and conductor in front of their car. The four cars of the design shown here were known as "Windsplitters" by P. & S.R. men. (Don Clouder Collection)

would try to resume their work, but the locos would then return and labor would be suspended.

There erupted a brawl of the first degree, and when barroom language and fists failed, rocks were used. Amid the melee the trolley wire fell, and it was only a mark of good fortune that no one was electrocuted. The P & S.R. men maneuvered two wagons loaded with sand onto the C.N.W. rails in a vain attempt to prevent the locomotives from doing their version of steam cleaning, but the two iron horses promptly converted the wagons to kindling.

By early afternoon, the battle had drawn some 3,000 spectators, mostly partisans of the electric road. Two more C.N.W. engines arrived with additional manpower from the Petaluma section gang, together with extra carloads of earth. Now the climax was at hand as the two steam spouters chugged past the war torn partisans of the P & S.R. At this moment, in a desperate attempt to stop the C.N.W., Director F. A. Brush threw himself across the C.N.W. rails. The engineer stopped his locomotive only inches short of short of sending Mr. Brush to a premature Great Reward.

Now began a physical encounter of a different sort. The steam men tried to pry Brush loose from the rails but he held on. The electric men tried, in return, to move the steam men and again a brawl ensued. This was too much for Chief Severson of the Santa Rosa Police. He arrived with a contingent of Santa Rosa's finest, together with a paddy wagon, and demanded that the "juice" line be allowed to cross C.N.W. steel. The Santa Rosa Police, however, were no intimidation to this lot, and after Chief Engineer Zook and other C.N.W. men were taken to court, the fight resumed until late afternoon. Then the exhausted men reached a natural truce, aided, no doubt, by word circulating through the throng that attorneys for the interurbans had applied to the Superior Court in San Francisco for a restraining order against the steam road. As Foster pulled into Santa Rosa from San Rafael shortly after five o'clock with no less than 150 additional hands, not to mention two Marin County deputy sheriffs who would, it was announced, arrest anyone interfering with the California Northwestern—and that included the Santa Rosa Police—he was handed the restraining order signed by Judge Hunt which the P. & S.R. had sought in San Francisco. According to that impeccable western railroad historian, Gilbert H. Kneiss, "Foster took it like a man," and called off his army of railroaders in respect to Judge Hunt's fiat.

Leaving nothing to chance, the men of the Petaluma & Santa Rosa Electric Railway were determined to allow the line for which they had fought so hard to live up to its name. They rigged up electric lights over the area and shortly after midnight the crossovers were in place and interurban service to the railway's namesake city became a reality.

By January 26, 1906, the short line had reached north from Sebastopol to Green Valley (later Graton), and by July 15 on to Forestville. This brought the total mileage to 35.82. Construction to this point had cost $1,077,396.10, a not inconsiderable sum for those times.

The road was laid using seventy-pound rail

The Battle of Santa Rosa is long past as Big White Car No. 61 rolls down Santa Rosa's 4th Street during the P. & S.R.'s halcyon years. (Jo Ann Shelburne Collection)

Passengers going to the Russian River resort areas during the 1920s could take the P. & S.R. to Forestville and then transfer to an auto stage such as this one headed for Guerneville. Windsplitter No. 51 has had her trolley poles changed for the return trip to Sebastopol. (Jo Ann Shelburne Collection)

Above, what is the conductor of No. 55 trying to do? Stop the car from running away? Generally speaking, platform men maintained their jobs with high dignity, even under a uniform of vest, shirt, and tie on a hot day in Sonoma County. (Jo Ann Shelburne Collection)

Right, this picture was probably taken during the latter 1930s, judging from the automobiles on the streets and the S.P. imprint on the P. & S.R.: marker numbers on the hood, pantographs instead of trolley poles, and the appearance of freight locomotive No. 100. (Jo Ann Shelburne Collection)

The P & S.R.'s northern terminus was at Forestville, and the station was typically short line: an open air passenger waiting platform, a small office, and a warehouse with a freight loading platform. P. & S.R. No. 61 is seen here in her latest livery of deep yellow. The two boxcars on the track to the right are home built. (Jo Ann Shelburne Collection)

P. & S.R. running in the open countryside of Sonoma County. However, due to the many flag stops along the line it was impossible for the Big White Cars to enjoy the speediest of timecards. (Jo Ann Shelburne Collection)

The Petaluma & Santa Rosa cars in their distinctive white paint. Four passenger motors of two different classes, line car No. 4, and a freight motor all appear at the old Sebastopol Station. (P. & S.R. photo/Edward Fratini Collection)

Pete Sciaroni, a car cleaner for the Sonoma County interurban, is seated inside No. 55. (Edward Fratini Collection)

mounted on redwood ties. The overhead was simple span, No. 0000 wire, feeding 600 volts. Power was purchased from the California Gas and Electric Corporation, aided by substations at Petaluma and Sebastopol.

The nerve center of the road then, as today, was located at Petaluma. Here was the steamer wharf for the *Gold*, as well as the car shops and offices. A passenger depot and freight warehouse completed the complex. Freight and passenger facilities were also located at Forestville, Graton, Sebastopol and Santa Rosa.

Many are the faded dreams of railroading. George Gould wanted to build a single road from the Atlantic to the Pacific; James J. Hill hoped to bring his Northern Pacific down the coast into California; Henry E. Huntington wanted to link California from Sacramento to San Diego with what would have been the vastest electric railroad network in the world; the Petaluma & Santa Rosa wanted to extend to San Rafael in the south, to Tomales in the west, to Healdburg in the north, and to Sonoma and Napa in the east. However, the effects of the earthquake of April 18, 1906, were of such Olympic proportions (Santa Rosa itself was burned) that these grand dreams never materialized.* Rather, the Sonoma County interurban served as a short line for both passengers and freight, and survives today as a freight-only, dieselized feeder in the Southern Pacific system.

The first four passenger carriers for the Petaluma & Santa Rosa Electric Railroad were Nos. 51, 53, 55, and 57, and bore the names of *Petaluma*, *Santa Rosa*, *Sebastopol*, and *Woodworth*. Costing $5,686.41 each, these four center-entrance cars were built by the American Car Company of St. Louis, Missouri. Prior to shipping them to California, the American Car Company had displayed them at the St. Louis Louisiana Purchase Exposition, where they were medalists. Such were the handsome proportions of these cars that the *Petaluma* was featured in the John Stephenson Company's catalogue of 1905 as a sample of that company's excellent craftsmanship.**

*They would eventually be accomplished through affiliations with the Northwestern Pacific and the Southern Pacific.

**To prevent confusion, it should be explained that the John Stephenson Company, Ltd., was acquired by the J. G. Brill Co. in 1904. In 1902, Brill also acquired the American Car Co. of St. Louis. However, Brill was hesitant about discontinuing trusted and reliable names in the carbuilding industry and as a consequence cars sometimes would be built under a different name than that which the catalogue might imply.

No. 67 in her "chicken house" white as she pauses in Petaluma. The picture was taken during a transition period of ownership, for No. 67's signboards say "Petaluma & Santa Rosa Railway" while the sign atop the warehouse reads "Petaluma & Santa Rosa R.R. Co." Sonoma County had only one interurban, however. (Charles A. Smallwood)

The P. & S.R. was never hesitant about promoting electric transportation services, particularly its freight service. Thus P. & S.R. rolling stock and buildings were frequently turned into billboards for the railway. (P. & S.R. photo/Charles A. Smallwood Collection)

In addition to the above mentioned passenger motors, the new road ordered six passenger motors from the Holman Car Company of San Francisco. These cars—which cost $3,595.00 apiece—were numbered 59, 61, 63, 65, 67, and 69, thus adhering to the company's plans to use odd numbers for passenger cars and even numbers for freight cars and locomotives.

The four American Car Company motors were by far the most distinguished of all passenger equipment on the P & S.R., with their acutely rounded dashes and bumpers. Their pilots, in reaching around their dashes, gave the illusion of giant walrus mustaches under the nose of an extended headlight.

Flatter in the dash, the Holman-built cars did share with the American builds another P & S.R. characteristic: a very high railroad-type roof. The resemblance ended, however, with the celestory windows: the Americans were arched while the Holmans were rectangular.

Originally the passenger equipment was painted brown, but later the management decided to paint the cars white, and in this color (or absence of color) they were the proudest looking and best remembered. Unfortunately, white was not to prove to be the safety factor that the white fronts on the Market Street Railway's cars were. It seems that there were a number of accidents at grade crossings by motorists who said they thought a Big White Car was a chicken house. Thus the Big White Cars were painted yellow with red trim.

In 1928 the P & S.R. received permission from the California State Railroad Commission to rebuild its passenger cars to one-man operation, in a move for economy. This was decided on the basis of declining passenger revenues. Since the trains usually consisted of a single car, a second man would only be required if a trailer were used, and even at that the trailers were discontinued the following year.

Unable to secure a franchise to operate through freight trucking from Sonoma County to San Francisco, the Sonoma Express Company contracted to ship its freight via the P. & S.R. Thus express motor No. 8 of the interurban railway came to be labeled Sonoma Express Company for a brief period. (Charles A. Smallwood Collection)

In January of 1907, when the Southern Pacific and the Santa Fe jointly bought out the California Northwestern and the North Shore and reorganized them into the Northwestern Pacific, the two class 1 railroads created a road which would provide a most effective competition for the P & S.R., ultimately dooming its independence. The N.W.P. carried its rail from Sausalito to Eureka and had a shorter water route from San Francisco than did the P & S.R. Moreover, the N.W.P. had a more direct route to Santa Rosa from Petaluma (traveling between Penngrove, Cotati, and Wilfred). Thus the electric line failed to show any profit until 1910. In 1907 a ten dollars per share assessment was levied on the stockholders. To make matters worse, the Petaluma Transportation Company began, in 1908, to operate a steamboat, the *Resolute*, on the Petaluma River, cutting into revenues. In spite of these early setbacks, the P & S.R. did extend its track by opening the 5.33-mile branch line from Liberty to Two Rock on July 28, 1913.

By 1914 the interurbans were making twelve round trips daily from Petaluma to Sebastopol, nineteen trips from Sebastopol to Santa Rosa, sixteen trips from Sebastopol to Forestville, and had reached the zenith of ridership with a passenger count of 757,759. This represented an increase of 137,540 over the 1907 figure of 620,219. The rise in popularity of the family automobile, however, cut so heavily into the number of fares that by 1931 the company's records showed only 162,742 riders and a decline in each year since 1914. After only 53,586 persons chose to ride the interurbans for the first six months of 1932, the company, faced with staggering costs accentuated by the Great Depression, gave up the passenger business for good.

The company had always seemed to be hit by the most costly of external forces (perhaps the Battle of Santa Rosa was an ill omen), such as its second steamboat, the *Petaluma I*, burning in March of 1914.* In 1916 a general strike of bay and river steamboat crews for fifty days (in their heaviest season) hurt the P. & S.R.'s river operations. By 1916, the railroad was on the fiscal ropes. Second mortgage bonds which had come due in 1915 were unpaid, and on its first mortgage bonds the company was unable to pay the interest. A reorganization took place on August 23, 1918, with the road dropping the word "Electric" from its name, becoming the Petaluma & Santa Rosa Railroad.

The new company purchased additional freight equipment and generally tried to upgrade the

Freight motor No. 1008 pulls a drag of homemade freight cars of 1913-14 vintage. From the very outset, freight operations played a principal part on the P. & S.R. (John Winding photo/Edward Fratini Collection)

A complimentary desk blotter of the 1920s ignores the passenger operation and instead promotes the freight services. Perhaps the courted businessmen were prosperous enough to own automobiles. (Edward Fratini Collection)

line. The first project was the construction of a spur track in Petaluma along the west bank of the Petaluma River. Other improvements were the purchase of a portable substation for the Forestville Branch for use during the fruit season (1925), reconstruction of trolley wire from two-pole simple span to single-pole catenary (1925), and a new passenger and freight depot at Santa Rosa (1927). Through the additions of sidings and spurs, trackage now totaled fifty and one-tenth miles, of which thirty-eight and one-tenth were main line.

Yet for all the energy and upgrading by the road's owners, losses continued to mount. In an economy move, in 1925 the money-losing passenger service on the Liberty to Two Rock Branch was eliminated. Seeking a further solution to their problems, the directors made inquiries to the Western Pacific in order to ascertain whether the W.P. would be interested in purchasing the Petaluma & Santa Rosa Railroad. This action, if fulfilled, would effect a long sought linkup between the Sonoma County traction line and the Western Pacific-owned Sacramento Northern. Had this inquiry been taken seriously enough by the lower officials to whom it was made, it might have given the (by now) Southern Pacific-owned Northwestern Pacific serious competition in the North Bay Area. However, the Southern Pacific did take the Petaluma & Santa Rosa seriously enough to take concrete action, and by January of 1932 the P & S.R. R.R. was bought out for ninety dollars per share (7,707 shares of common stock, 600 shares of preferred), to become a subsidiary of the Northwestern Pacific. The ownership remains unchanged to this day.

While the new management eliminated the money-draining passenger service,** the freight linkups were made more efficient by rerouting and exchanging track to suit the convenience of both the P. & S.R. in particular and the Espee in general. Also abandoned at this time was the Sebastopol branch.

The Petaluma & Santa Rosa Electric Railway had wanted to develop a strong freight business from the beginning, and therefore the new line wasted no time in acquiring freight locomotives and cars. In 1907, the railroad purchased thirty-two freight cars from the Santa Fe. Further, two crude oil tank cars were home built. These, along with others, gave the ambitious little road a total of fifty-five freight cars.

Freightwise, the farmers of Sonoma County had long supported the P. & S.R., and it may be reliably estimated that the overwhelming bulk of

*See Chapter Ten for additional data on riverboats and ferryboats.
**In 1932, passengers accounted for only five percent of P. & S.R. revenue.

No. 502 on a trestle outside of Petaluma with a refrigerator car from Pacific Fruit Express and five freight cars outshopped by the P. & S.R. (P. & S.R. photo/Charles A. Smallwood Collection)

the Sonoma County-to-San Francisco l.c.l. freight business originated on this railroad. The animosity toward the steam roads, which had its roots in the days when promises of steam train service were many but few were kept, was heightened by the Battle of Santa Rosa. Thus, produce and poultry (Petaluma long being known as the Egg Capital of the World) could be loaded on P. & S.R. freights, transferred to P. & S. R. steamers bound for San Francisco's Pier 9, and bypass the N.W.P.'s rails entirely.

For a number of years the P. & S.R. acted as the carrier for the Sonoma Express Company, which also worked in competition with the N.W.P. The Sonoma Express Company was an express carrier which was prevented by law from operating its own express vehicles. An early view of P & S.R. Express Motor No. 8 shows it bearing advertising for the Sonoma Express Company, much as the Sacramento Northern and other railroads carried the familiar red shield of the Railway Express Company.

In the years following World War II, it was apparent that to retain electrification, a major overhaul would be needed. The overhead was

In this later photo, No. 1008 has been completely rebuilt, sports a pantograph rather than a trolley pole, and has a slave, or booster unit, behind her as she rumbles along. (Tom Gray)

worn and the locomotives were no longer adequate. The decision was then made to utilize the diesel-electric locomotive. (This decision, incidentally, coincided with plans to eliminate electrification of all Southern Pacific lines, as witness the decline of electrification on other Espee properties.) By 1947 the Petaluma & Santa Rosa's catenary was down, the last remaining locos were headed for their funeral in Sacramento, and electric railroading in the North Bay Area was ended.

Under the ownership of the Southern Pacific, P. & S.R. locos not only discarded their trolley pole in favor of pantographs, but also adopted S.P.-type train markers, shown here next to the headlamp. (Stephen D. Maguire Collection)

Occasionally heavy winter rains brought the P. & S.R. roadbed close to the waterline, such as in this scene out of Sebastopol on the way to Santa Rosa. In such circumstances the high iron was preferable to mud roads. (Edward Fratini Collection)

Poised like knights ready for battle, freight motors 506, 1010, and 1004A await orders in their Petaluma yards. Behind No. 1010 is line car No. 8 and behind 1004A is slave unit 1004B. (Stephen D. Maguire Collection)

Petaluma & Santa Rosa Rolling Stock

Passenger Motors

51 Class
Seated 50. Named *Petaluma*, *Santa Rosa*, *Sebastopol*, and *Woodworth*, and numbered 51, 53, 55, and 57, respectively. Nos. 51, 53, and 55 received Brill MCB trucks in 1921. Nos. 51 and 53 were retired in 1933; Nos. 55 and 57 were retired in 1941 after being used since 1933 as inspection cars. Nicknamed the "Windsplitters" because of their sharply rounded dashes.

Builder: American Car Company
Year: 1904
Length: 47′9″
Weight: 41,200 lbs., less motors
Trucks: Brill 27E-2
Controller: K28
Body: Double-end, center entrance, wood
Motors: Four G.E. 70; 40 h.p.

59 Class
Numbered 59, 61, 63, 65, 67, and 69. Seated 50. No. 63 was taken off her wheels and used as a shed, later taken to California Railway Museum at Rio Vista Junction. No. 69 was converted to a passenger trailer prior to 1909. Remainder retired in 1933.

Builder: Holman
Year: 1904
Length: 44′
Weight: 35,035 lbs.
Motors: Four G.E. 70; 40 h.p.
Trucks: Brill MCB 14B
Controller: K28
Body: Double-end, wood

Passenger Trailers

No. 69
No. 69 was the same as Passenger Motor No. 69, although de-motorized. In later years No. 69 was converted to a baggage-express trailer.

Builder: Holman
Year: 1904

71 Class
Seated 48. Numbered 71 and 73. Both cars were retired in 1929. These cars were unusual in that they were both open trailers, and had only a screen covering as high as the belt rail.

Builder: Holman
Year: 1905
Length: 44′
Weight: 22,400 lbs.
Trucks: Rigid arch bar

Express Motor

No. 8
Purchased shortly after 1915. In 1917 the trolley poles were removed and No. 8 was converted into a line car, becoming No. 4.

Builder: Holman
Body: Wood
Length: 35′10″

Express Trailers

No. 01
Rebuilt from Line Car No. 4. During rebuilding the side windows were removed. No. 01 spent its last years as a shed, eventually being taken off her wheels.

Builder: Holman, rebuilt in Petaluma & Santa Rosa Shops

No. 69
No. 69 was converted to use as an express trailer when No. 8 was altered for line car duties.

Builder: Holman
Year: 1904
Trucks: Arch bar

PETALUMA AND SANTA ROSA RAILROAD COMPANY

1926   No 336

PASS Jack T. Bate
ACCOUNT Pacific Coast Traffic Agent
           Missouri-Kansas-Texas Ry.Co.
BETWEEN All Stations

UNTIL DECEMBER 31
UNLESS OTHERWISE ORDERED AND SUBJECT TO CONDITIONS ON BACK

PRESIDENT AND GENERAL MANAGER

Below, swan song for P. & S.R. passenger service was in March of 1941. Freight motor No. 506 teams with four relics from the Northwestern Pacific to make a railfan special. Behind No. 506 is passenger-baggage combo No. 354, followed by four wooden coaches. Shortly after this trip, the four N.W.P. pieces will go to the scrap pile. Leaning out of the baggage door with camera in hand is railfan Ray Hannah. (Stephen D. Maguire Collection)

Beyond the reaches of the P & S.R.'s riverboats, Nos. 1008A and 1008B pull a freight train across Petaluma Creek in November of 1938. (Wilbur C. Whittaker)

Freight Motors

1002 Class

These four vehicles, originally numbered 1002, 1004, 1006, and 1008, began as motor flats, or motorized flatcars with wooden control cabs in the centers. In the 1920s they were rebuilt to steeple cabs. In 1928 Nos. 1002 and 1006 had their superstructures removed and their controls taken off. They were then wired for multiple unit operation and renumbered 1004B and 1008B, respectively, and used as M.U. slave units. At the same time, Nos. 1004 and 1008 were rewired for M.U. running and were renumbered 1004A and 1008A, respectively. All were scrapped in 1947.

Builder: Holman
Year: 1904
Length: 34'0"
Weight: 32,500 lbs.
Truck arrangement: B - B
Motors: Four G.E. 70; 160 total h.p.; tractive force 13,720

1004A Class

In 1928 freight motors 1004 and 1008 were rebuilt and rewired for M.U. operation. In 1946 they were retired and in 1947 they were scrapped at Sacramento.

Builder: Petaluma & Santa Rosa Shops
Year: 1928
Weight: 52,000 lbs.
(Other data same as 1002 Class)

1004B Class

In 1928 freight motors 1002 and 1006 were stripped of their superstructures and rewired for M.U. non-control operation, or slave units. In 1946 they were retired and in 1947 they were scrapped at Sacramento.

Builder: Petaluma & Santa Rosa Shops
Year: 1928
Body: Weighted flatcars with electrical equipment for M.U. with 1004A Class

No. 1010

No. 1010 was a steeple cab which was built utilizing the electrical and running gear as well as the flat body of the original line car. She was sold to the Municipal Railway of San Francisco (Muni No. 501), bought back in 1930. Retired in 1946 and scrapped in 1947.

Builder: Petaluma & Santa Rosa Shops
Year: 1915-1917
Length: 36'0"
Weight: 48,400 lbs.
Motors: Four G.E. 70; 40 h.p.
Controller: K28

No. 502

Purchased secondhand in 1920 from Kansas City-Keys Valley Railroad. Retired in 1946 and scrapped in 1947.

Builder: American Car Company
Year: 1917
Length: 30'
Weight: 78,900 lbs.
Motors: 300 h.p.
Trucks: B - B

No. 504

Purchased secondhand from the abandoned Ocean Shore Railroad in 1921. Retired in 1946 and scrapped in 1947.

Builder: Ocean Shore Railroad Shops
Year: 1917
Length: 44'4"
Weight: 80,000 lbs.
Trucks: B - B

Baldwin-Westinghouse built this much-traveled freight loco for the S.P. in 1912, and after the end of P. & S.R. electrification she finished her career in Iowa. (Stephen D. Maguire Collection)

On a weed-choked dead track, former passenger motor number 69 sits, her usefulness at an end and waiting for the scraper's torch. The time is July 1938 but her signboard still proclaims "Electric Transportation is a Necessity."

November of 1938 saw one of the oddest cars ever to roll over the rails of the Bay Area's interurbans. In need of an overhead line car to service the trolley wires, the ever resourceful company shops fitted out a boxcar with platform and trolley pole and towed it behind one of the passenger motors which had been retired from revenue service. (Wilbur C. Whittaker)

In December of 1937 No. 01 performs her last service for her owners—a tool shed! She has seen duty previously as a baggage-express motor, line car, and baggage-express trailer. (Stephen D. Maguire Collection)

Above, on January 7, 1947, freight motors 1008A and 1008B pull one of the last freights under the P. & S.R. trolley wire. Shortly afterward, these motors will take their Last Ride to Sacramento for scrapping. (Stephen D. Maguire Collection)

Left, by April 6, 1941, Windsplitter No. 55 had long since ended her passenger service. Although she still has her seats, trolley pole mounts, and trim lines, she is relegated to company service. (Stephen D. Maguire Collection)

No. 506

Builder: Petaluma & Santa Rosa Shops
Year: 1923
Length: 30′10″
Weight: 93,000 lbs.
Trucks: B - B

Built with body from ex-Sacramento Northern No. 1000 and running gear and electrical equipment from the Ocean Shore R.R. Scrapped in 1947. No. 506 pulled the last train carrying passengers over the P. & S.R.—a railfan special using Northwestern Pacific R.R. passenger cars on April 6, 1941.

Note: In 1921 the Ocean Shore R.R. went bankrupt and sold two of its three locomotives to the P & S.R., Nos. 51 and 53. Which of these two became P. & S.R. No. 504 and which one was stripped for parts with which to build No. 506 is unknown.

No. 100

Builder: Baldwin
Year: 1912
Weight: 121,000 lbs.
Horsepower: 1,000
Tractive Force: 21,600 lbs.
Trucks: B - B; 36½″ wheels

Leased in years 1933-1941 from Southern Pacific (S.P. No. 100). Sister loco to S.P. electric Nos. 101-102. Sold by S.P. to Waterloo, Cedar Falls & Northern in Iowa.

Line Cars
Original Car

Builder: Holman
Year: 1904

Originally this car was a flatcar with a tower mounted on it and used for construction of the P.& S.R. Sometime prior to 1909 it was fitted with the trucks and electrical gear from de-motorized No. 69. Rebuilt to Freight Motor No. 1010 around 1916-1917.

No. 4

Builder: Petaluma & Santa Rosa Shops
Year: 1915-1917
Length: 35′10″

Converted from Express Motor No. 8 between 1915 and 1917. Later rebuilt to Express Trailer No. 01.

No. 8

Builder: Petaluma & Santa Rosa Shops
Length: 28′7″
Weight: 22,500 lbs.
Trucks: Arch bar
Body: Converted from wood boxcar

Built by P. & S.R. to handle line car duties when No. 4 reverted to express service. Retired at end of electrification of P. & S.R.

The area between Petaluma, Sebastopol, and Santa Rosa was for many years known as the "Poultry and Egg Capital of the World." Indeed, for many years there was a veterinarian in Petaluma who specialized in treatment of chickens! Support for the electric railroad by the poultry farmers is evident in this freight receipt. (Jo Ann Shelburne Collection)

Chapter Eight
The Country's Longest Interurban

Sacramento Northern Railway

On January 21, 1951, San Franciscans were treated to an unusual sight—a single-truck streetcar, in Sacramento Northern livery, traveling on the city's streetcar tracks. Unusual? Perhaps so, but the Sacramento Northern Railway seemed to thrive on the unusual. Consider these items: the only interurban-carrying ferryboat in the United States; electric power drawn from third rail, trolley pole, and pantograph, and using no less than three different voltages; the nation's longest interurban line, running almost 180 miles between Oakland and Chico; extensive bridges and trestles; the last local streetcar service in California to charge a five-cent fare. Since these items alone should whet the appetite of any true traction fan, let us return to where it all began, in June of 1905 in the town of Chico, California.

The small town of Chico was a most unlikely place to begin what would eventually become the nation's longest interurban, but in the living room of a Victorian mansion in Oakland, owned by one Henry A. Butters, articles of incorporation were drawn up for the Northern Electric Company. This company, fathered by Butters, David S. Edwards, Alpheus W. Clement, Charles A. Rose, and Adolph Loessel, all men of great vision, was to build an electrified railway from Chico to the state capital of Sacramento. River steamers would connect with the trains and transport passengers and freight the rest of the way to San Francisco.

Butters was a dynamic figure in the history of Northern California, as well as no stranger to electric railways. Having been involved in mining operations in Colorado, he turned to the building of the first electric railway in South Africa (Capetown) in company with Cecil Rhodes and John Hays Hammond. This venture was so successful that the company went on to build the first street railways in Geneva, Lisbon, Mexico City, and Valpraiso. It was the earnings from the Geneva venture that helped finance the Northern Electric.

Against this background, the Northern Electric began with but ten of 30,000 shares of stock subscribed (at $100 per share) and nothing as yet in the treasury. Stage one had been accomplished. Stage two was to acquire the Chico Electric Railway, which had been converted from mule power only the year before, and begin construction from Chico southward toward Sacramento.

(While most of the interurbans under study here were either owned or influenced by the Southern Pacific, the Sacramento Northern and predecessors were intertwined with the interests of George Gould, even to the point of eventually being taken over by Gould's Western Pacific. Fitting it was that the largest industry in Chico, the Diamond Match Company, owned by Gould, gave the road its initial impetus. The Northern Electric's first railway was run to the Diamond Match Company's plant. In that factory was built the road's first piece of motive power: flat motor No. 701, nicknamed by the crews as "Old Maude." Diamond Match would also supply the timber and cutting for the Northern Electric's trolley poles and ties.)

Actual construction of the Northern Electric Railway was begun in October of 1905 in Oroville and by January 29, 1906, the tracks had been laid to Oroville's new covered bridge over the Feather River. With the completion of the Chico-Oroville line on April 11, 1906, a fair crowd (including a probable number of V.I.P.'s) rode Niles-built passenger-baggage combo No. 100 over the new rails to celebrate the event. Fourteen days later, the line was opened for revenue service, with Niles cars for passengers and "Old Maude" for freight.

The big passenger station in Chico was home to the handsome Niles cars with their graceful arched windows. This picture is a postcard view. (Stephen D. Maguire Collection)

Harry A. Mitchell, general manager of the Oakland, Antioch & Eastern, is at the right on the rear platform of the *Moraga* while on a stockholders' special train pulled by No. 1015 in 1913. The setting is Redwood Canyon. (Randolph Brandt Collection)

Northern Electric No. 100 at the head of a two-car train in Chico in 1907. So new was the railway that street paving was still unfinished. (Stephen D. Maguire Collection)

O.A. & E. No. 1002 was one of the two original cars on the South End. She is shown here between Meinert and Gavin on the Walwood Branch.

No. 1001 running solo in S.N. days. Unlike No. 1002, she underwent some major rebuilding.

It is said by some historians of electric railroading that the wooden interurban cars from Niles Car Company were the handsomest and most photogenic of all. Indeed, it is rare to find a Niles car which did not make a good subject for a photographer. Designed with railroad-type roofs, tall arched windows, and tongue-and-groove vertical siding with curved corners, they were easily recognizable to any student of interurban carbody design.

From the very outset, road construction was of the highest standards. The rails were laid according to the criteria of the steam railroads, and the overhead trolley wire was by direct suspension, supported by cross spans and brackets. Perhaps part of this can be attributed to the N.E.'s hiring of Frank J. Ross as Superintendent. Ross had had prior experience in the traction field as manager of the Sacramento Street Railway (later owned by the Pacific Gas & Electric Company).

The next section to be built—the line to Marysville—was highlighted by a steam vs. electric war, albeit not as violent as that of the Battle of Santa Rosa. To begin with, it was rumored that Butters was in league with John Martin of the North Shore R.R., when in reality, Martin had plans of his own with his projected California Midland, which would run from Marysville to Auburn and Nevada City using electric power. Moreover, the Western Pacific had its own plans for running through Marysville to Sacramento, and competition with the Northern Electric was not a part of those plans.

After some rather deft maneuvering of franchise applications for street operations in Marysville, an agreement for shared trackage was

END OF AN ERA

Last Sacramento Northern Passenger
Train in Contra Costa County
Between Walnut Creek and Port Chicago

SUNDAY, APRIL 12, 1964

〜〜〜SOUVENIR COUPON〜〜〜

Sponsored by
WALNUT CREEK JAYCEES
in co-operation with
Bay Area Electric Railroad Association
and
Northern California Railroad Club

LEAVE WALNUT CREEK   12:30 PM

(Ray Hannah Collection)

An Oakland, Antioch & Eastern train with Nos. 1003, 1020 and *Moraga* crossing Lake Temescal sometime before 1915. (Robert Hannah photo/Randolph Brandt Collection)

reached with the California Midland. This left the N.E. and the W.P., together with their citizen and journalist allies, to fight it out, and so they did. On January 12, 1907, the Northern Electric sent a crew of some one hundred men to connect its tracks to its newly laid rail in Marysville. The Western Pacific, meanwhile, had also reached Marysville and laid its rail across the N.E.'s right-of-way. It was the job of the electric crew to cross the steam road's steel. They didn't cross it—they merely tore it up and went merrily on their way.

Saturday, July 20, 1907, saw the first Northern Electric trains reach Sacramento from Marysville, and under steam power at that. The N.E. could take no chances of losing its franchise rights by default and therefore used its steam locomotive (purchased originally for construction purposes) in order to ensure a maiden run.

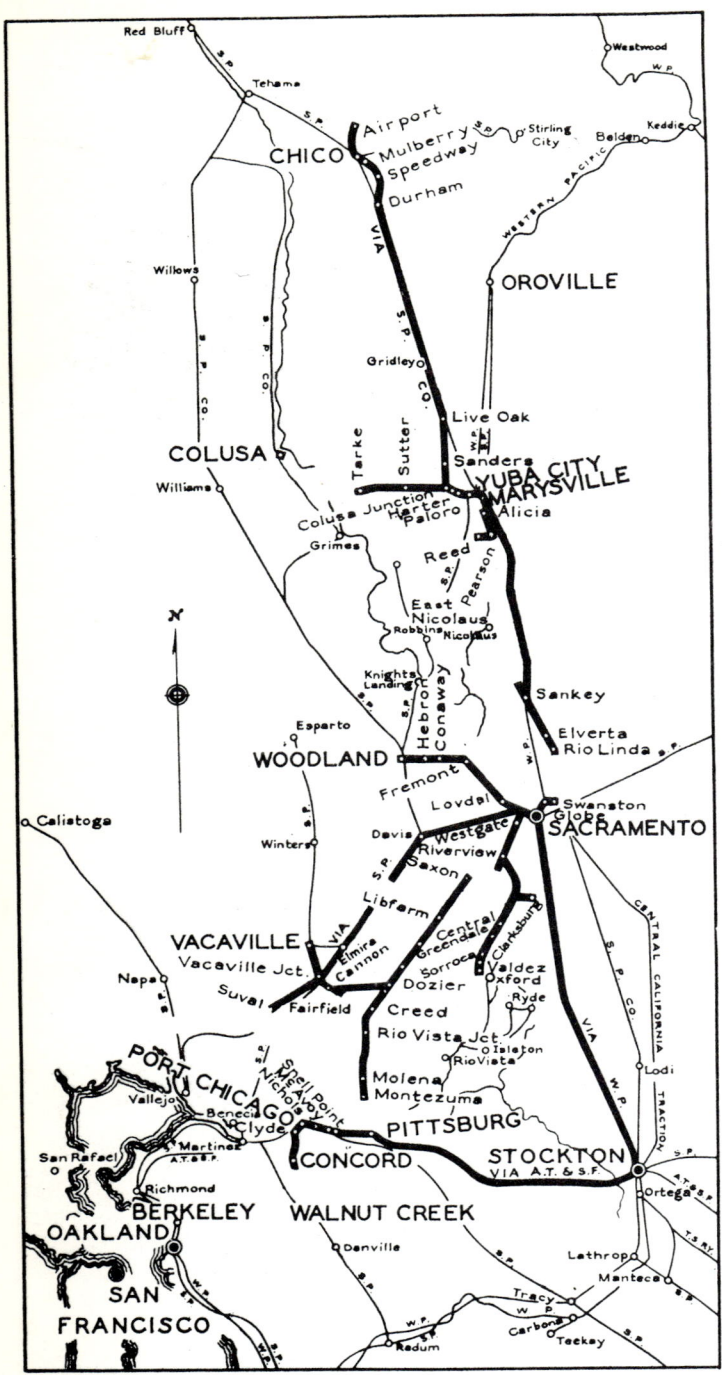

SACRAMENTO NORTHERN RAILWAY

During the Sacramento Northern's de-electrification period, trackage rights were secured from other railroads until the S.N.'s once continous mainline was a series of sections. Even more fragmented today, the S.N. is now fully integrated into the Western Pacific's system. (Courtesy of Western Pacific Railroad Co.)

From that point on, the Northern Electric continued to advance its tracks. To Yuba City (1907). To Hamilton City (September 12, 1907). To Woodland (July 4, 1912). To Colusa (June 13, 1913). To Swanston (1914). And the isolated Vacaville Branch to Willotta (1914). Never fulfilled, however, were the original plans to complete the road to Red Bluff. Because of this, the Mulberry Shops—carshops of the N.E.—remained at the N.E.'s tag end and not in the center.

On June 20, 1918, the Sacramento Northern Railroad Company was incorporated. Eleven days later, on July 1, the Sacramento Northern bought the Northern Electric at auction, and gave to American interurban railroading one of the industry's most prestigious names.

The new Sacramento Northern instituted a variety of changes, some minor, two major. The minor changes included a new painting scheme for the cars (from orange to Pullman green), adoption of single-truck, one-man, Birney Safety cars for local streetcar service, and two place name changes (Tres Vias to Oroville Junction and Heyman to Colusa Junction). The major changes were through parlor car services to Oakland and the building of a union traction terminal at Sacramento.

Interestingly, in 1922 the Interstate Commerce Commission claimed jurisdiction over the Sacramento Northern despite protests that the road was primarily an electrically powered interurban line. The I.C.C.'s reasoning was based upon the S.N.'s heavy freight hauls, its connections with the transcontinental railroads, and the exchange of freight cars. The I.C.C. discounted any reference to motive power, as its main concern was the railroad and its operation.

The founders of the Northern Electric had always intended to be able to schedule passengers all the way to San Francisco with a minimum of passenger transfers, but distances and a water barrier always seemed to stand in the way. With the completion of the Oakland, Antioch & Eastern Railway from Oakland to Sacramento, through train service to Oakland (with connections to the Key System's ferries to San Francisco) was not only feasible but desirable.

Accordingly, the beginnings of through train service began with an agreement between the O.A. & E. and the S.N. to exchange parlor cars so passengers traveling through would not have to get off and transfer at Sacramento, but could ride

From the 40th and Shafter shops emerged repaired cars, rebuilt cars, and new cars. Without much elbow room, 40th and Shafter still managed to get in a lot of railroading. Featured are two classes of freight locos, a passenger trailer, and a passenger-baggage combo. (Stephen D. Maguire Collection)

through on the same car; a slightly higher tariff was charged passengers who used the parlor car service. O.A. & E. parlor cars were the *Moraga* and the *Sacramento*, and the Sacramento Northern furnished *Alabama* and *Bidwell*.

The parlor cars were the last word in luxury aboard a western interurban. Equipped not only with observation platforms (except for the *Alabama*), but with first-class appointments and dining facilities as well, they were the equal of any accommodations for railway passengers in the United States, and certainly an inducement to ride the interurbans during the heyday of the Southern Pacific's competing steam services to Sacramento.

To facilitate connections between the traction companies, a union traction terminal was jointly built in Sacramento by the Central California Traction, the Sacramento Northern, and the successor to the Oakland, Antioch & Eastern, the San Francisco-Sacramento Railroad.

On December 23, 1921, the Sacramento Northern was taken over by the Western Pacific and a corporate union with the San Francisco-Sacramento R.R. (advertised as the Sacramento Short Line) was imminent.

Five years the junior of the Northern Electric, the Oakland, Antioch & Eastern had its beginnings as the Oakland & Antioch Railway, incorporated January 13, 1909, for the purpose of linking the state capital with Oakland via high speed electric trains as well as branch line services. Incorporators for the O. & A. were: A. W. Maltry, S. L. Napthaly, Allan Pollock, Walter Arnstein, F. E. Brooks, H. A. Mitchell, F. W. Smith and J. Napthaly. Capital stocks of twenty thousand shares with par value of one hundred dollars each were issued.

While Sacramento was the long distance objective, the immediate intent was to use an electrically powered railroad to conquer the Coast Range Mountains, which had long separated Oakland from the Central Valley of California and had prevented any large scale commerce between the farmers of the rich delta regions of Contra Costa County and the expanding communities of Alameda, Berkeley and Oakland. True, the Santa Fe and the Southern Pacific did offer some service, but that was round-and-about at best, and at the worst never solved the problem of handling potential commuter traffic. With construction beginning in 1910, it was hoped that

The long climb up the hill to Havens was such that for safety reasons every train had to have at least two motors in its consist. No. 1014 heads Train #6, bound for Sacramento, at Valle Vista. (Tom Gray)

All aboard! A seven-car train, with parlor-observation car *Moraga* on the rear, makes up *The Comet*, S.N.'s crack train for Sacramento. (Charles A. Smallwood)

One of the most beautiful cars ever to travel on interurban rails in California was *Bidwell*, a Niles coach rebuilt to a parlor-observation car at Mulberry Shops in Chico. *Bidwell* is shown running with the *Meteor*, companion train to *The Comet*, in August 1941. At the head end is 1014 and in the middle is 1005. (Stephen D. Maguire)

these problems would be bested. In time they would.

From the onset, the Oakland & Antioch's (and later titles to the same railroad) fortunes were linked with two other traction companies: the Central California Traction and the Key System. Electrified at 1200 volts, the Oakland & Antioch used Central California Traction express motors on its work trains. This led to early ill-founded rumors that the new interurban line would divert its tracks to Stockton and attempt to reach Sacramento via C.C.T. rails. Actual construction never substantiated the rumor, however, except to say that had a connection of this sort ever been effected, there is no telling what impact it would have had on the fortunes of electric railroading. That subject, though, will be treated later.

More so than the Central California Traction, however, the Oakland & Antioch's relations with "Borax" Smith's Key Route spelled success. Connections with the Key Route's ferryboat fleet would mean that passengers would travel from Contra Costa County to San Francisco with a minimum of inconvenience. The use of the Key System rails and franchise rights would take the new interurbans into the City of Oakland itself. The Key System's lines (particularly the C Line-Piedmont via 40th Street) would provide excellent feeder service to its yards and depot at the intersection of 40th Street and Shafter Avenue in Oakland. Later, the Key System's San Francisco-Oakland Terminal Railway would handle freight shuttle service connection with the Sacramento Northern. It was logical, then, that the resurrection of the Key System by BART would include portions of the original routes, and, in part, actual right-of-way.

Providing not only the use of right-of-way, in March of 1965 the Sacramento Northern delivered the first piece of rolling stock to BART: Test Track Car "C," nicknamed *Clara*. Shortly afterward, the S.N. completed delivery of Test Track Cars "A" and "B," thus providing a semblance of orderly transition to the Bay Area's passenger rail service.

Construction of the interurban railway, which was done by the White Engineering Company of New York, centered around the cutting of a 3,200-foot tunnel from Havens to Eastport which made possible the negotiation of the hills to the east of Oakland. This tunnel was truly an engi-

There were few residents on Shafter Avenue when this six-car train was bound for Sacramento. The newsboy at lower right doesn't look too prosperous. (Charles A. Smallwood)

No. 1019 pauses on Shafter Avenue, Oakland, prior to turning into the yards at 40th Street. (Stephen D. Maguire Collection)

neering marvel, for while it cut through rock on the east side, it nonetheless encountered extremely wet and unstable ground on the Oakland (west) side due to its proximity to the Hayward Fault Zone, the source of many earthquakes in Northern California. This problem was countered by using reinforced concrete lining to prevent swelling of the walls and floor. The tunnel was equipped with fire doors, but due to excellent construction and maintenance they were never used, nor even needed.

The roadbed used seventy-pound rail, adequate for the time. The electric overhead was catenary, using 0000 contact wire, and the new railway employed the latest in electric block signal systems. The South End, as the Oakland-Sacramento portions of the Sacramento Northern came to be called, never used a third rail as did the North End, the Sacramento-Chico segment.

Two Holman-built passenger motors, Nos. 1001 and 1002, gave the O. & A. its first passenger equipment, but before they were placed in service, the railroad had become the Oakland, Antioch & Eastern Railway.

The "Antioch" part of the Oakland, Antioch & Eastern name soon lost significance as the rails progressed northward, separating the namesake city from its branch line ending at Pittsburg, some five miles to the west. Further, the speculation of the interurban going to Stockton was quashed as the trackage turned northward from Walnut Creek to Concord, to Bay Point (now Port Chicago), eastward to Mallard and Pittsburg, and by ferry from Mallard to Chipps Island to embark on a northerly direction to Sacramento.

The reason for the rumors concerning the O. A. & E. going to Stockton, or even who started them, has never been clearly ascertained, but the most plausible explanation is that it was to ward off any ideas that the Northern Electric might have had *vis-a-vis* an extension from Sacramento to Oakland/San Francisco. No matter. The two roads eventually merged under the stewardship of the Western Pacific, which held one-third interest in the Central California Traction anyway.

North of Pittsburg the O. A. & E. encountered its first water barrier on the run to Sacramento: Suisun Bay. Original plans called for a bridge, but as work on the piers began, it was decided to use a ferry instead, perhaps because one condition for permission to build a bridge would have been allowing other railroads access as well. The interurban's first ferry was named the *Bridget*, which was replaced by the *Ramon* after a fatal fire. The north ferry slips were at Chipps Island, and from there the interurbans crossed the Montezuma Slough on a wooden swing bridge. Following this, the trains rolled over the two-mile-long Arcade Trestle.

The electric interurban, after traveling almost due north from Chipps Island, turned northeasterly at Creed and continued in an almost straight line until reaching Saxon. There the rails turned due east and crossed the three-mile-long Lisbon Trestle toward Lisbon.

North of Lisbon was the Oxford Branch, which ran southward from Riversview to Oxford. The mainline, however, continued north toward Sacramento, entering the city over the Northern Electric's tracks on the M Street Bridge.

On September 13, 1913, service was opened to Sacramento, and completion of branch line trackage followed. Apparently the Sacramento North-

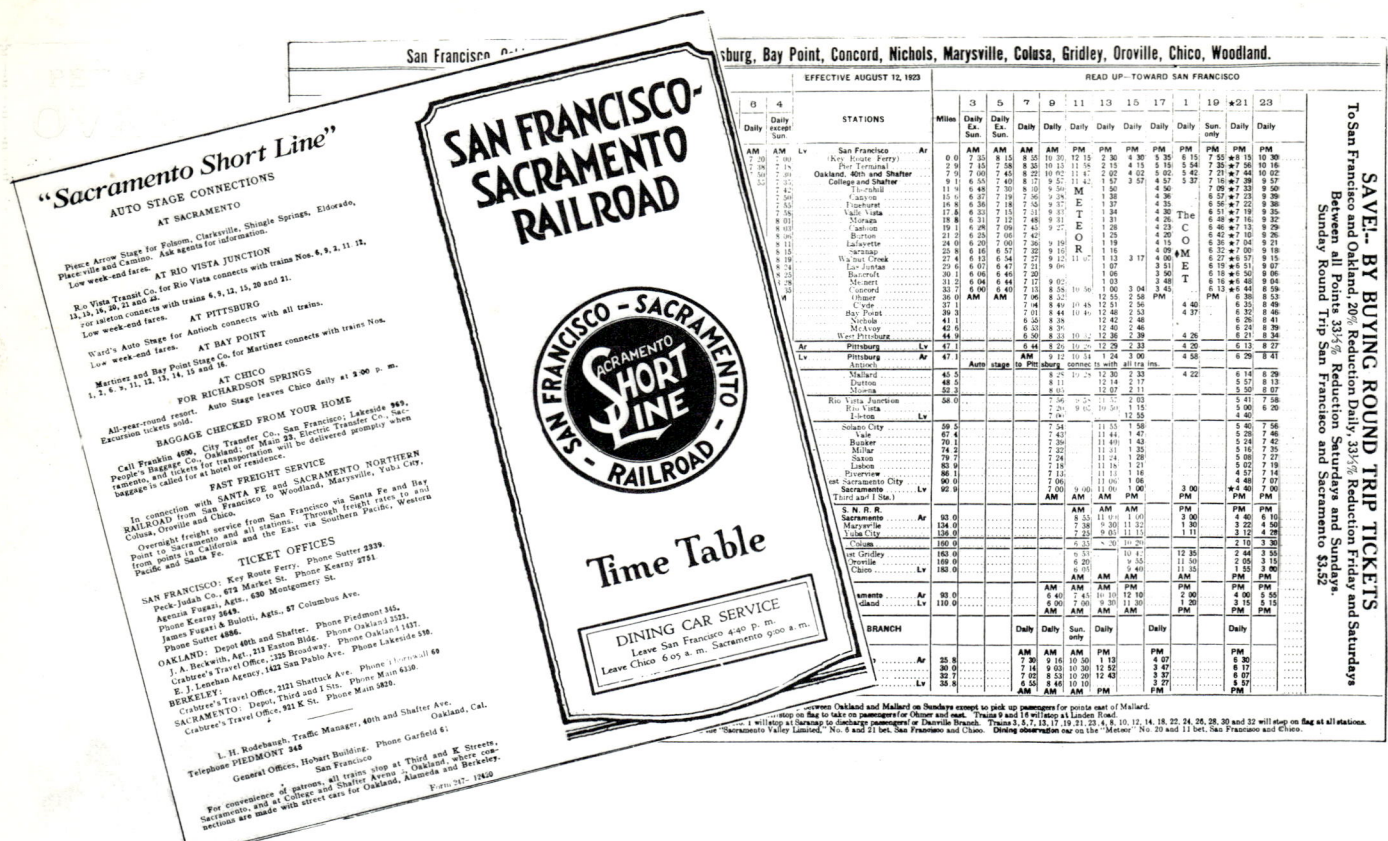

ern's reticence in using the number thirteen for car numbering didn't extend to opening days!

The Pittsburg Branch was completed in September of 1913, with service beginning on the fifth of that month. Motor No. 1001, the O. A. & E.'s first piece of passenger motive power, inaugurated service, becoming a fixture for many years on this branch.

On March 2, 1914, the Danville Branch was opened, running southeasterly from Saranap (Originally called "Ramon Junction," it was renamed Saranap in honor of Sara, the wife of Sam Napthaly, a director of the O.A. & E. Hence, Sara-Nap or Saranap.) to Danville, a distance of about eight miles. This work was done by a subsidiary corporation known as the San Ramon Valley Railroad, Inc.

The next branch line was the short-lived Dixon Branch (See Chapter Eleven).

The hopes of the Vallejo & Northern (See Chapter Eleven) were encompassed in the Vacaville Branch which ran cars westerly from Creed to Vacaville Junction and then branched out farther to Vacaville on the north and Fairfield to the southwest. This had been an isolated branch of the Northern Electric but became a South End connection with the laying of track from Creed in 1930.

Returning now to the City of Oakland, the O. & A. established its nerve center at 40th and Shafter. While certainly not the heart of Oakland (The Southern Pacific/I.E.R., on the other hand, had its major transfer point at 14th and Franklin Streets.) it was nevertheless served well by the Key Route's C Line interurbans and streetcars.

Offsetting much of the good will generated from use of the Key Route's rails were the tracks of the O. A. & E. on Shafter Avenue. The running of both passenger trains and freight on Shafter Avenue's single track quickly aroused the enmity of the street's residents, an attitude which persisted up to and including the last day of operations, February 28, 1957.

(Perhaps it can be considered a backhanded compliment to the surveyors and engineers who laid out the roadbed for the trip through Oakland and beyond, but while parts of the old right-of-way have been subverted for automobile use, other sections are being incorporated by the Bay Area Rapid Transit District [BART].)

While this picture shows a good mix of North End and South End equipment, it also demonstrates how interurban trains became an increasing annoyance to motorists. Train #2 in Sacramento in January of 1939 was no exception. (Stephen D. Maguire Collection)

In 1940 the town of Chico, northernmost reach of the Bay Area's interurbans, was still host to the photogenic Niles cars. This three-car train still looked good after thirty-four years of service. (Stephen D. Maguire Collection)

From 40th and Shafter, the route proceeded to College Park, to Rockridge, to Temescal, to Thornhill, through the Montclair District, through the tunnel from Havens to Eastport, then on to Canyon, Pinehurst, Valle Vista and Moraga. At Havens, northbound motors got their first rest after the strain of pulling both varnish and freight up no less than a four percent grade in the Lake Temescal region. From Moraga, the interurbans stopped at St. Mary's College, Burton, Lafayette, Saranap, Walnut Creek and points north.

A rule on the Oakland Hills section stipulated that every train had to have at least two cars or motors in its consist. The origin of this requirement was a serious accident early in the life of the route, in which a gondola car became disengaged from a locomotive and rolled freely downhill for two miles. It was stopped only by the smashup method, involving a Key Route streetcar and a real estate office. The gondola hit the streetcar and was derailed, sending it into the real estate office. The office was demolished. The accident aside, a brace of heavy duty hogs was a necessity to haul freight trains up that four percent climb.

While operating in the Key Division, or Oakland west of 40th and Shafter, it was necessary to conform to Key System voltages and signal systems. Since the South End was electrified at 1200 volts and the Key at 600 volts, the O. A. & E. motive power was equipped to operate on either voltage. Thus South End motors were fitted out both with trolley poles for 1200-volt running and pantographs for 600-volt running with the changeover occurring at 40th and Shafter. They were also fitted out with tripper arms for use on the Key Pier. North End motors, on the other hand, never faced this problem, and therefore were not equipped to work both ends. While there had been plans to refit North End combos for this purpose, the Great Depression left the Sacramento Northern short of the necessary funds.

In 1939, when the S.N. began to use the Bay Bridge, further adjustments had to be made in the current collection systems. It was agreed to run the Key System trains over the bridge at 600

En route to Oakland, Train #27, headed by No. 1014, sweeps past an army of swimmers and sunbathers at Lake Temescal in 1940. (Tom Gray Collection)

The highlight of the Sacramento Northern came when passengers could ride directly into San Francisco without having to transfer to the Key Route's ferries. Train #3 was the first train of the day to arrive from Chico, completing the longest interurban run in America. Bert Martin is motorman on Train #3 on January 30, 1939. (State of California Toll Bridge Administration)

volts, using the outside third rail. The Sacramento Northern and the Interurban Electric Railway were to use their pantographs to pick up current from the overhead at 1200 volts. This meant that any motors, whether North End or South End, which had third rail shoes for the 1200 volts of the North End could not be used on the Bay Bridge.

Whereas the North End was notorious for its use of wooden cars from the Niles Company, the South End was equally known for the big steel cars from the Hall-Scott Motor Car Company and the wood and steel cars from Wason, Holman, and Cincinnati Car Company. The end bulkheads had a square look, square or rectangular windows, and an appearance of solidity which was reinforced by the sturdy steel sides and arch roofs. Amazingly, this design was never copied on other roads; amazing because carbody designs were rarely confined to one railway.

As with most of the Nation's interurban systems, and certainly for most of the systems encompassed in this volume, the Great Depression and the horseless carriage combined to bring about the demise of passenger service. The use of the Bay Bridge to bring passengers directly into downtown San Francisco was a last-ditch attempt by the Sacramento Northern to recoup passenger patronage, which had been dwindling for some years, but the same bridges which enabled the trains to come directly into San Francisco also eased the way for automobiles. Commuter traffic from Contra Costa County to San Francisco had not reached the volume it is today and the S.N.

Track 6 was the domain of the Sacramento Northern in the Transbay Terminal, and Train #3, having freshly arrived from Chico at 1:40 P.M., is now designated DH-3, meaning the train is now a "deadhead" and out of revenue service. Sharing the terminal with the S.N. is the Key System on Track 4 and the I.E.R. on Track 3. (State of California Toll Bridge Administration)

asked the Public Utilities Commission of the State of California for permission to bow out as a passenger carrier. So it came to pass that combo No. 1009 headed the last S.N. Train #10 for Sacramento on a sad August 26, 1940. Commuter services continued from Pittsburg to San Francisco until June 30, 1941, when the Sacramento Northern hauled its final varnish, except for a single round trip on the two succeeding Saturdays between 40th Street and Shafter Avenue in Oakland and Pittsburg, with the trains designated as Train #6 eastbound and Train #27 westbound. Combo No. 1014 performed these last rites.

Gone now were the name trains *Comet* and *Meteor* which made the ninety-three-mile trip from San Francisco to Sacramento in three hours and fifteen minutes, including fifteen minutes on the Key System's ferryboats and ten minutes on the Sacramento Northern's ferry *Ramon*. Gone were the deluxe parlor cars *Alabama*, *Bidwell*, *Moraga*, and *Sacramento*. Gone were the eighty-five-cent dinners for which one menu offered pineapple salad, choice of club steak or lamb chops, omelette of minced ham, hash-browned potatoes, hot biscuits, apple pie, and a choice of coffee, tea or milk. All that remained were the cold economics of railroading which indicated that freight was more profitable to haul than people.

The only remaining passenger business of the Sacramento Northern was the streetcar service, and even the diminutive streetcars had their own final moments of glory, for in 1951, S.N. No. 62, a four-wheel Birney, had the distinction of making the last streetcar run down San Francisco's Market Street to the Ferry Building, under the auspices of the Bay Area Electric Railroad Association. Conversely, ex-Municipal Railway of San Francisco No. 178 had the honor of making the final streetcar run between Yuba City and Marysville, a trip which was also sponsored by the B.A.E.R.A.

Despite the appearance of loco No. 650 on the cover of the December, 1953 issue of *Railroad Magazine*, it was all too obvious by 1950 that the big electric locomotives were doomed in favor of dieselization. The opening of the Southern Pacific's bridge across the Carquinez Strait in 1930 meant a faster carding than the S.N., still using the *Ramon*, could muster. Freight runs from the electric overhead had begun their retreat

In January of 1957, the Bay Area Electric Railroad Association sponsored a railfan special over the S.N.'s tracks—the final passenger trip for the interurban railway. Motor No. 1005 is pulling ex-Salt Lake & Utah No. 751. Today both cars are at the California Railway Museum and sometimes still run together for old times' sake. (Stephen D. Maguire Collection)

in the face of acquisition of diesel-electric locomotives which first appeared in 1946. With more and more diesel power coming to the S.N.'s roster, the electrification was cut back section by section.

The most dramatic ending of an electrified stretch of high iron on the Sacramento Northern occurred at 2:59 P.M. on Tuesday, July 24, 1951, when a twenty-one-car trainload of steel with steeple cab No. 650 on the head end was crossing the Lisbon Trestle. At once the entire trainlength of trestle collapsed—pile bent by pile bent, like a row of dominoes. When rebuilt, the Lisbon Trestle was not electrified, nor was any of the trackage north of the Sacramento River retained as electric except for the Marysville-Yuba City run. In 1954, the United States Coast Guard condemned the *Ramon* and she was retired from service. Sacramento Northern trains, with diesel-electrics on the head ends, were rerouted over the Western Pacific's and Santa Fe's tracks between Sacramento and Pittsburg via Stockton.

In 1957, the last scheduled freight train under electric power on the South End pulled out of the 40th and Shafter complex in Oakland to begin the farewell climb through the Oakland hills. This nine-car consist, with loco No. 652 on the point, was manned by engineer Les Paul, conductor Walter Butterfield, and brakeman Charles Dowd. O. H. Schindler was the engineer on helper locomotive No. 653 at the rear. The overhead was then taken down between Oakland and West Lafayette. Electric operations were cut back to Walnut Creek in 1958, and in 1964 the trackage between Walnut Creek and Concord was discontinued in order to allow the Bay Area Rapid Transit District to absorb the old right-of-way for test track, and later, mainline purposes. This section of the S.N. lives on today under the auspices of BART.

By 1960, a map of Sacramento Northern electrification showed only the rails between Marysville and Yuba City, and for switching duties only at that. Reduced to using locomotives 653 and 654, it was only a matter of time before they too would leave the S.N. roster. Loco No. 652 was kept at this time in the Western Pacific's Sacramento Shops (Mulberry was long gone) to be cannibalized for spare parts. In April of 1965, the last electric trains ceased to run, and all overhead was de-energized.

Parent Western Pacific, wielding a sharp blue pencil, eliminated much of the S.N.'s trackage that was unprofitable, and in its stead obtained trackage rights from other roads where necessary, thus reducing a once proud mainline to strictly a feeder service, and a profitable one at that. Today the S.N. Ry. carries on an important function as a major link between W.P. and the marketplace. While locos and cabooses often bear the heralds of the S.N., sometimes locomotives in Tidewater Southern (See Chapter Eleven) or W.P. livery appear on Sacramento Northern's tracks as part of the Western Pacific's motor pool system.

Box motor No. 602 came to the S.N. from the O.A. & E. Strictly a local product, she was outshopped by Holman in San Francisco in 1912. (Stephen D. Maguire Collection)

SACRAMENTO NORTHERN'S SACRAMENTO TERMINALS

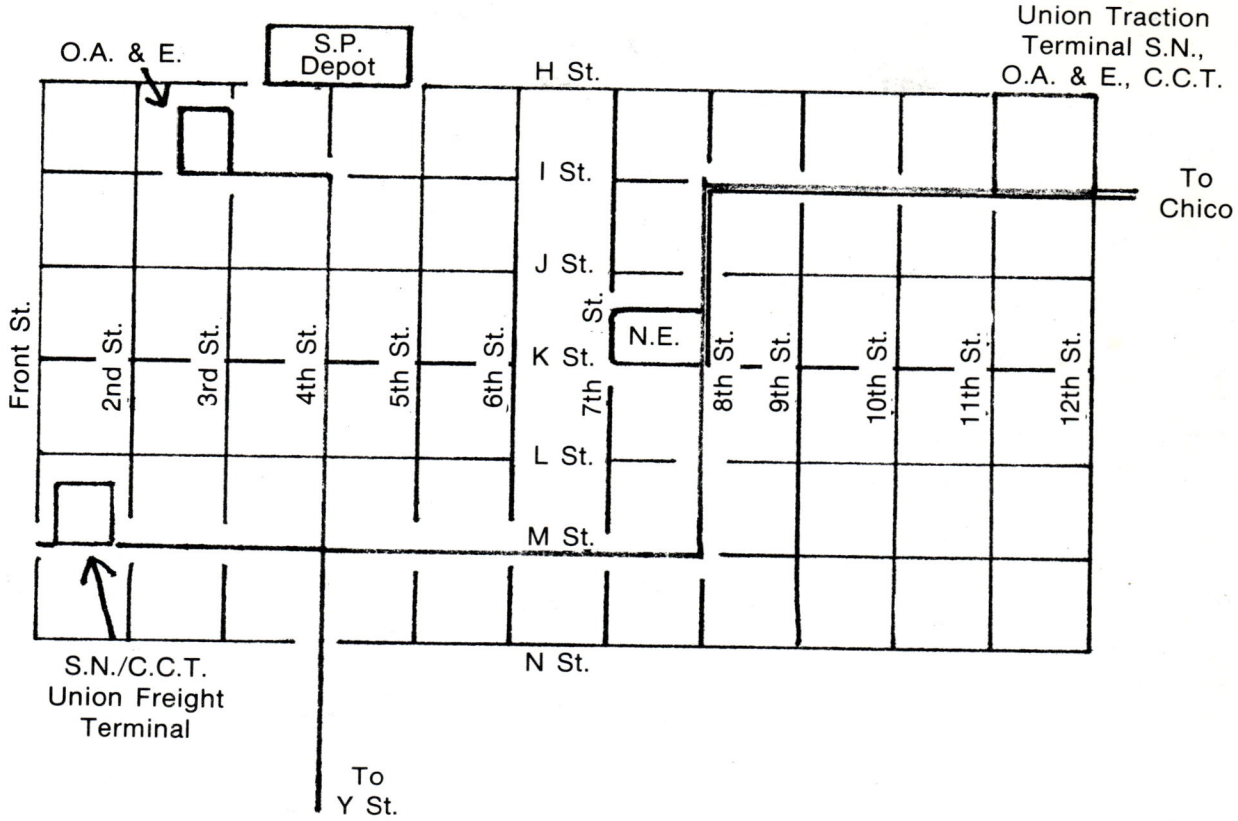

Northern Electric and Sacramento Northern trains arrived from Chico via C Street, 15th Street, I Street, thence to respective terminals.

Oakland, Antioch & Eastern and Sacramento Northern trains arrived from San Francisco over the M Street Bridge (to left of map, not shown).

Freight trains rumbling down city streets were the cause of much citizen antagonism toward freight-hauling interurbans in the United States. The residents along Shafter Avenue in Oakland did not shed many tears when this trackage was abandoned. (Stephen D. Maguire Collection)

Juice hog No. 440 shuttles a cut of freight cars on Oakland's 40th Street. For many years the S.N. shared this trackage with the Key System's C Line-Piedmont. (Tom Gray)

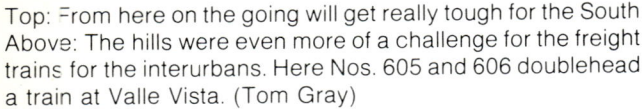

Top: From here on the going will get really tough for the South

Above: The hills were even more of a challenge for the freight trains for the interurbans. Here Nos. 605 and 606 doublehead a train at Valle Vista. (Tom Gray)

Above: The hills were even more of a challenge for the freight trains for the interurbans. Here Nos. 605 and 606 doublehead a train at Valle Vista. (Tom Gray)

Above right: Streetcar No. 62 came to the S.N. from San Diego. On December 14, 1947, the S.N.'s streetcars were the last in California to charge a five-cent fare. (Stephen D. Maguire Collection)

Above: No one knew how many miles No. 228 had traveled by the time S.N. service was routed directly into San Francisco, but she was still a proud vehicle as she stood guard with a Hall-Scott-built motor on Track 6.

Sacramento Northern's Rolling Stock During Electric Period

The Sacramento Northern carried an extensive roster, rivalled only by the Key System among the eight Bay Area interurban lines. This was largely due to the proliferation of trackage, as well as to the fact that the S.N. was a merger of two roads, each of which was a bona fide interurban railway in its own right. Add to this the constant building and rebuilding programs carried on by both the North and South Ends, and we arrive at a list encompassing numerous classes and subclasses.

This list deliberately omits freight cars and cabooses, but is forced to list the streetcars inasmuch as they were used for intercity purposes and ran on interurban trackage over rights-of-way.

100-102 Class
Passenger-Baggage Combo

Builder: Niles
Year: 1906
Length: 56'
Weight: 90,000 lbs.
Motors: Four Westinghouse 121A; 90 h.p.
Wheels: 36"
Body: Wood
North end

No. 100 made N.E.'s first run on April 11, 1906; No. 100 wrecked in 1935; No. 102 wrecked in 1912; No. 101 made the farewell trip between Chico and Sacramento on October 30, 1940.

103-105 Class
Passenger-Baggage Combo

Builder: Cincinnati Car Company
Year: 1906
Length: 58'6"
Weight: 84,000 lbs.
Motors: Four Westinghouse 121A; 90 h.p.
Gear Ratio: 24:51
Trucks: Baldwin 741; 36" wheels
North End

Originally passenger motors numbered 203-205; rebuilt and renumbered in 1912; the only N.E. cars with spoked wheels; all were destroyed at Chico in 1941.

106-109 Class
Passenger-Baggage Combo

Builder: St. Louis Car Company
Year: 1906
Length: 51'4"
Weight: 86,000 lbs.
Motors: Four Westinghouse 121A; 90 h.p.
Gear Ratio: 24:51
Trucks: Baldwin 246
Body: Wood and steel
North End

Originally built as part of an order for Philadelphia & Western Railway, they were purchased at the same time as U.R.R. Nos. 1-12, numbered 250-253 and used as passenger motors. In 1912 they were rebuilt into passenger-baggage combos and renumbered. No. 251 was numbered No. 10 of Marysville & Colusa R.R., later N.E. 109; No. 251 was numbered No. 1 of Sacramento & Woodland, later N.E. 108; No. 106 was rebuilt into a freight switcher in the 1920s; No. 107 was rebuilt into a one-man car in 1938; No. 109 made last revenue run to Colusa. All were scrapped in 1940.

125-130 Class
Passenger-Baggage Combo

Builder: N.E. shops from Niles specifications
   (Always considered Niles cars.)
Year: 1909
Length: 58'
Weight: 88,000 lbs.
Motors: Four Westinghouse 323; 100 h.p.
Gear Ratio: 24:51
Trucks: Baldwin 246; 36" wheels
Body: Wood
North End

These cars were rebuilt from time to time, sometimes being rebuilt again. Thus photographs often show variances in window arrangements. Nos. 128 and 130 were scrapped in 1938, the remainder in 1941. Built exactly according to Niles specifications, they had the same wood and steel bodies as did the bona fide Niles cars.

1001-1002 Class
Passenger-Baggage Combo

Builder: Holman Car Company
Year: 1911
Length: 45'
Weight: 60,000 lbs.
Trucks: Brill 27 MCB-1
Body: Wood and steel
South End

No. 1001 rebuilt in 1913 with added section in middle; new length: 56'8", new weight: 76,000 lbs. No. 1002 was rebuilt in 1914 into an inspection car; rebuilt again in 1915 into a combo. Both were destroyed in 1941.

1003-1006 Class
Passenger-Baggage Combo

Builder: Holman
Year: 1912
Length: 58'
Weight: 87,300 lbs.
Motors: Four Westinghouse 322E; 120 h.p.
Trucks: Baldwin 79-308
Body: Wood and steel
South End

No. 1006 carried the first passengers between Oakland and Bay Point; originally equipped with Brown Roller Pantograph, later converted to U.S. 121-A Westinghouse type. Vestibules rebuilt in 1914. Nos. 1003 and 1004 were destroyed in 1941; Nos. 1005 and 1006 to Key System in 1942. No. 1005 to B.A.E.R.A. in 1951.*

1007-1010 Class
Passenger-Baggage Combo

Builder: Cincinnati Car Company
South End

These cars were actually a subclass of the 1003-1006 Class. They featured the squarish look in front. Oddly, the design was never duplicated on any other interurban. Nos. 1007-1008 were destroyed in 1941; No. 1009 to Maint. of Way 80; No. 1010 was destroyed in 1951 by Key System.

1011-1014 Class
Passenger-Baggage Combo

Builder: Wason
South End

Also a subclass of 1003 series. No. 1011 was at the head of the first S.N. train across the Bay Bridge in 1939. No. 1014 made the farewell passenger run in 1941.

1015-1018 Class
Passenger-Baggage Combo

Builder: Cincinnati Car Company
South End

Similar to 1007-1010 Class. No. 1017 was originally a trailer until assignment to the Dixon Branch. Outfitted with controls pieced together from spare parts, she had a bad electrical fire and had to be towed back to Oakland for extensive repairs. No. 1016 and 1017 were scrapped in 1941; Nos. 1015 and 1018 were scrapped by Key System in 1951.

*Preserved by the B.A.E.R.A. at its museum.

Builder: Central Pacific Shops
Year: 1873
Length: 60'0"
Weight: 78,000 lbs.
Motors: Four G.E. 205
Gear Ratio: 16:58
Trucks: Baldwin 79-30B; 37" wheels
Controller: Westinghouse C6A
Body: Wood
South End

Builder: Niles
Year: 1906
Body: Wood and steel
North End

Builder: Hall-Scott Motor Car Company
Year: 1913
Length: 59'0"
Weight: 101,780 lbs.
Motors: Westinghouse 322E
Trucks: Baldwin 79-30B
Controller: Westinghouse 15A2
Body: Steel
South End

Builder: Niles
Year: 1906
Length: 58'0"
Weight: 64,000 lbs.
Body: Wood and steel
North End

Builder: Southern Pacific
Year: 1880s
Length: 60'
Weight: 52,000 lbs.
Trucks: Southern Pacific
  (1204 trucks from Baldwin)

*Preserved by the B.A.E.R.A. at its museum.

1051 Class
Passenger-Baggage Combo

Acquired from Southern Pacific in 1913, No. 1051 was first used as a construction motor on the Dixon Branch and others until assigned to the Danville Branch. Ungainly, she was nicknamed "the Alligator" by crews. Used almost exclusively on the Danville Branch, she was dismantled at the 40th and Shafter shops in 1924 when the Danville Branch was abandoned. Trucks, motors, and other parts were used in construction of No. 607.

200-202 Class
Passenger Motors

The passenger motor did not figure greatly in Northern Electric's plans or operations. Rarely did the North End head a train with a passenger motor, and this class more often was used in the middle of a train of three or more cars, again a rarity. No. 201 was rebuilt into a combo in 1915, and retired in 1937. No. 202 was so badly damaged in a wreck in 1913 that in 1914 her trucks and underframe were used in building parlor car *Bidwell*. No. 200 was the only car of this class to survive until 1940 without alteration.

1018-1020 Class
Passenger Motors

Originally built as passenger trailers, the Hall-Scotts were intended to be pulled behind locomotives. This plan was shelved due to the weight of locos on the Key Pier. All were motorized in 1915 with 1018 being renumbered from 1026 on December 5, 1926. Nos. 1019 and 1020* were converted to M.W. 301-302 in 1940. No. 1018 became the property of the Toll Bridge Authority in 1940, then was sold to Key System (Key System No. 499) and scrapped by the Key in 1951.

220-229 Class
Passenger Trailers

Nos. 220, 221, and 223 remained in original condition until scrapping in 1940. Nos. 222, 224, 226, and 228 were given South End controls after merger, but had to run "dead" on North End track thereafter due to differences in controls. Nos. 227 and 229 were rebuilt into combos in 1919, being renumbered 131 and 132. All were destroyed in 1941.

1201-1206 Class
Passenger Trailers

Purchased by O.A. & E. in 1913. Nos. 1202, 1203, and 1204 had railroad roofs removed and arch roofs added in September of 1919; all others kept their original roofs. They were occasionally cut off from the rest of the mainline train to continue the run on a branch. Nos. 1202 and 1204 were equipped with controllers. Nos. 1201, 1204, and 1205 were scrapped in 1938. Nos. 1202, 1203 were sold in 1941 to Diamond Match Co. where they were cut down to flat cars. No. 1206 was scrapped at the end of passenger operations by S.N.

Builder: Pennsylvania Railroad
Year: 1880s?
Length: 62′2″
Weight: 70,000 lbs.
Body: Wood
South End

Builder: Holman
Year: 1906
Length: 52′1″
Weight: 50,000 lbs.
Trucks: Baldwin 79-30B
Body: Wood and steel
South End

Builder: Hall-Scott Motor Car Company
Year: 1913
South End

Builder: Cincinnati Car Company
Year: 1913
South End

Builder: Pennsylvania Railroad
Year: 1895
Length: 54′
Weight: 60,000 lbs.
North End

Builder: St. Louis Car Company
Year: 1905
Length: 63′9″
Weight: 96,400 lbs.
Trucks: 1 Hedley, 1 Baldwin
North End

1207 Class
Passenger Trailer
This car may have been built in 1890; purchased by O.A. & E. in 1916. Scrapped at Chico in 1938.

1208-1210 Class
Passenger Trailers
Purchased from defunct Ocean Shore R.R. in 1916, they were equipped for use as motors, but did not have motors themselves. No. 1210 was lengthened to 63′7″. No. 1208 was sold to Diamond Match Co. in 1941 and cut down to a flat car (D.M. No. 22). 1209-1210 were destroyed at Chico in 1941.

1021-1025 Class
Passenger Trailers
Sisters to passenger motors 1018-1020, they retained their appearance until the end. All were sold to the Western Pacific in 1941 for branch line use.

1026 Class
Passenger-Baggage
Originally numbered 1018 and sister to 1015 Class. Rebuilt into a passenger-baggage trailer in 1928 and destroyed in 1941.

90 Class
Express Trailer
Purchased in 1907 from Pennsylvania R.R. In 1912 converted to serve as a traveling showcase for electrical machinery and appliances under sponsorship of Pacific Gas & Electric Co. To MW 90 in 1930, destroyed in 1935.

Parlor-Observation Cars
Alabama
The *Alabama* was built by St. Louis Car Co. for Henry Huntington, President of P.E., and was his own personal car. Used on P.E. trackage until P.E. was sold to S.P. Kept in storage on Huntington's estate until 1920 when it was sold to Sacramento Northern. A huge steel car, it contained every luxury of the day, and was easily the most distinguished private car ever to run on interurban trackage. Originally equipped with four 200 h.p. motors, *Alabama* had a theoretical speed of 120 m.p.h.! Destroyed by an accidental fire in 1931.

Builder: Northern Electric Shops, Chico
Year: 1913
North End

Bidwell

The *Bidwell* was built from the wreckage of N.E. No. 202, and is said by experts to be the most photogenic car on the entire S.N. roster. Named for General John Bidwell, Chico's founder. *Bidwell* served until the end of passenger service and was sold to a private individual at Wheatland, California.

Moraga

Builder: Wason
Year: 1913
Length: 57'1"
Weight: 65,000 lbs.
Trucks: Baldwin 79-30B
Body: Wood and Steel
South End

Double-ended *Moraga* was originally equipped with motors, but was demotorized in 1918. Motors went to No. 1026. In 1927 *Moraga* was rebuilt as single-end. She was fitted out with controls for backup purposes only; the only parlor car on the S.N. roster which was originally built for that purpose. Scrapped in 1941.

Sacramento

Builder: Cincinnati; rebuilt as parlor car by O. A. & E.
Year: 1913
Length: 66'0"
Weight: 84,900 lbs.
Trucks: Brill MCB 27
Body: Wood and steel
South End

Sacramento began life as a passenger-baggage combo, original number 1016. Rebuilt by O. A. & E. as a parlor car before entering service. Rebuilt again in 1920 and lengthened to 76'0". However, this made *Sacramento* not only too long to be used on North End curves, but to be moved out of the 40th and Shafter shops as well. Ten feet had to be cut out of her center before she could be sent to the main line. In service to the end, *Sacramento* was scrapped in 1941.

In addition to the above-mentioned passenger equipment, the Sacramento Northern maintained a diverse collection of freight equipment. A brief summary is given here, omitting such appendages as freight cars, cabooses, and maintenance-of-way cars. The S.N. did not use motorized work cars.

No. 701: Nicknamed "Old Maude" by N. E. trainmen, No. 701 was built at the Diamond Match Company plant in Chico. Used in construction of Northern Electric. Scrapped in 1935.

Nos. 402-405: Work motors built by N.E. as follows: 402 and 403 in 1907, 404 in 1908, 405 in 1914. Nos. 402 and 403 were destroyed in 1947, No. 404 was destroyed in 1950, No. 405 was sold in 1954.

No. 410 (ex-1010): No. 1010 was built by Northern Electric as a combination box motor and locomotive. Indeed, this massive (82 tons) loco was able to do the job since all electrical gear was under the floor. First built in 1911, she was later shortened and after merger was renumbered 410. Destroyed in 1954.

No. 420: Greatly resembling No. 410 in appearance, No. 420 was built by Northern Electric in 1915 and destroyed by S.N. in 1952. To all intents and purposes, Nos. 410 and 420 could be considered box cab locomotives.

Nos. 601-602: Both were inherited by Sacramento Northern from the South End after merger. No. 601 was built by American Car Co. and No. 602* by Holman, both in 1912. Both were converted to maintenance-of-way in 1948, being renumbered MW 82 and MW 83, respectively.

No. 607: A wood and steel box motor built by the San Francisco-Sacramento R.R. shops at 40th and Shafter, Oakland, in 1924. Badly damaged from warehouse fire in 1938, she was placed in storage until scrapping in 1941.

Nos. 1000-1001: A pair of steeple cab locos built in N.E.'s Mulberry Shops in Chico in 1906. Both strongly resembled Pacific Electric 1600. No. 1000 was sold in 1923 to Petaluma & Santa Rosa R.R. while sister 1001 was destroyed in 1915 as a result of a wreck.

*S.N. cars so noted are preserved by the B.A.E.R.A. at their museum.

No. 430: Also a steeple cab locomotive, was built by General Electric in 1918 and went out of service for scrapping in 1957.

Nos. 440-442: This trio of steeple cabs was outshopped by Baldwin-Westinghouse in 1918, 1920, and 1920, respectively, for the North End. No. 440 was leased during World War II to Oakland Terminal Ry. Nos. 440 and 442 were scrapped in 1955 while No. 441 was destroyed during the previous year.

Nos. 650-654: No. 650, except for weighing 126,000 lbs. to the others' 123,000 lbs., was in all respects a sister to 651-4. They were built by General Electric as follows: 650-1, 1923; 652-3, 1928; 654, 1930. Except for "Old Maude" and Nos. 1000-1001, No. 654 was the only locomotive ordered for the North End which was not renumbered, partly due to delivery date. Nos. 653 and 654 were the last holdouts against dieselization with No. 652 providing transfusions of spare parts. Nos. 650-651 were taken out of service and destroyed in 1957. In April 1965, No. 654 pulled the last electric freight run—not only on the Sacramento Northern but in the State of California. Nos. 652 and 653 pulled the last scheduled electric train out of Oakland. In 1965, Nos. 652 and 654 were presented to the Bay Area Electric Railroad Association's museum in Rio Vista Junction where they are kept in running condition.

Nos. 660-661: Outshopped by Baldwin-Westinghouse for the North End in 1927, they lasted exactly thirty years on the Sacramento Northern, being destroyed in 1957.

Nos. 603-604: These two steeple cab locomotives, built by Baldwin-Westinghouse in 1912, were delivered to the Oakland, Antioch & Eastern and served faithfully until scrapping in 1957. In 1953 they were renumbered 643 and 644, respectively.

Nos. 605-606: Built by Baldwin-Westinghouse in 1914. As built, they possessed a set of pony wheels at each end which enabled them to negotiate curves at high speeds. As with Nos. 603-604, they possessed a single trolley pole and pantograph to enable them to operate on both 600 and 1200 volts as needed. Later, No. 605 had her pony wheels removed, leaving No. 606 the S.N.'s only 2B = 2B locomotive. Both were destroyed in 1957.

The South End never operated local streetcar service and as such never owned any streetcars. Northern Electric did, however, and actually ran its streetcars from city to city. While not true interurban cars, they do merit consideration. The Sacramento Northern was the last rail transit service in California to charge a five-cent fare.

Nos. 21 and 22 were purchased from St. Louis Car Company in 1904, and came to Northern Electric via Chico Railway Company. Cars 25-28 were also St. Louis builds, constructed as follows: 25-27, 1906 (Northern Electric); 28, 1911 (Vallejo & Northern Railway). In mint condition, they strongly resembled Pacific Electric's California types which had been converted from narrow to standard gauge, even to the point of having curved end windows on each bulkhead. Nos. 50 and 51, built by St. Louis, had one open end with longitudinal seats.

The Birney Safety Car was designed by Charles O. Birney in the years prior to World War I as the answer to the electric railways which had to maintain streetcar service where traffic was light. Generally using only one set of trucks, they were short and were not famous for a smooth ride. Yet, they were economical, because they used less electric power, were one-man, and did not take much room in the carbarns.

Nos. 60 and 61 were Birneys, purchased new from American Car Company in 1918. Nos. 62-68 were also Birneys, purchased secondhand from San Diego Electric Railway. No. 62* had the distinction of being the only Birney ever to run in San Francisco. Birneys No. 69 and 70 were purchased secondhand from the San Jose Railroads in 1936, and were distinguished by their "Ubangi" anti-climbers.

Streetcars 70-73 were purchased secondhand from the United Railroads of San Francisco. As single truck, California type, all cars of that class were sold as fast as possible by the U.R.R., as the company was going all-out on a modernization program after the 1906 Fire and Earthquake. Thus, in 1907, the N.E. purchased Nos. 70-73. Although 70 and 71 were scrapped in 1915, they must have been a good buy since Nos. 72 and 73 found new life on the Union Traction Company's rails in Santa Cruz.

As the Greek plays depict both Triumph and Tragedy, so do the cars of the Sacramento Northern. Triumph in their long life, Tragedy that so many of them were deliberately destroyed.

Chapter Nine
Wine Country and Geysers

San Francisco, Napa & Calistoga Railway

Charles A. Smallwood remembers the Napa Valley Route. Not merely because he is a railfan and historian, but because he was its final passenger. Shortly before his retirement as shop superintendent for the San Francisco Municipal Railway's famed cable car system, he talked with the author about the Napa Valley Route, as the San Francisco, Napa & Calistoga Railway was called. Smallwood remembered them as "good cars... well built." This was the veteran mechanic talking. In reply to the author's remark that it was too bad they couldn't have held out for awhile longer, he became the wistful railfan: "You have to go back to conditions of that time. People were just using their automobiles more and more."

The Napa Valley Route was conceived on December 3, 1901, when J. W. and H. F. Hartzel applied for a franchise to operate an electric interurban railroad in Napa Valley, and was born on April 24, 1902 with the granting of the franchise. The railroad was incorporated on that day as the Vallejo, Benicia & Napa Valley Railroad.

With full intention to operate as far as Lake County, the railroad began grading on December 3, 1903, between Napa and Vallejo, completing it on July 16, 1904. On May 29, 1905, the first piece of rolling stock on the new line arrived from the American Car Company. A work motor strongly resembling a flatcar with a small wooden shed on top, finished by a roof-dwarfing pantograph, the car was used in construction of the railroad; her final duties on the Napa Valley Route would be to assist in its demolition.

On July 2, work had progressed enough for a trial passenger trip to be made. On Independence Day of 1905, the official opening of the rails from Vallejo to Napa Station took place, followed by regular freight and passenger service, powered by 750 volts of alternating current—the only railroad in the Bay Area to use a.c.—on July 20 and August 7, respectively.*

Mention must be made at this point of the Napa Valley Route's decision to employ a.c.—backed by Westinghouse, rather than direct current which was advocated by General Electric. In those years, d.c. was favored for use on electric motors because of its smoother operating efficiency. The drawback, however, was loss of current on the transmission lines. Alternating current, on the other hand, allowed for longer lines with less power loss, eliminating the need for the additional substations which would be demanded by d.c.

Apparently the founders of the Napa Valley Route had further plans when they elected to use a.c. First, the line had always intended to extend the rail service north of Calistoga into Lake County and for years had entertained hopes of reaching Sacramento and other Bay Area cities as well. These distances would have made a.c. transmission quite reasonable. Perhaps the Napa Valley Route felt that it would be cheaper to provide power for its trains with a.c. and not have to equip the line with expensive supporting equipment.

At this time, however, it was being demonstrated on eastern railroad electrifications that d.c. above 600 volts was more practical—so practical that, after 1910, 1200 to 1500 volts d.c. became standard for new interurban lines, and no a.c. systems were established after that year.

---

*The only other interurban in California to use alternating current was the Visalia Electric which operated in ~~Madera~~ County. [Tulare]

133

Steam trains of the Ferries & Cliff House R.R. provided San Franciscans with transportation from Presidio Avenue out California Street to the Cliff House in the 1890s. Fireman John Francis Guerin is on the right of F. & C.H. R.R. No. 8. The open car in back of the loco will later go to the Vallejo, Benicia & Napa Valley R.R. (John J. Crowley, Jr. Collection)

In this postcard scene, V.B. & N.V. is posed on Georgia Street in Vallejo. (Stephen D. Maguire Collection)

In years to come, the use of alternating current on the Napa Valley Route would prove to be more of a hindrance than a help inasmuch as no interurban could interchange electric equipment with the road—even if the rails had made connection with the other lines (principally the Petaluma & Santa Rosa and the Sacramento Northern).

On June 6, 1906, a new corporation was formed, naming itself the San Francisco, Vallejo & Napa Valley Railroad, the purpose of which was to extend railroad service northward up the Napa Valley, and on October 12th of the same year, grading was completed as far as St. Helena.

By August 23, 1907, the interurbans were running as far as the Veterans' Home in Yountville, and three big handsome cars built by the Niles Car Company were in service. On New Year's Day, 1908, St. Helena was linked by the growing interurban network.

On February 28, 1910, the Vallejo, Benicia & Napa Valley Railroad was absorbed into the San Francisco, Vallejo & Napa Valley Railroad, paving the way for the reorganization on November 10th of the following year when the San Francisco, Napa & Calistoga Railway took over the S.F.V. & N.V.R.R.

Construction to Calistoga began in January 1912 and the first service to the road's namesake town began on September 2nd. With this extension, the Napa Valley Route had reached the zenith of its north-south trackage. From the hot springs and geysers of Calistoga through lush farmlands (featuring some of the finest vineyards in the world), down to San Pablo Bay, the cars of the S.F.N. & C.R.R. worked a respectable timecard, even by today's standards. After all, from North Main Street in Napa to Main and Pope Streets in St. Helena in forty-three minutes with two scheduled and six flag stops in between is not exactly crawling!

On June 19, 1913, the Napa Valley Route experienced possibly the worst wreck involving interurbans in the Bay Area. Train #6, the *Calistoga Flyer*, was seventeen minutes late leaving Vallejo since the ferry from San Francisco could not meet its schedule due to bad tides. New train orders were given to Train #6, but because southbound Train #5 had left on time from Calistoga and only two minutes late from Napa, the crew was not given instructions to cover the emergency. On a single track blind reverse curve north of Vallejo near the community of Flosden,

In this early day view at the Vallejo Pier, V.B. & N.V. No. 7 is coupled to two trailers from the Ferries & Cliff House R.R. No. 7 is using a bow collector for picking up electric current from the overhead wire. Widely used in Europe, bow collectors were extremely rare in North America. Railroads using alternating current were also rare—only twenty-eight in all. But then the Napa Valley was a most unusual interurban. (Randolph Brandt Collection)

the *Calistoga Flyer* crashed head on with Train #5, killing thirteen people and injuring many more. Passenger motor No. 41, the lead car on Train #6, was demolished.

The effects of the 1913 wreck were to reverberate for years to come, since the railroad's revenues not only had to pay for all scheduled expenses, but for the costs of litigation as well. Despite periods of relative prosperity, the expenses resulting from this wreck put such a severe crimp in the financial structure that projected expansions never took place, and route mileage never succeeded 44.697.

In 1918 the Napa Valley Route achieved the pinnacle of financial success as each passenger car earned $25,000. One month showed 478 commutes sold between Napa and Mare Island. Traffic was so heavy that Key Route trailer No. 533 had to be leased to handle the increase in service demands due to the heavy wartime activity at Mare Island Naval Shipyard during World War I.

Passengers were the priority on the S.F.N. & C.R.R., with the bulk of the freight business being concentrated in the Vallejo-Mare Island sector. The Napa Valley Route carried all of Napa County's R.P.O. mail (the mail was carried to and from San Francisco on the connecting Monticello steamers where it was sorted en route), and two car trains, including an R.P.O. car, were not uncommon.

Freight service to Mare Island (over a newly built causeway) began on September 20, 1920, at which time it was probably little realized that this short shuttle service would eventually be the salvation of the road.

In 1922, the track across the Vallejo marsh was relaid and straightened in order to facilitate the freight runs. Together with track relaying, the big freight hog, No. 99, was built at the company's shops in Napa. No. 99 was jointly owned by the Napa Valley Route and the Sacramento Northern, although always carried on the S.F.N. & C.R.R. roster. The old Vallejo & Northern cut was Sacramento Northern property and it was this combination which handled the interurban's main freight runs, rather than the Vallejo-Calistoga trackage. Later years would see this stretch plied by diesel-electric locomotives long after passenger operations had ceased.

At Vallejo, passengers bound for San Francisco connected with the Monticello Steamship Company's steamboats. The Monticello steamers were later taken over by Southern Pacific-Golden Gate Ferries, Ltd., which eventually abandoned the service. To the north, passengers who wished to

With one foot on the step, the motorman of No. 8 of the Vallejo, Benicia & Napa Valley Railroad Company poses for a photograph in Vallejo. The front window arrangement of five panes, the two end panes curved, was popular on early California interurbans, particularly in Southern California. (Randolph Brandt Collection)

travel beyond Calistoga transferred to the Spiers Auto Stage Line. The auto stage traveled to the various resort areas north of Calistoga, past Mount St. Helena to the region surrounding Clear Lake.

In 1924 and again in 1927, applications were made to operate competitive bus lines in the Napa Valley. They were denied by the California Railroad Commission because the existing railroad service by both the Southern Pacific and the Napa Valley Route was deemed adequate.

By 1927, it had become obvious that the highways were eating into the interurbans' market, and line after line was fading from the once prosperous interurban scene. This was happening not only in California but across the nation as well. Some lines, including street railways in cities as well as interurbans, attempted to forestall the inevitable as they experimented with motor buses. To all of this, the San Francisco, Napa & Calistoga was no exception. On October 4, 1927, a subsidiary corporation was formed and bus operation to supplement interurban service began under the name of Napa Valley Bus Company.

With street operations in Vallejo abandoned in 1925 in favor of the old Vallejo & Northern cut (see Chapter Eleven), the Napa Valley Route in 1930 ended them in Napa as well, resorting to the use of Southern Pacific trackage around the city rather than face the high cost of strengthening the Francis Bridge over the Napa River.

The year 1932 opened with a foretaste of doom as the carbarn and powerhouse at Napa burned to the ground, totally destroying passenger motors 40 and 51 as well as combo No. 60. The January 22nd holocaust caused all rail service on the San Francisco, Napa & Calistoga to cease, and it was not until May 29 that the trains rolled again under the catenary as far as St. Helena. Service to Calistoga was not resumed until July 1, 1933. Meanwhile, the Napa Valley Bus Company filled in for the stricken interurban. The disastrous fire, coming during the darkest hours of the Great Depression, only served to seal the proverbial

Officially she was freight motor No. 98, but to employees of the Napa Valley Route she was simply "The Pig." Absolutely ugly and without any graceful features, she was nonetheless an efficient work piece. Here "The Pig" is helping to build the Napa Valley Route. Her last assignment will be to help tear it down. (Randolph Brandt Collection)

coffin on this once prosperous interurban line, and on November 23, 1934, the Napa Valley Route went into receivership with Clyde E. Brown acting as receiver.

A last-ditch attempt to keep the big electric trains running was made on the first of March, 1936, when the road was taken over by the San Francisco & Napa Valley Railroad. But by that time the construction of the Golden Gate Bridge, together with the San Francisco-Oakland Bay Bridge and the Carquinez Bridge, had signaled the end of an era. On September 12, 1937, the Southern Pacific-Golden Gate Ferries, Ltd., gave up the ghost and ended steamer service forever between the Clay Street Pier in San Francisco and the docks in Vallejo. Eight days later, the S.F. & N.V.R.R. tossed in the passenger towel, ending both R.P.O. and passenger operations.

Only one more passenger run was ever made. On February 13, 1938, a farewell excursion run was made between Vallejo and Napa under the auspices of the Electric Railway Historical Society of California, after which the overhead line between Napa and Calistoga was torn down. The rails and catenary between Napa and Mare Island Naval Shipyard remained for freight runs only.

The catenary, however, was on borrowed time. In February of 1942, with America at war, the Napa Valley Route was converted to diesel-electric by request of the United States Navy, since, it was claimed, the catenary interfered with crane operations. This was just as well, for the electric locomotives were simply not up to the strength demanded of heavy wartime traffic. Their ability to haul but ten freight cars per trip caused combo motor No. 62 to be pressed into locomotive duties.

March of 1942 saw the Napa Valley Route leasing three steam locomotives: Amador Central No. 6, a 2-6-2; Southern Pacific No. 1677, a 2-6-0; and Western Pacific No. 122, a 4-6-0. Since the steam-powered locomotives could pull as many as fifty cars per trip, their value was obvious.

With the arrival of diesel locomotives Nos. 30 and 40, the three steam locomotives were returned to their owners, but the sands of the clock for the last of the electrics had virtually run out. In November of 1942, locomotive No. 99 dropped the pantograph for the last time and thus closed the book on electric railroading in the Napa Valley. The Napa powerhouse was then sold.

The Napa Valley Route's last piece of motive power, diesel-electric No. 50, arrived in March of

Take a wooden Niles car, fit her out with a large pantograph, load her underside with electrical equipment for alternating current, and you still have a handsome Niles car. No. 42 was photographed at Napa. (Charles D. Savage photo/Tom Gray Collection)

1943. Diesel-electric No. 40 was sold in 1947 to the Sacramento Northern and renumbered No. 141. Nos. 30 and 50 continued for many years thereafter.

In the era of all diesel-electric motive power, the locos were labeled "Navy Yard Freight," and any references to a once prosperous interurban line were obliterated. Utilizing some Sacramento Northern trackage (actually the old Vallejo & Northern franchise), service was conducted strictly between Vallejo and Mare Island. In August, 1956, the United States Navy paid $190,000 for possession of the little short line. The purchase price was divided between the Sacramento Northern and the San Francisco & Napa Valley.

Charles A. Smallwood remembers the Napa Valley Route. He is retired now and so is the San Francisco, Napa & Calistoga Railroad.

San Francisco, Napa & Calistoga Rolling Stock

The roster of the Napa Valley Route consisted of no less than nine carbuilders. Their products ranged from rebuilt passenger trailers from a San Francisco steam dummy line to the stately wooden interurbans from Niles Car Company. Included were Nos. 62 and 63, whose claims to fame were as the last conventional passenger interurbans built before the Great Depression put a virtual end to the industry.

The Napa Valley Route, for most of its life, used pantograph current collectors. In its infancy, however, the line first employed trolley poles and later bow collectors. A bow collector is an elongated loop of metal, flattened on the end,

These two all-steel cars represent the first heavy duty cars on the Napa Valley Route. The full name at the time—San Francisco, Napa & Calistoga—usually deferred to the line's nickname. (Stephen D. Maguire Collection)

In April of 1937, No. 61 is at the Vallejo Pier with No. 56 in tow. By this time the Monticello Steamship Line is a property of Southern Pacific-Golden Gate Ferries, Ltd., and the Brewster green cars of the Napa Valley Route are hanging on for dear life. In September of this same year both will be gone. (Stephen D. Maguire Collection)

Strictly utilitarian was the only way to describe baggage-express motor No. 100, the second of the line to bear that number. Here she is in front of the carbarn at Napa. (Randolph Brandt Collection)

with the flat part resting against the trolley wire. While popular on streetcars in Europe, bow collectors were rarely used on railways in the United States. The Napa Valley Route was the only road in California to use them, and at that for only a short period before conversion to the more efficient pantographs.

While under the aegis of the Vallejo, Benicia & Napa Valley, the road's carpainting scheme strongly reflected that of the Pacific Electric in Southern California. P.E. influences were further found in the type of lettering, in the end signboards on the cars, and in the fact that the first three motors were combination open and enclosed vehicles, thus catering to the warm California climate. When outshopped from the carbuilders, the Niles cars were painted Brewster green with gold trim. This became the permanent car color scheme for the Napa Valley fleet.

Whereas the cars from Niles gave away none of their handsome proportions in Napa Valley service, they certainly had more than their share of bad luck on this line. Of a total of twelve cars from Niles, two were destroyed in wrecks, one was heavily damaged in a wreck, two were destroyed by fire, and one—the last car built by Niles to operate in California—was destroyed by vandalism. Another Niles car was given the dubious honor of making the farewell run in 1936.

The arrival of Nos. 62 and 63 marked the last delivery of conventional interurban cars from the carbuilders in America. Unfortunately this was not due to increased business but rather to replace equipment lost in the disastrous carbarn fire. (Stephen D. Maguire Collection)

Nos. 60 and 61 came to the Napa Valley Route from the Visalia Electric by way of Pacific Electric, giving them the distinction of being the only interurban cars to operate on California's only two a.c.-powered railways. (Charles A. Smallwood)

Nos. 62 and 63 when they were first delivered from the St. Louis Car Co. of St. Louis, Missouri. (Charles A. Smallwood)

Passenger Motors
6-8 Class

Builder: American Car Company
Year: 1905
Length: 48'0"
Weight: 74,000 lbs.
Motors: Four Westinghouse 106; 75 h.p.
Controllers: HLF
Gear Ratio: 19:63
Trucks: 23B-M.C.B.
Body: Wood; originally semi-open, later fully enclosed

Seated 48. Nos. 6 and 7 were rebuilt and renumbered 49 and 47, respectively, in 1916. No. 6 was dismantled in 1937; No. 7 was dismantled in 1938; No. 8 was rebuilt to a trailer and renumbered 48 in 1916.

40-42 Class

Builder: Niles Car Company
Year: 1907
Length: 56'0"
Weight: 90,000 lbs.
Motors: Four Westinghouse 132A; 100 h.p.
Controllers: 251C
Trucks: Baldwin 84-30
Body: Double end, wood

Seated 62. Placed in service in 1908. Nos. 40, 42 were rebuilt to passenger-baggage combos in 1913. No. 41 was destroyed in a wreck in 1913. Named *San Francisco*, *Napa*, and *St. Helena*, respectively.

50-51 Class

Builder: Niles Car Company
Year: 1909
Length: 56'0"
Weight: 96,000 lbs.
Motors: Four Westinghouse 132A; 100 h.p.
Controllers: 251C
Body: Double end, wood

No. 50 headed the first train to Calistoga, September 2, 1912. No. 50 was badly damaged in a 1913 wreck and was rebuilt to a control trailer. No. 51 was destroyed in a 1932 carbarn fire. Seated 44.

A three-car train consisting of Nos. 62, 63, and 56 in 1936. It is said by some that the Napa Valley Route traveled through some of the prettiest country in Northern California—from San Pablo Bay through the valley which featured some of the finest vineyards in the world to the land of warm springs and geysers. In this picture grapes and wild flowers abound. (Charles D. Savage photo/Tom Gray Collection)

61 Class

Builder: Moran Shipbuilding Company
Year: 1910
Length 56'3"
Weight: 97,000 lbs.
Motors: Four Westinghouse 132C; 100 h.p.
Controllers: 251C
Body: Steel

Seated 67. Originally Visalia Electric No. 203, later to Pacific Electric No. 1045. To Napa Valley Route in 1921. Converted to trailer in 1922.

Passenger-Baggage Combos
40, 42 Class

Builder: Niles Car Company
Year: 1907
Length: 56'0"
Weight: 96,000 lbs.
Motors: Four Westinghouse 132A; 100 h.p.
Controllers: 251C
Trucks: Baldwin 84-30
Body: Wood

Seated 46. Placed in service in 1908; rebuilt to passenger-baggage combos in 1913. No. 40 was destroyed in a carbarn fire in 1932. No. 41 was destroyed in a wreck at Flosden in 1913. Salvage of No. 41 was used to rebuild No. 50 into a control trailer after the Flosden crash.

Builder: Niles Car Company
Year: 1907
Length: 56'0"
Weight: 65,000 lbs.
Motors: Four Westinghouse 132A; 100 h.p.
Controllers: 251C
Trucks: Baldwin 84-30
Body: Wood

Builder: Niles Car Company
Year: 1907
Length: 56'0"
Weight: 96,000 lbs.
Motors: Four Westinghouse 132A; 100 h.p.
Controllers: 251C
Trucks: Baldwin 84-30
Body: Wood

Builder: Moran Shipbuilding Company
Year: 1910
Length: 56'3"
Weight: 97,000 lbs.
Motors: Four Westinghouse 132C; 100 h.p.
Controllers: 251C
Body: Steel, arch roof

Builder: Moran Shipbuilding Company
Year: 1910
(Rest of data same as 60 Class)

Builder: St. Louis Car Company
Year: 1932
Length: 54'6"
Weight: 102,000 lbs.
Motors: Four Westinghouse 132A; 100 h.p.
Controllers: 251C
Trucks: Baldwin 84-30
Body: Steel, arch roof

Builder: Mahoney Brothers
Year: 1888
Length: 48'0"
Weight: 42,500 lbs.
Body: Wood, deck roof

43-44 Class
Seated 44. Placed in service in 1908. No. 43 was retired and scrapped in 1938. No. 44 was retired and partially dismantled in 1933.

45-46 Class
Seated 44. Placed in service in 1908. No. 45 was damaged beyond repair in a collision with a gravel truck in 1929 and scrapped. No. 46 made the farewell run in 1937 and then was scrapped.

60 Class
Seated 57. No. 60 was originally Visalia Electric No. 103; sold to Pacific Electric in 1918 and renumbered P.E. 1364. To Napa Valley Route in 1919. Ruined in a 1932 carbarn fire.

61 Class
Seated 57. Rebuilt from trailer No. 61 in 1932. Scrapped in 1942.

62-63 Class
Seated 37. St. Louis Job #1562 was for these two cars which were the last conventional interurban cars built in the U.S.A. No. 62 was pressed into service as a freight locomotive in the last of the electric era. Both cars were consigned to scrap but then were sold in 1943. No. 62 was sold to Weyerhauser Timber Co. as No. 706. No. 63 was sold to Pacific Lumber Co. With Napa Valley, both cars used salvaged Niles cars' equipment.

Passenger Trailers
9-10 Class
Originally built for the narrow-gauge Ferries & Cliff House R.R. in San Francisco, they were sold to Pacific Electric in 1902 and modified for interurban-type operation. Purchased by Napa Valley Route in 1905 for $3,415.99. Sixty seats.

The Napa Valley Route was usually single-tracked, but occasionally there would be a passing siding to give the illusion of a double-tracked heavy duty interurban road. (Charles D. Savage photo/Tom Gray Collection)

Three Niles cars in one train. The flags mounted at the end of No. 43 and people walking around indicate it might be a special. (Stephen D. Maguire Collection)

Although the Napa Valley Route was intended to go as far as Lake County, this station at Calistoga was as far as the line ever went and Lake County is still waiting for its first railroad. Train #7 is waiting to return to Vallejo. (Stephen D. Maguire Collection)

No. 63 did not always run with a trailer as this photo indicates.

On March 20, 1941, Niles car No. 42 is being stripped of her electrical equipment but not her good looks. Even though the passengers had vanished from her rails she was still being maintained in good order. (Stephen D. Maguire Collection)

Builder: Niles Car Company
Year: 1907
Length: 56′0″
Weight: 54,000 lbs.
Body: Wood

Builder: American Car Company
Year: 1905
Length: 48′0″
Weight: 52,000 lbs.
Body: Wood

Builder: S.F.N. & C. Company Shops
Year: 1913
Length: 56′0″
Weight:
Controllers: 251C
Trucks: Brill 27-MCB-3X
Body: Wood

Builder: Niles Car Company
Year: 1913
Length: 56′0″
Weight: 62,000 lbs.
Body: Wood

Builder: Moran Shipbuilding Company
Year: 1910
Length: 56′3″
Weight: 97,000 lbs.
Body: Steel

Builder: American Car Company
Year: 1905
Length: 46′0″
Weight: 60,000 lbs.
Motors: Four Westinghouse 107; 50 h.p.
Controller: HLF
Gear Ratio: 15:60
Body: Wood

Builder: Niles Car Company
Year: 1907
Length: 54′6″
Weight: 85,000 lbs.
Motors: Four Westinghouse 132A; 100 h.p.
Controller: 251C
Body: Wood

43-44 Class
    Seated 64. Rebuilt to passenger-baggage combos in 1913.

48 Class
    Rebuilt from passenger motor No. 8 in 1916; dismantled in 1938. Seated 33.

50 Class
    Seated 62. Put together from the salvage of the 1913 Flosden wreck. The smashed ends of Nos. 41 and 50 were discarded while the two good ends were joined together. No. 50 was given new trucks during rebuilding and kept old controllers, making her the only control trailer in the Napa Valley fleet. Scrapped in 1938.

52-53 Class
    Seated 62. No. 52 was sold to Weyerhauser Timber Co., renumbered 705. No. 53 was sold to Bay Area Electric Railroad Association in 1945. Burned by vandals while in storage in 1959. No. 52 is under private ownership at Dunsmuir, California.

61 Class
    Seated 57. Originally Visalia Electric motor No. 203; sold to Pacific Electric in 1918 and renumbered P.E. No. 1045. Sold to S.F.N. & C. in 1920 and de-motorized. Used as a trailer until rebuilt into a combo in 1932.

Baggage Motor
101 Class
    Originally No. 1, renumbered in 1907. When delivered from carbuilders, No. 1 was painted white, thus earning the nickname "Snowball." Scrapped in 1938.

Baggage-Express Motors
100 I Class
    Converted to mail and express motor No. 500 in 1922.

Builder: Maguire-Cummings
Year: 1922
Motors: Four Westinghouse 132A; 100 h.p.
Controller: 251C
Body: Steel

100 II Class
Sold in 1942 to Pacific Lumber Company.

Mail and Express Trailers
55 Class

Builder: McKeen Motor Car Company
Year: 1908-1911 (Exact date unknown)
Length: 31'0"
Weight: 42,000 lbs.
Body: Steel

Acquired secondhand from the Southern Pacific; junked in 1938.

500 Class

Builder: Niles Car Company
Year: 1907
Length: 54'6"
Weight: 52,000 lbs.
Body: Wood

In 1922, No. 100 I was converted to a mail and express motor, No. 500, but in 1924 was de-motorized and used thereafter as a trailer until scrapping in 1942.

R.P.O. Trailer
56 Class

Builder: J. G. Brill
Year: 1929
Length: 55'0"
Weight: 56,000 lbs.
Trucks: Brill MCB 3
Body: Steel

No. 56 met all the standards of the Railway Post Office and handled the R.P.O. mail for the Napa Valley until abandonment in 1938, whereupon she was sold to the Huntington & Broadtop R.R. in Pennsylvania. Wrecked in 1957.

Electric Freight Locomotives
No. 98

Builder: American Car Company
Year: 1905
Length: 46'0"
Weight: 60,000 lbs.
Motors: Four Westinghouse 107; 50 h.p.
Gear Ratio: 16:50
Body: Motor flat

Originally a wooden motor flat without an assigned number; nicknamed "the Pig." Numbered 98 in 1907. Superstructure completely rebuilt with steel in 1922. Scrapped in 1943.

No. 99

Builder: S.F.N. & C. Company Shops
Year: 1922
Length: 31'7"
Weight: 106,000 lbs.
Motors: Four Westinghouse 132A; 100 h.p.
Control: Westinghouse Unit Switch
Gear Ratio: 16:57
Trucks: Baldwin 84-30A
Body: Steel

Built with motors and auxiliary gear from No. 61. Sold in 1942 to Mutual Engineering, South San Francisco, California. Scrapped in 1948. No. 99 was jointly owned by Sacramento Northern and Napa Valley Route, although always carried on the latter's roster.

Miscellaneous Cars

No. 501: Bunk Car (home built from box car)
Nos. 502-514: Box Cars
No. 533: Key Route trailer leased during 1917-1918

Nos. 600-607: Flat Cars
No. 603: Tower Car
No. T1: Weed Killer and Tank Car

Chapter Ten
The Water Routes

Due to the topography of San Francisco Bay, most interurbans were forced to operate some kind of ferryboat service to bring passengers into San Francisco, as well as to carry the large number of excursionists from the population center of San Francisco to the recreational areas of Marin, the East Bay, and the Napa Valley. Of all the routes and lines which actually brought passengers into the city, only the Market Street Railway Company's #40 Line never had a water connection.

The earliest known ferry service on the waters of San Francisco Bay was provided by a British immigrant by the name of John Reed, who in 1826 transported patrons about the Bay in his small sailing vessel, originating in the Bay Area what would eventually become the largest ferry flotilla in the world.

Given the large population, the propensity for growth, and the absence of bridges, ferrying in the Bay Area was an absolute necessity for generations, and the fleets served well. So beloved did they become that when no longer needed by their operators they sometimes found new life in other forms, such as a floating restaurant, an office building, a shopping center, and in one case, a floating nightclub. A trio survived north of the city limits of Sausalito, and even in their decayed condition they evoke memories of the years when transbay travel was leisurely and unhurried by today's standards, and yet the ferries were the last word in rapid transit in their halcyon days.

Let it not be forgotten, however, that ferryboat travel was not without its hazards. Dense fogs, particularly at night, made the possibility of collision with another ship a constant nightmare for masters and pilots who held the responsibilities for guiding their vessels without such a modern precision as radar. More than one ferryboat lies sunk in the mud at the bottom of the Bay as silent testimony. Moreover, ships' firemen had to take care to prevent boiler explosions on the old steamers, and the crews had the added responsibility of seeing that landlubber passengers did not lean too far over the rail and come eyeball to eyeball with a more aquarian creature.

There were a number of ferry landings outside of San Francisco, but within the city itself, the Ferry Building, at the foot of Market Street, was the first major one and over the years handled the bulk of the ferry trade. From here departed not only the Key Route's boats and the river steamers bound for Petaluma, Vallejo, and Sacramento, but the Southern Pacific's ferries for their East Bay Interurbans as well as their transcontinental trains. Built in 1898 at a cost of one million dollars of Colusa sandstone to replace the old wooden ferry sheds, San Francisco's Ferry Building was for years the second busiest passenger terminal in the world. Serving an estimated 50,000,000 patrons a year during the 1920s and early 1930s, the activity here was exceeded only by London's Charing Cross Station. The building's 235-foot clock tower, designed after the Moorish Giralda (bell) Tower in Seville, Spain, has served for generations as a beacon to travelers arriving in San Francisco from the east side of the Bay.

Automobile ferries bound for Berkeley and Sausalito had their ferry slips at the foot of Hyde Street on the city's northern shoreline. Today the Hyde Street Pier houses the floating exhibits of the San Francisco Maritime Museum, including the former Northwestern Pacific ferryboat *Eureka*.

Of the various passenger accommodations aboard the ferryboats, perhaps the best remembered were the short-order food counters where a traveler could have a snack en route. Since a

World War I hasn't erupted yet and already the ferry traffic is straining the streetcar facilities at the Ferry Building. From the line of cars the single loop is inadequate; later second and third loops will be added and it will still be hectic.

Ferry traffic from the interurban trains as well as from the transcontinental railroads made San Francisco's Ferry Building the second busiest terminal in the world during the 1920s and 1930s. An estimated 50,000,000 passengers per year entering its portals necessitated three loops for streetcars coming from Market Street. This did not include the streetcars from Mission and Union Streets or the cable cars on the Sacramento-Clay and California Street lines. Leaving San Francisco in the background are boats from the Key Route (left) and Southern Pacific (right).

ferry trip took only about twenty minutes, there was seldom enough time for a full course dinner, but millions of commuters over the years began their day with a breakfast of "coffee and...", or on the Key Route's boats, their much touted "Key Route Corned Beef Hash."

Over the years, regular passengers formed social groups aboard the ferries which were dedicated to conversation, chess, checkers, or a friendly game of cards. Periodically these groups would celebrate a member's birthday on board, complete with gifts and a chorus of "Happy Birthday." Another favorite pursuit was the reading of the daily paper and doing the crossword puzzle to a background symphony of ships' whistles, bells, and paddlewheels churning the water to the accompaniment of the San Francisco foghorns and the chatter of seagulls.

And woe unto the unsuspecting stranger who happened to inadvertently occupy the seat of a *regular* patron! For this "crime" a punishment was more than once affixed with a frightful stare from the supposed owner, and in some extreme cases, a verbal warning as well. So much for ferryboat conduct.

The ferries often carried a large number of football fans to games in either San Francisco or Berkeley, with the passengers transferring to the Berkeley-bound interurbans to watch the University of California's Golden Bears, or to the San Francisco streetcars which would take them to either Ewing Field or Kezar Stadium for the home games of the University of San Francisco Dons, St. Mary's College's Galloping Gaels, the University of Santa Clara's Broncos, or the football season's finale, the East-West Shrine Game, also played in San Francisco.

Nor was football the only sport served by the ferryboats. There was also the "Ferryboat Series" of baseball games between the then Pacific Coast League Oakland Oaks and the San Francisco Seals, with a Sunday doubleheader being split between the two cities, one game in the morning and the other in the afternoon.

(Several Class 1 railroads and independent ferry companies maintained ferry fleets in the Bay, but we will concern ourselves only with the companies which operated in conjunction with electric interurban service.)

The largest fleet of ferries was operated by the Southern Pacific Railroad, which not only acquired several boats from its predecessor, the

The *Santa Clara* of the S.P. and a Key Route boat were the only two ferries in the Ferry Building's slips when this photo was snapped. The large building in back of the *Santa Clara* is the headquarters of the Southern Pacific, and the Fairmont Hotel breaks the city's skyline in the center.

Central Pacific, but inherited a few with its purchase of the South Pacific Coast Railroad in 1887. Later the Southern Pacific merged its ferry services with the automobile-carrying Golden Gate Ferry, to form a subsidiary known as the Southern Pacific-Golden Gate Ferries, Ltd. While this combined operation ran both passenger and automobile ferries, their main function was carrying passengers who connected with the interurbans. The Southern Pacific-owned fleet also served the steam-powered (and later diesel-electric) trains which embarked from and terminated at the Oakland Mole. Since the S.P. service was so heavily linked to the steam train service, it is hard to draw a line of demarcation between interurban and transcontinental ferry connections. As they offered connections to the Class 1 trains, these were the last passenger ferries on the Bay.

The Key System began its ferry service on September 24, 1903, with the first of its screw propeller steamers, the *San Jose* and the *Yerba Buena*. Unfortunately for photographers, the Key System painted its boats in the same orange paint it used on its interurbans, a paint scheme which worked to their disadvantage when it came to being photographed in black and white. Later, the ferries were painted white, whereupon they were photographed as often as those of other companies.

Our third fleet of ferries carried passengers to the trains—both steam and electric—in Marin County under the ownership, and predecessor ownerships, of the Northwestern Pacific Railroad. As with the Southern Pacific, the N.W.P. ferry service preceded railroad electrification by a number of years, and five of the N.W.P.'s

In this classic picture of ferryboat activity, the *Alameda, Berkeley, Edward T. Jeffrey,* and *Thoroughfare II* occupy the Ferry Building's slips. (Bert Ward photo/Tom Gray collection)

Should the adage that a picture is worth a thousand words be true, the author is content to let Albert Tolf's cartoon speak for itself. (From *In Old San Francisco* by Albert Tolf)

ferries preceded the interurbans. In 1923 the N.W.P. rebuilt its *Ukiah* into what would be the last walking beam steamer on the Bay: the *Eureka*. The *Eureka* is still afloat at San Francisco's Maritime Museum, one of the few ferryboats approximating its original condition.

The relationship of the Monticello Steamship Company with our study of electric interurbans in the Bay Area was its connection with the Vallejo, Benicia & Napa Valley Railroad and its successor, the San Franciscan, Napa & Calistoga Railroad, otherwise known as the Napa Valley Route. Beginning on July 4, 1905, the steamers of the Monticello fleet commenced operations between the San Francisco Ferry Building and Vallejo. R.P.O. mail destined for the S.F. N. & C., as well as mail for San Francisco from the Napa Valley, was sorted aboard the Monticello boats. These speedy vessels had the longest runs in terms of time and distance of any of the Bay's ferry fleets, and amazingly enough, considering the hazardous course, one of the best safety records. The company was sold to the Golden Gate Ferry in 1927, and in 1929 the operation was taken over by the newly formed Southern Pacific-Golden Gate Ferries, Ltd., which abandoned the San Francisco-Vallejo steamers in 1937.

While not actually operating steamers of its own, the Northern Electric maintained connections with the California Transportation Company's riverboats which would bring passengers to San Francisco via the Sacramento River, utilizing steamers *Fort Sutter* and *Capital City*. To facilitate these connections, the N.E. maintained for a number of years a name train called *The Steamer Special*. The California Transportation Company briefly tried to compete with the river steamers of the Petaluma & Santa Rosa Railroad, but later bowed out and sold its *Fort Bragg* to the P. & S.R., whereupon she became the *Gold II*.

The Petaluma & Santa Rosa Electric Railway's first piece of equipment was the stern paddlewheeler *Gold I*. Built in 1883, purchased in December of 1903, *Gold I* burned at Petaluma on November 8, 1920.

The second boat had been built in 1884 and christened the *Resolute*. Upon purchase by the railway in 1911 from the Petaluma Transportation Company, she was renamed the *Petaluma I*.* She was sunk in a fire on March 22, 1914.

The third vessel of the P. & S.R. was the one purchased from the California Transportation Company whose name was changed from *Fort Bragg* to *Gold II*. Built in 1899, she was taken out of service in 1935 and dismantled in 1940.

The road's last steamer, and incidentally the last stern paddlewheeler to operate on San Francisco Bay, was the *Petaluma II*, built in 1914. She was taken out of service in 1950 and sold in 1951.

All of the P. & S.R.'s boats were of the stern paddlewheel variety, and had one of the most difficult runs on the Bay. From San Francisco, they plied the Bay to the Petaluma Creek and up the creek to Petaluma, location of the company's docks and rail connections. The river steamers made the thirty-nine-mile trip in four to five

---

*A previous river steamer, owned by Charles Minturn—an early North Bay transportation entrepeneur—was named *Petaluma*, and after purchase by the Sausalito Land & Ferry Company she was renamed *Petaluma of Saucelito*. Taken over by the North Pacific Coast Railroad, she was again renamed, this time becoming the *Tamalpais I*. At no time did she have any connection to either the P. & S.R. or to any electric interurban.

hours. The sixteen-mile course on the Petaluma Creek was a most demanding one with no less than ninety-five course changes. The longest stretch took six minutes and the shortest thirty seconds! Then, too, the channel in some places was only six feet deep, while the boats had a draft of four and one-half feet. Thanks to excellent masters, there was only one serious mishap other than the fires. On October 16, 1947, the *Petaluma II* stove a hole in her hull. Two weeks later she was back in service. In 1950, Captain Jack Urton skippered the *Petaluma II* on her last trip, ending 103 years of steamboat navigation on California's inland waterways.

The Petaluma & Santa Rosa also maintained three tugboats: *Golden Eagle*, *Antler*, and *Coos Bay*, all now out of service.

Originally, the P. & S.R.'s riverboats carried passengers as well as freight, but after the ridership dropped from a high of 8,761 in 1907 to a meager fifteen in 1935, passenger service was discontinued.

The Richmond-San Rafael Ferry opened for business on May 1, 1915 with the *Ellen*, running a course from Castro Point in Richmond to the old North Pacific Coast R.R. pier at Point San Quentin. Simultaneously, the Key System extended its recently acquired Richmond streetcar tracks to the Richmond-San Rafael Ferry pier. After a month of service, the *Ellen* was condemned and in July of 1916 the company began anew with the newly built automobile ferry *Charles Van Damme*. For the next forty years, this line plied the waters between Contra Costa and Marin Counties, providing the only transportation between the two. In 1956, the line went out of existence, choosing not to compete with the new bridge of the same name and route. (More on the bridge later.)

In earlier years, in deference to two partners who couldn't agree whether to paint the boats red or white, the R.-S.R.'s boats were repainted annually; one year red and the alternate year white. In later years they were only painted white, retaining that scheme until retirement.

One reason for the line's popularity was its active solicitation of automobile business, while the Northwestern Pacific—possibly in an effort to keep automobiles out of Marin County—disdained such traffic and only agreed to carry autos on a "space available" basis. Therefore, to get to Marin from Richmond, one had to drive to Oakland, take the S.P. ferry to San Francisco, and then gamble on a ride to Sausalito.

Later, the Richmond-San Rafael Ferry had the *City of Richmond* built and in 1924 the last side wheeler built on San Francisco Bay, the *City of San Rafael*, was placed in service.

As for the Richmond-San Rafael Bridge, it is designated by the California State Division of Highways as part of Highway 17—the same highway which contributed to the demise of interurban service on the Peninsular Railway and cut into Key System patronage as the asphalt ran its course on the eastern shore of San Francisco Bay.

The smallest fleet was that of the Oakland, Antioch & Eastern, and its successor, the Sacramento Northern. It consisted strictly of car ferries, used to transport the interurbans from Mallard to Chipps Island. The first boat was the *Bridget*, built for the O.A. & E. in 1913. The name derived from an anticipated bridge across Suisun Bay and was a slang contraction of "bridge it." Powered by a gasoline engine, *Bridget* developed a leak, caught fire, and was destroyed in 1914.

Bridget's replacement, the *Ramon*, entered service on January 3, 1915. Initially, the *Ramon* offered coffee shop facilities for passengers. *Ramon* survived all passenger service of the Sacramento Northern by thirteen years, finally being laid off by the S.N. on April 7, 1954.

The Southern Pacific's shipyards in the background performed all types of work on San Francisco Bay's ferries; here the *Newark* is in for repairs.

In the 1920s, the conventional passenger-carrying ferries were facing heavy competition from the automobile-carrying boats of the Golden Gate Ferries. The Northwestern Pacific R.R., which heretofore had not encouraged the automobile-carrying trade, found it was losing so much business to the Golden Gate Ferries that two new automobile ferries, the *Mendocino* and the *Santa Rosa*, were placed in service in 1927, with the *Redwood Empire* following suit two years later. In addition, the Monticello line converted the *Calistoga* to an auto carrier. The Southern Pacific, anticipating the increased volume of auto traffic, ordered a number of automobile ferries: *El Paso, Fresno, Klamath, Lake Tahoe, Melrose, New Orleans, San Mateo, Shasta, Stockton, Thoroughfare II,* and *Yosemite*. It must be emphasized that while these vessels were primarily automobile carriers, they were nonetheless a part and parcel of the total ferryboat operations which were in conjunction with the Bay Area interurban railways. Still, like the interurbans, the ferries themselves were to be rendered obsolete by the automobile, and the automobile-carrying ferryboats merely hastened their own demise.

The *Sierra Nevada* is docked at the Alameda Mole to connect with the Big Red Trains of the S.P. (Tom Gray Collection)

The *Santa Clara* was one of Espee's two twin-stacked ferries. Without a doubt, she is a graceful vessel as she steams toward Oakland. (Wilbur C. Whittaker)

Not quite as ornate as the Alameda Mole, but with an ample supply of trim nonetheless, the old Key Pier hosts the *Yerba Buena I.* (Alameda-Contra Costa Transit District)

Combined Roster of Ferryboats and Riverboats

Cal.Trans.Co. = California Transportation Co.
Key System = Key Route, Key System
M.S.L. = Monticello Steamship Line
N.W.P. = Northwestern Pacific Railroad
P. & S.R. = Petaluma & Santa Rosa Railroad
Rich.-S.R. = Richmond-San Rafael Ferry
Sac.Nor. = Sacramento Northern Railway (including Oakland, Antioch & Eastern)
Southern Pacific = Southern Pacific Railroad
S.P.-G.G.F. = Southern Pacific-Golden Gate Ferries, Ltd.
*Riverboat

Vessel:	*Alameda II*	*Amador*	*Arrow*
Operator:	Southern Pacific	Southern Pacific	M.S.L.
Builder:	Southern Pacific	Patrick Tiernan	Puget Sound
Year:	1913	1869	1903
Length:	273'	199'	147'
Hull:	Double end, steel	Double end, wood	Single end, wood
Tons:	1,320	897	318
Engine:	Steam	Steam	Steam
Propulsion:	Side wheel	Side wheel	Screw
Disposition:	Scrapped 1945	Burned 1915	Retired 1924

Vessel:	*Asbury Park*	*Bay City*	*Berkeley*
Operator:	M.S.L.	Southern Pacific	Southern Pacific
Builder:	William Cramp & Sons	William Collyer	Union Iron Works
Year:	1903	1878	1898
Length:	297'	247'	279'
Hull:	Single end, steel	Double end, wood	Double end, steel
Tons:	3,016	1,283	1,883
Engine:	Steam	Steam	Steam
Propulsion:	Twin screw	Side wheel	Screw
Disposition:	Renamed *City of Sacramento* 1925	Dismantled 1929	Sold 1958, used as floating trade fair; towed to San Diego Maritime Museum 1973

Mailed in 1907, this postcard shows one of the Key Route's first ferryboats, the steamer *San Francisco*.

On April of 1938, the Golden Gate Bridge was open and more and more people were driving instead of riding the trains and ferries. As the *Cazadero* steams into her San Francisco berth, no passengers are visible on her decks. (Wilbur C. Whittaker)

Built to replace the old pier destroyed in the 1933 fire, the new Key Pier has the *Hayward* in her slip. Out from the land fill work is just beginning on the Bay Bridge which will doom the Key's ferryboats and ultimately the interurbans as well. The land fill is now part of the Bay Bridge complex. (Alameda-Contra Costa Transit District)

The *Mendocino*, along with sister ships *Santa Rosa* and *Redwood Empire*, was supposed to give the Northwestern Pacific a competitive position in the auto ferry business, but the Golden Gate Ferries had been there first and the *Mendocino* finished her days bearing the name of merged rivals.

Because the Key System insisted on painting its ferries orange to match its trains, they were never as photogenic as the white vessels of other fleets. But even under less than ideal conditions, it was hard to take a poor photo of a N.W.P. boat. Note the contrast between the *Yerba Buena* of the Key and the *Tamalpais* of the N.W.P., both the second to bear their respective names. (Bert Ward photo/Tom Gray Collection)

Vessel:	*Bridget*	*Calistoga*	*Capital City*°
Operator:	Sac.Nor.	M.S.L.	Cal.Trans.Co.
Builder:	Moore & Scott	Maryland Steel Co.	James Robertson
Year:	1913	1907	1910
Length:	173.4'	298'	220'
Hull:	Double end, wood	Single end, steel	Single end
Tons:	594	2,680	1,139
Engine:	Gasoline	Steam	Steam
Propulsion:	Screw	Screw	Stern wheel
Disposition:	Fire May 17, 1914	Scrapped 1941	Renamed *Port of Stockton*, sold 1942.

Vessel:	*Cazadero*	*Charles Van Damme*	*City of Richmond*
Operator:	N.W.P.	Rich.-S.R.	Rich.-S.R.
Builder:	John W. Dickie	James Robertson	James Robertson
Year:	1903	1916	1921
Length:	228.5'	152.8'	168'
Hull:	Double end, wood	Double end, wood	Double end, wood
Tons:	1,682	342	408
Engine:	Steam	Steam	Steam
Propulsion:	Side wheel	Side wheel	Side wheel
Disposition:	Scrapped in 1942	Vacated 1958, used as floating night club in Sausalito	Sold 1939

Vessel:	*City of Sacramento*	*City of San Rafael*	*Claremont*
Operator:	M.S.L.	Rich.-S.R.	Key System
Builder:	See *Asbury Park*	James Robertson	John W. Dickie
Year:		1924	1907
Length:		172'	189'
Hull:		Double end, wood	Double end, wood
Tons:		484	1,138
Engine:		Steam	Steam
Propulsion:		Side wheel	Screw
Disposition:	Sold 1942	Retired, beached at Sausalito	Sold 1924 to G.G. Ferry, renamed *Golden Way*

The *Capital City* was fully representative of California's riverboats, and would not take a back seat to boats of the Mississippi, Missouri, Ohio, or any other river in the land. She and her sister, the *Fort Sutter*, took Northern Electric passengers from Sacramento to San Francisco and return, and in so doing gave the name *Steamer Special* to the N.E. train which met the boats. (Roy Graves Collection/Bancroft Library)

This classic single ender, *James M. Donahue*, is approaching Tiburon with her passengers forward on the main deck ready to disembark. (Wilbur C. Whittaker)

Launched as the *Ukiah* in 1890, this boat was rebuilt into the *Eureka* in 1922, and served well into the 1950s. In November of 1939, as the largest ferryboat on the Bay, *Eureka* steams toward Sausalito with her walking beam turning the paddlewheels full speed ahead. Today she serves as a permanent floating exhibit at the Hyde Street Pier in San Francisco. (Roy Graves photo/Marin County Historical Society)

The *Napa Valley* of the Monticello Steamship Line was once a trim and graceful single ender. In this picture she has been rebuilt to carry autos and is flying the colors of the Southern Pacific-Golden Gate Ferries, Ltd. Three vessels of the former Monticello fleet so rebuilt were the only ferries on San Francisco Bay to carry passengers on the texas, or third, deck. No passengers were ever carried on the hurricane, or top, decks.

Vessel:	*El Capitan*	*Ellen*	*El Paso*
Operator:	Southern Pacific	Rich.-S.R.	Southern Pacific
Builder:	Central Pacific R.R.	Unknown	Bethlehem Steel Co.
Year:	1868	1883	1924
Length:	194'	133'	234'
Hull:	Double end, wood	Double end, wood	Double end, steel
Tons:	982	328	1,953
Engine:	Steam	Steam	Steam
Propulsion:	Side wheel	Side wheel	Screw
Disposition:	Sold 1925	Condemned and broken up 1919	To Rich.-S.R. 1939, retired 1956

Vessel:	*Encinal*	*Eureka*	*Fernwood*
Operator:	Southern Pacific	N.W.P.	Key System
Builder:		Southern Pacific	John W. Dickie
Year:	1888	Rebuilt from *Ukiah* 1923	1908
Length:	244'	277'	294.3'
Hull:	Double end, wood	Double end, wood	Double end, wood
Tons:	2,014	2,420	789
Engine:	Steam	Steam	Steam
Propulsion:	Side wheel	Side wheel	Screw
Disposition:	Dismantled 1930	On exhibit, San Francisco	To G.G. Ferry, renamed *Golden Era* 1924

Vessel:	*Fort Sutter*°	*Fresno*	*Garden City*
Operator:	Cal.Trans.Co.	Southern Pacific	Southern Pacific
Builder:	James Robertson	Bethlehem Steel Co.	William Collyer
Year:	1912	1927	1879
Length:	219.2'	242.5'	243'
Hull:	Single end	Double end, steel	Double end, wood
Tons:	1,139	2,486	1,080
Engine:	Steam	Diesel-electric	Steam
Propulsion:	Stern wheel	Screw	Side wheel
Disposition:	Sold 1942	To Puget Sound, renamed *Willapa* 1937	Retired 1929

The *Fort Sutter* and her sister vessel, *Capital City*, carried San Francisco-bound passengers from Sacramento after the transfer was made from the interurbans of the Northen Electric Railway. To some old-timers this was the only way to travel—especially on a balmy evening in the hot Sacramento Valley. Through connections to Oakland aboard the San Francisco-Sacramento Railroad and eventual merger to form the Sacramento Northern ended this riverboat connection. (Roy Graves Collection/Bancroft Library)

Vessel:	*General Frisbie*	*Gold I°*	*Gold II°*
Operator:	M.S.L.	P. & S.R.	P. & S.R.
Builder:	G.R. Whidden & Co.	Marucci	
Year:	1900	1883	1899
Length:	187′	155′	155′
Hull:	Single end, wood	Single end, wood	Single end, wood
Tons:	670	334	317
Engine:	Steam	Steam	Steam
Propulsion:	Screw	Stern wheel	Stern wheel
Disposition:	Sold 1927	Destroyed by fire 1920	Abandoned 1940

Vessel:	*Golden Age*	*Golden Bear*	*Golden Coast*
Operator:	S.P.-G.G.F.	S.P.-G.G.F.	S.P.-G.G.F.
Builder:	General Engineering	General Engineering	Ex-*Harry E. Speas*, ex-*Yerba Buena I*
Year:	1928	1927	
Length:	226.8′	226.8′	
Hull:	Double end, wood	Double end, wood	
Tons:	779	779	
Engine:	Diesel-electric	Diesel-electric	
Propulsion:	Screw	Screw	
Disposition:	Sold 1937 to Puget Sound, renamed *Klahanie*	Wrecked 1937	Retired 1937

Stern paddlewheels churning, the *Gold I* approaches the steamer landing in Petaluma where her freight will be loaded aboard the trains of the P. & S.R. Her cargo is located on the main, or first, deck, while her passengers are up in the cabin, or second, deck, and may transfer to the Big White Cars to Sebastopol, Santa Rosa, or Forestville. (Edward Fratini Collection)

Nary a curve in her, the *Ramon* is carrying a complete interurban train across the choppy waters of Suisun Bay. Fully equipped with overhead trolley wires, the *Ramon* and her predecessor, the *Bridget*, were the only interurban-carrying ferries in the Bay Area. (Stephen D. Maguire Collection)

Vessel:	*Golden Dawn*	*Golden Era*	*Golden Gate*
Operator:	S.P.-G.G.F.	S.P.-G.G.F.	S.P.-G.G.F.
Builder:	Rebuilt from *San Francisco*	Rebuilt from *Fernwood*	James Robertson
Year:			1923
Length:			206.5'
Hull:			Double end, wood
Tons:			598
Engine:			Diesel-electric
Propulsion:			Screw
Disposition:	Retired 1937	Retired 1937	Dismantled 1938

Vessel:	*Golden Poppy*	*Golden Shore*	*Golden State*
Operator:	S.P.-G.G.F.	S.P.-G.G.F.	S.P.-G.G.F.
Builder:	General Engineering	General Engineering	General Engineering
Year:	1927	1927	1926
Length:	226.8'	226.8'	226.8'
Hull:	Double end, wood	Double end, wood	Double end, wood
Tons:	779	779	780
Engine	Diesel-electric	Diesel-electric	Diesel-electric
Propulsion:	Screw	Screw	Screw
Disposition:	To Puget Sound, renamed *Chetzemoka* 1937, sunk off Straits of Juan de Fuca May 31, 1977	To Puget Sound, renamed *Elwha* 1937	To Puget Sound, renamed *Kehloken* 1937

Vessel:	*Golden Way*	*Golden West*	*Hayward*
Operator:	S.P.-G.G.F.	S.P.-G.G.F.	Key System
Builder:	Rebuilt from *Claremont*	James Robertson	Los Angeles Shipbuilding
Year:	1924	1923	1923
Length:		214.1'	225'
Hull:		Double end, wood	Double end, steel
Tons:		594	1,653
Engine:		Diesel-electric	Turbo-electric
Propulsion:		Screw	Screw
Disposition:	Retired 1937	To San Diego 1939, renamed *North Island*	Dismantled 1947

Vessel:	*James M. Donahue*	*Klamath*	*Lake Tahoe*
Operator:	N.W.P.	S.P.-G.G.F.	Southern Pacific
Builder:	William Collyer	Bethlehem Steel Co.	Moore Dry Dock Co.
Year:	1875	1925	1927
Length:	208'	234'	251'
Hull:	Single end, wood	Double end, steel	Double end, steel
Tons:	730	1,952	2,468
Engine:	Steam	Steam	Diesel-electric
Propulsion:	Side wheel	Screw	Screw
Disposition:	Dismantled 1924	To Rich.-S.R. 1939, retired 1956, used as floating office building, San Francisco	To Puget Sound, renamed *Illahee* 1937

Vessel:	*Marin*	*Melrose*	*Mendocino*
Operator:	N.W.P.	Southern Pacific	N.W.P.
Builder:	Rebuilt from *Requa*	Southern Pacific	Bethlehem Steel Co.
Year:	1912	1908	1927
Length:		274'	251'
Hull:		Double end, wood	Double end, steel
Tons:		2,662	2,467
Engine:		Steam	Diesel-electric
Propulsion:		Side wheel	Screw
Disposition:	Scrapped 1935	Dismantled 1931	To Puget Sound, renamed *Nisqually* 1937

Vessel:	*Monticello*	*Napa Valley*	*Newark*
Operator:	M.S.L.	M.S.L.	Southern Pacific
Builder:	E. Sorenson	Bethlehem Steel Co.	William Collyer
Year:	1892	1910	1877
Length:	126'	231.2'	268'
Hull:	Single end, wood	Single end, steel	Double end, wood
Tons:	175	2,189	1,237
Engine:	Steam	Steam	Steam
Propulsion:	Screw	Screw	Side wheel
Disposition:	Out of service 1909	To Puget Sound, renamed *Malahat* 1942	Rebuilt as *Sacramento* 1923

The *Gold II*, shown here at the Petaluma steamer landing, was very similar in design to the first *Gold* and the *Petaluma II*. (Jo Ann Shelburne Collection)

Vessel:	*New Orleans*	*Oakland II*	*Peralta*
Operator:	Southern Pacific	Southern Pacific	Key System
Builder:	Bethlehem Steel Co.	Central Pacific R.R.	Moore Dry Dock Co.
Year:	1924	Rebuilt from *Chrysopolis*, 1875	1927
Length:	234'	265'	256'
Hull:	Double end, steel	Double end, wood	Double end, steel
Tons:	1,952	1,672	2,075
Engine:	Steam	Steam	Turbo-electric
Propulsion:	Screw	Side wheel	Screw
Disposition:	To Rich.-S.R., renamed *Russian River* November 1938	Destroyed by fire 1941	Destroyed by fire 1933, to Puget Sound and rebuilt as M.V. *Kalakala*

Vessel:	*Petaluma I*°	*Petaluma II*°	*Piedmont*
Operator:	P. & S.R.	P. & S.R.	Southern Pacific
Builder:	Turner	James Robertson	Central Pacific R.R.
Year:	1884	1914	1883
Length:	134.2'	184.4'	257.1'
Hull:	Single end, wood	Single end, wood	Double end, wood
Tons:	264	448	1,169
Engine:	Steam	Steam	Steam
Propulsion:	Stern wheel	Stern wheel	Side wheel
Disposition:	Fire 1914	Sold 1950	Dismantled 1944

Vessel:	*Ramon*	*Redwood Empire*	*Russian River*
Operator:	Sac.Nor.	N.W.P.	Rich.-S.R.
Builder:	O. A. & E.	Moore Dry Dock Co.	ex-*New Orleans*
Year:	1914	1927	
Length:	202.7'	251'	
Hull:	Double end, steel	Double end, steel	
Tons:	775	2,467	
Engine:	Gasoline	Diesel-electric	
Propulsion:	Screw	Screw	
Disposition:	Retired 1953	To Puget Sound, renamed *Quinault* 1937	Retired 1956

Steaming out of San Francisco for Petaluma, the *Petaluma II* was the last stern wheel riverboat to sail California's waters. After retirement in 1950, she was towed to Jack London Square in Oakland to serve as a floating restaurant. However, after many years of safely making one of the most dangerous trips in the Bay Area, she fell victim to a fire and was a total loss. (Roy Graves Collection/Bancroft Library)

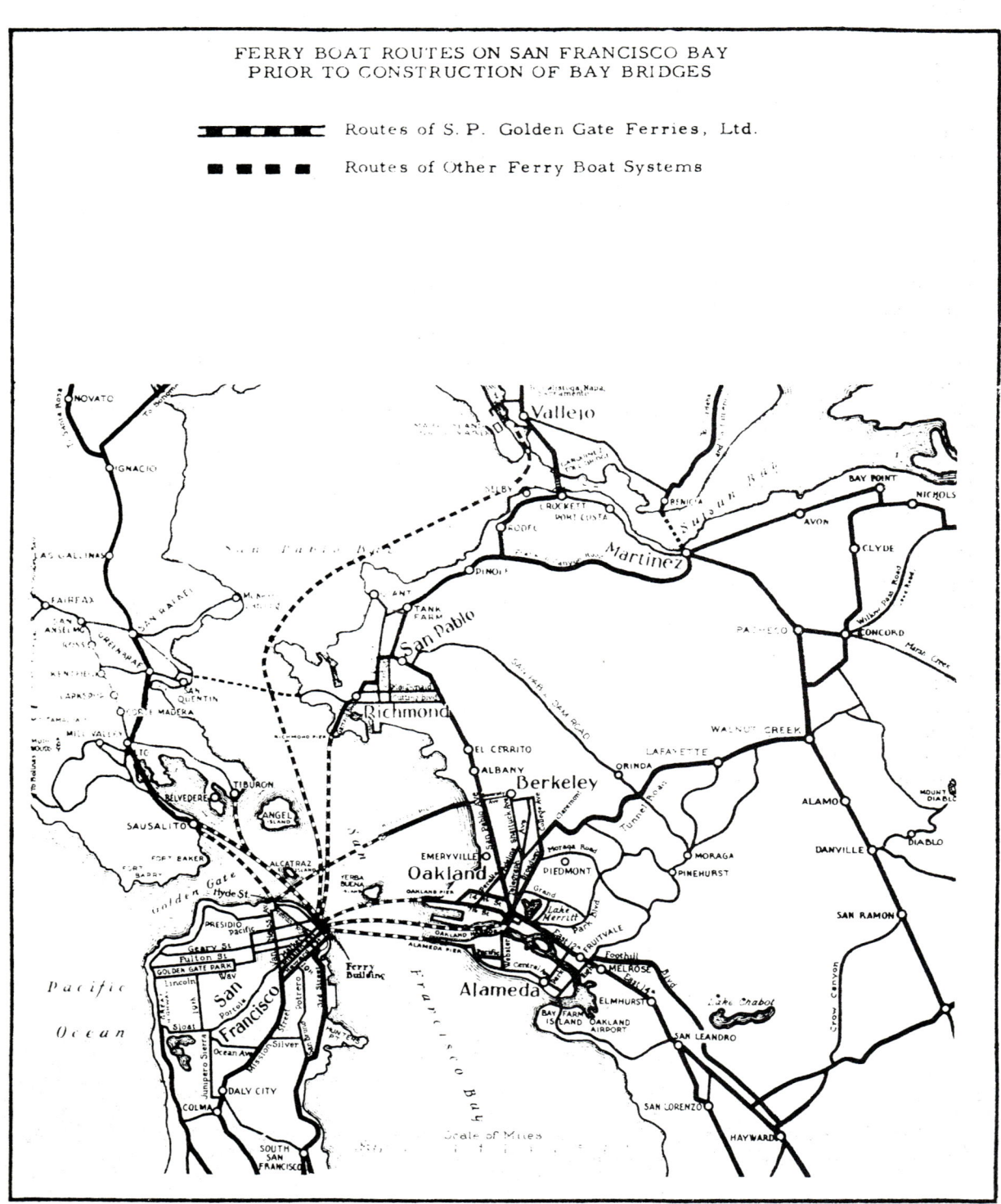

Lanes traveled by San Francisco Bay's famed ferryboat flotilla. (Courtesy of Golden Gate Bridge, Highway and Transportation District)

Vessel:	*Sacramento II*	*San Francisco*	*San Jose*
Operator:	Southern Pacific	Key System	Key System
Builder:	Southern Pacific	John W. Dickie	John W. Dickie
Year:	Rebuilt 1923 from *Newark*	1905	1903
Length:	268'	180'	175.5'
Hull:	Double end, wood	Double end, wood	Double end, wood
Tons:	2,254	612	630
Engine:	Steam	Steam	Steam
Propulsion:	Side wheel	Screw	Screw
Disposition:	Sold 1956	To G.G. Ferry 1924, rebuilt, renamed *Golden Dawn*	Badly burned 1919, sold later *Sonoma Valley*

Vessel:	*San Leandro*	*San Mateo*	*Santa Clara*
Operator:	Key System	Southern Pacific	Southern Pacific
Builder:	L.A. Shipbuilding	Bethlehem Steel Co.	Southern Pacific
Year:	1923	1922	1915
Length:	225'	216.7'	273'
Hull:	Double end, steel	Double end, steel	Double end, steel
Tons:	1,653	1,782	2,282
Engine:	Turbo-electric	Steam	Steam
Propulsion:	Screw	Screw	Side wheel
Disposition:	To U.S. Maritime Commission in World War II, later Southern Pacific, last ferry on San Francisco Bay, made final run on July 30, 1958, sold by Southern Pacific	To Puget Sound 1940	Scrapped 1945

The first *Gold* was the first vessel of the Petaluma & Santa Rosa R.R. She was lost in a fire at Petaluma and sunk, and today her remains can still be seen at low tide. (Roy Graves photo/Marin County Historical Society)

Vessel:	*Santa Rosa*	*Sausalito*+	*Sehome*
Operator:	N.W.P.	N.W.P.	M.S.L.
Builder:	General Engineering	John W. Dickie	
Year:	1927	1894	1877 as stern wheel, rebuilt 1889 as side wheel, rebuilt 1914 to screw
Length:	251'	236'	192'
Hull:	Double end, steel	Double end, wood	Single end, wood
Tons:	2,468	1,766	692
Engine:	Diesel-electric	Steam	Steam
Propulsion:	Screw	Side wheel	Stern wheel, side wheel, screw
Disposition:	To Puget Sound, renamed *Enetai* 1937	Out of service 1934	Sunk December 14, 1918

Vessel:	*Shasta*	*Sierra Nevada*	*Sonoma Valley*
Operator:	Southern Pacific	S.P., Key System	Rich.-S.R.
Builder:	Bethlehem Steel Co.	Moore & Scott	Rebuilt from *San Jose*
Year:	1922	1913	1928
Length:	216.7'	218'	
Hull:	Double end, steel	Double end, steel	
Tons:	1,782	1,578	
Engine:	Steam	Steam	
Tons:	1,782	1,578	
Engine:	Steam	Steam	
Propulsion:	Screw	Screw	
Disposition:	To Puget Sound 1940	To Rich.-S.R. 1947, later to San Pedro	Scrapped 1947

Vessel:	*Stockton*	*Tamalpais II*	*Thoroughfare II*
Operator:	Southern Pacific	N.W.P.	Southern Pacific
Builder:	Bethlehem Steel Co.	Union Iron Works	Southern Pacific
Year:	1927	1901	1912
Length:	251'	224'	278'
Hull:	Double end, steel	Double end, steel	Double end, wood
Tons:	2,468	1,631	2,620
Engine:	Diesel-electric	Steam	Steam
Propulsion:	Screw	Side wheel	Side wheel
Disposition:	To Puget Sound, renamed *Klickitat* 1937	Scrapped 1946	Dismantled 1935

Vessel:	*Tiburon*	*Transit*	*Treasure Island*
Operator:	N.W.P.	Southern Pacific	Key System++
Builder:	S.F. & North Pacific	Central Pacific R.R.	Bethlehem Steel Co.
Year:	1884	1876	1911
Length:	215'	310'	248.5'
Hull:	Double end, wood	Double end, wood	Double end, steel
Tons:	1,284	1,566	1,720
Engine:	Steam	Steam	Steam
Propulsion:	Side wheel	Side wheel	Side wheel
Disposition:	Vacated 1924	Dismantled 1934	To Martinez-Benicia Ferry 1940

+Not to be confused with ferry by name of *Saucelito*.

++Ex-*San Pedro*, purchased from Santa Fe Railway in 1939, to Navy during World War II, scrapped in 1946.

Vessel:	*Ukiah*	*Yerba Buena I*	*Yerba Buena II*
Operator:	N.W.P.	Key System	Key System
Builder:	S.F. & North Pacific	John W. Dickie	Moore Dry Dock Co.
Year:	1890	1903	1927
Length:	291'	175.4'	256'
Hull:	Double end, wood	Double end, wood	Double end, steel
Tons:	2,564	616	2,075
Engine:	Steam	Steam	Turbo-electric
Propulsion:	Side wheel	Screw	Screw
Disposition:	Rebuilt as *Eureka* 1923	To G.G. Ferry, renamed *Harry E. Speas* 1924	To Army Transport Service during World War II, scrapped in 1950s

Vessel:	*Yosemite II*
Operator:	Southern Pacific
Builder:	Bethlehem Steel Co.
Year:	1923
Length:	216.7'
Hull:	Double end, steel
Tons:	1,782
Engine:	Steam
Propulsion:	Screw
Disposition:	To Rio de la Plata, Uruguay, 1939, renamed *Argentina*, later sunk

The camera of Will Whittaker was as adept at capturing ferryboats as interurban trains. The *Tamalpais II* is arriving from Marin County, the *Yerba Buena II* from Oakland, and the *Berkeley* is leaving San Francisco for Oakland. Three ferries, three companies, all in one picture! But the Bay Bridge in the background is about to reduce the ferry service to the East Bay to only those few boats necessary to service the transcontinental trains. (Wilbur C. Whittaker)

Steaming toward San Francisco with a boatload of automobiles, the *Klamath* is no help to the interurbans and their ferry services. But then the Bay Bridge is about to make short work of the *Klamath*, and today she is a floating studio and office building at San Francisco's Pier 3. (Wilbur C. Whittaker)

San Francisco's skyline has changed dramatically since the days when the ferryboat *Klamath* plied the Bay's waters. San Francisco is no longer one of the world's busiest seaports and the *Klamath* is permanently moored at Pier 5 and serves as a floating office building.

Chapter Eleven
Other Lines

It would be impossible—if not actually unfair—to engage in a project of this kind without including several of the other railroad lines which either paralleled, connected with, or were related to the network of interurbans in the San Francisco Bay Area. Although often diminutive in operations, these lines cannot be overlooked, as they were, albeit sometimes indirectly, associated with the interurban railways either through ownerships, supplementary service, connecting service, or outright competition.

True, many were neither suburban nor interurban lines, and certainly Class 1 service and freight-hauling short lines were not in any sense of the word interurban services. Yet these roads admirably filled in the gaps where the interurbans failed to serve, such as between San Rafael and Petaluma, Oakland and San Jose, and San Mateo and Palo Alto. Moreover, although short line freight switching operations were certainly not interurbans, their inclusion is mandatory as they were either an arm of an interurban road or else were the final repositories of the castaway equipment of an interurban railroad.

For purposes of clarification, streetcar lines with actual connections to the eight interurban lines of the Bay Area are included. Often these car lines served to complete the journey of the interurban rider, and occasionally they shared the same tracks with the interurbans.

In the process of presenting capsule comments—rather than entire chapters—to these railways, there is no intention to slight these roads in any way. Each in its own way was important, and, as service was either cut back or abandoned, the public was shortchanged as the possibilities of a unified rapid transit network became that much more remote. Unfortunately, the pattern of railway abandonments has not called for restoration.

Alameda Belt Line
The Alameda Belt Line is a short switching line jointly purchased from the City of Alameda in 1924 by the Atcheson, Topeka & Santa Fe and the Western Pacific. It remains under that ownership today.

Auto Stages
From time to time in this volume the reader will note references to so-called auto stages. These were generally what could be described as automobiles with extended seating capacities. Finding great favor due to their economical operation for small groups of passengers, they were used extensively prior to the 1930s to supplement railroad service to what then could be considered remote areas.

As improvements in motor buses were made and the use of private automobiles increased, the auto stages declined in both popularity and operations.

Burlingame Railway
In 1913, the Burlingame Railway was formed to connect with the United Railroads' #40 Line in Burlingame, and the short (1½ miles) route went from Broadway Station to the top of Hillside Drive. A single car, powered by storage batteries, comprised the rolling stock.

The Burlingame Railway was intended as a real estate promotional venture and never as a full-fledged street railway. It ceased running in 1917.

California Midland
The California Midland was an aspiration of John Martin of the North Shore R.R. Intended as a 1200-volt, third-rail line from Marysville to Auburn and Nevada City, it lost out on a franchise application to the Northern Electric for street service in Marysville. The 1906 earthquake disaster precluded the railroad's ever becoming a reality.

California Wine Association

In 1911, the California Wine Association constructed an electric railway for transfer purposes in its gigantic winery in Richmond. The road had two freight motors, Nos. 501 and 52. The origins of No. 501 are unknown, while No. 52 had been No. 52 on the Ocean Shore R.R. With the advent of Prohibition, the winery was closed and the two motors were placed in a storage shed where they remained, unused, until the property was taken over by the United States Navy at the beginning of World War II. The Navy scrapped both pieces in 1942.

Central California Traction

This 1200-volt d.c. line was chartered on August 7, 1905, and began operations on August 29, 1910, between Stockton and Sacramento. It provided a high grade freight and passenger service over a 55.68-mile main line, connecting with the Sacramento Northern in Sacramento and the Tidewater Southern in Stockton, often sharing rolling stock on a rental basis.

The C.C.T. also operated local streetcars in Stockton and Sacramento, but relinquished streetcar operations after 1928. Power collectors were third rail as well as trolley pole. On January 1, 1928, the road came under the joint ownership of the Southern Pacific, Santa Fe, and Western Pacific.

Marysville & Colusa R.R.

The Marysville & Colusa Railroad was incorporated May 6, 1910, under the imposing title of The Northern Electric Railway Marysville-Colusa Branch, to build the Northern Electric's branch line from Marysville to Colusa. After completion, N.E.'s No. 109 was lettered Marysville & Colusa No. 10 in order to comply with franchise requirements. N.E. No. 105 also served this road.

Mt. Tamalpais & Muir Woods Railway

Advertising itself as the "Crookedest Railroad in the World," the Mt. Tamalpais and Muir Woods Railway opened for business on August 26, 1896, and continued running until abandonment some thirty-four years later. Negotiating a tortuous course from the Northwestern Pacific depot in Mill Valley up the slopes of Mt. Tamalpais to an elevation of 2,400 feet in less than nine miles, the little railway's motive power was steam locomotives of the type used on logging railroads; indeed, most of the locos were, at one time or another, veterans of logging operations.

Throughout its lifetime, the Mt. T. & M. W. Ry. served residents of the Bay Area, who enjoyed not only a railroad ride of roller coaster proportions, but were also afforded, from the 2,586-foot summit of Mt. Tamalpais, a spectacular view of San Francisco Bay.

For a number of years the Mt. T. & M. W. Ry. offered local "streetcar" service from the N.W.P. depot down Blithedale Canyon as far as the Lee Street Station through the use of a passenger car coupled to a diminutive four-wheel steam locomotive, and later a gas car. Plans to electrify this service never materialized.

An extension was later built which went to the famed redwood groves of Muir Woods, thus offering Marin County visitors a choice of woods or mountains, all on one short railway line.

Municipal Railway of San Francisco

The Muni, as generations of San Franciscans have called the Municipal Railway, began service in December of 1912 with the electrification of the Geary Street cable car line. For a number of years thereafter, it expanded its services, chiefly by inaugurating new lines. The intended purpose of the Muni was, in compliance with the City Charter of 1900, to eventually unify the multitude of street railways under a single ownership.

The Muni assumed the freight switching duties of the Ocean Shore Railroad upon the latter's abandonment, and in order to carry out these operations, the road purchased steeple cab No. 1010 from the Petaluma & Santa Rosa Railroad, repainting her in the standard Muni colors of the time: grey with gold trim and a tile-red roof. No. 1010 was renumbered to M.Ry. 501. Ocean Shore switching duties lasted from 1920 to 1927, and after 1927, No. 501 was stored in the Geary Carbarn until May of 1930 when the P. & S. R. repurchased her for $1,100.

The Muni provided highly effective competition to the Market Street Railway for a number of years until 1944, when the M.S.Ry., bankrupt and worn out, sold out to the city-owned system. With this sale went title to the #40 Line to San Mateo, and the City of San Francisco found itself running an interurban line.

The Muni tried to run its new P.C.C.-type streetcars on the #40 Line, but these cars were unsuitable for high speed running, and the experiment failed. Further traffic congestion on Mission Street in San Francisco, a lack of right-of-way into downtown, and subsequent abandonment of the streetcars on Mission Street caused the Muni to discontinue the interurban line in 1949.

In 1952, the Muni ended all private street railway service in San Francisco by purchasing the California Street Cable Railroad Company, and while today most of its lines have been converted to either motor bus or trolley bus operations, the Muni still operates five streetcar lines and three cable car lines.

Oakland-Sacramento Service (Southern Pacific)

Among the earliest trains scheduled by the Central Pacific after the completion of the transcontinental railroad were those between Oakland and the new state capital at Sacramento.

For generations, politicians from the Bay Area, S.P. executives from the corporate headquarters on Market Street in San Francisco, as well as petitioners and lobbyists—not to mention the general public—rode the Espee, whose lists included as many as eleven trains daily between Oakland and Sacramento, graced by such name trains as *El Dorado*, *The Governor*, *The Legislator*, *The Senator*, and *The Statesman*. A bar car and a diner were regular fixtures on these trains.

The Oakland-Sacramento trains made their crossings of Suisun Bay on a train ferry in the like manner of competitor Sacramento Northern, but when the Port Costa-Benicia Bridge was opened for service, the ferry was abolished and the S.N.'s timecards slipped behind those of the Espee.

With the building of the Martinez-Benicia Bridge, the S.P. eliminated the slower ferry, but conversely when the Sacramento Northern's trains began to use the San Francisco-Oakland Bay Bridge for direct routing from San Francisco to Sacramento, the passengers still had to be ferried across Suisun Bay on the *Ramon* while Sacramento-bound San Franciscans on the S.P. still had to take the ferries to the Oakland Mole.

The demise of this interurban competition was, in the main, caused by the general decline of railroad passenger service, but state regulatory authorities compelled the Southern Pacific to retain this run despite a bleak financial ledger for passenger trains.

However, bridges and highways ate into the S.P. rail service in the same manner as the interurban service, and by 1962, only *The Senator* was carrying on tradition. All S.P. passenger services to Sacramento ended with the forming of Amtrak, the government agency established to maintain rail passenger service, even at public subsidy.

Oakland-San Jose Service (Southern Pacific)

Sharing its northern terminus at the Oakland Mole with such crack varnish trains as *The Overland Limited*, *St. Louis Express*, *Pacific Limited*, *The Oregonian*, and in later years the *Shasta Daylight* and *The City of San Francisco*—not to mention the Southern Pacific's East Bay interurban trains—was the Espee's steam train service to San Jose from Oakland. Such was the importance of railway travel in the pre-Nimitz Freeway (Highway 17) age that a typical train board at the Oakland Mole would list five trains daily from which an Oaklander could alight at San Jose; three trains in the morning and two more in the afternoon.

Why this section was never electrified to coordinate with the S.P. East Bay interurbans has never been fully explained, although one theory has it that by the time the Southern Pacific had decided to electrify its East Bay operations in 1911, the railroad was still conscious of the anti-Southern Pacific sentiment which had propelled Hiram Johnson into the Governor's Chair. The theory is that if "Borax" Smith had been able to advance his Key Route to San Jose, and the S.P. electrified its Oakland-San Jose run, it would have brought extremely unfavorable legislation from the Statehouse as well as possibly adverse rulings from the courts—particularly in view of the national popularity of reformers within the Republican Party such as Johnson of California, Theodore Roosevelt of New York and Robert LaFollette of Wisconsin.

On the other hand, the S.P. installed the last interurban system in the Bay Area and probably did not feel any additional construction expenses were warranted. Further, it is doubtful if anyone—much less the Espee—could ever have envisioned the day when such electric rail service would become a necessity in order to avoid traffic strangulation from automobiles and other highway users.

Oakland Terminal Railway

Jointly owned by both the Atcheson, Topeka & Santa Fe and the Western Pacific, what is today the Oakland Terminal Railway was once the interurban passenger division of the Key System. The Key System's 1929 reorganization left the transit company in the hands of the Railway Equipment and Realty Co., Ltd. This corporation then divided its operations into four subsidiary companies: Key System, Ltd. (passenger trains east of Keel Station—near where the Bay Bridge Toll Plaza now stands—and some freight switching in the West Oakland area), Key Terminal Railway, Ltd. (ferries and freight west of Keel Station), East Bay Street Railway, Ltd. (streetcars), and the East Bay Motor Coach Lines, Ltd. (buses). In 1938, the Key System, Ltd., was renamed the Oakland Terminal Railroad and assigned the freight switching chores of the Key System, while the Key Terminal Railway, Ltd., was renamed the Key System, Ltd., and assigned to passenger service only. In 1942, the Oakland Terminal Railroad was sold to the Santa Fe and the Western Pacific and its name was changed again, this time to Oakland Terminal Railway.

In order to reach certain harbor areas, the O.T.Ry. acquired use of the old Interurban Electric Railway overpass to the Bridge Yard, and today the O.T.Ry. continues to use some ex-Key System track.

While under the Key System, freight motors 1000 and 1001 were used, along with steam locomotive No. 4. No. 4 was later sold to the Santa Fe, being renumbered A.T. & S.F. No. 24. In 1944, Santa Fe No. 24 was sold again, this time to Modesto & Empire Traction Company. Freight motor No. 1000 was scrapped in 1947 while No. 1001 is at the California Railway Museum at Rio Vista Junction, California.

Ocean Shore Railroad

On May 18, 1905, the Ocean Shore Railroad began its ill-starred life. Intended as an electric interurban between San Francisco and Santa Cruz, the railroad was snake-bit from the onset by labor disputes, washouts, and wrecks, not to mention general inefficiency. The trolley wire never left San Francisco, and probably never would have been erected there except to satisfy franchise requirements. Consequently, the only electric operations came from freight switching duties. The road did share one stretch of track with the Municipal Railway's "H" Line, giving the Muni the distinction of being the only local streetcar service in California to run on "steam railroad" tracks. As such, "H" Line cars had to be equipped with railroad marker lamps.

Since the electrification never left San Francisco, the road operated "temporarily" all of its life with steam power. While in the act of declaring bankruptcy, the line was stuck during a labor dispute and never ran again. Operations ceased on August 16, 1920.

The O.S.R.R. owned only three pieces of traction equipment, all steeple cabs:

No. 51
B-B trucks; purchased in April, 1907; 350 h.p.; originally using a pantograph current collector, it was later replaced with a trolley pole; rebuilt in 1919; sold to the Petaluma & Santa Rosa in 1921.

No. 52
B-B trucks; purchased in September, 1907, 500 h.p.; trolley pole; sold to the California Wine Association in 1920; scrapped in 1942.

No. 53
B-B trucks; purchased in March of 1910; 350 h.p.; trolley pole, sold to the Petaluma & Santa Rosa in 1920.

Richmond-Hayward Line (Key System)

What must rank as one of the longest streetcar lines in California was the #1 Line of the Key System's Oakland Traction Company, running from Richmond to Hayward. This long line had its inception when incorporated as the Richmond Railway & Navigation Company on August 13, 1900. Four years later, on July 7, 1904, the first streetcars commenced operations, under the name East Shore and Suburban Railway, the franchise having been sold prior to its first run.

On September 20, 1914, the line was sold again, this time being consolidated with the Oakland Traction Company, the pre-1929 name for the streetcar arm of the Key System. The Oakland Traction Company then commenced through streetcar service to Richmond from Oakland, and on May 1, 1915, extended the Richmond streetcar service to the Richmond ferry slips to greet the picturesque red and white boats of the Richmond-San Rafael Ferry.

In 1932, the line to the ferry pier was discontinued, and the Key System effected other cutbacks in Richmond's streetcars. However, on October 1, 1932, the Key merged the Oakland-Richmond and the Oakland-Hayward lines into one streetcar route, designating it the #1 Line, and thus created through service from Hayward to Richmond.

168

The Richmond cars used several rights-of-way, including underpasses, to avoid crossing the rails of the Class 1 railroads. Therefore, one might designate the #1 Line as an interurban except for the fact that only streetcars were ever used by the Key on this run. "Suburban service" might be a more accurate term. In latter years, the old Richmond yards were used as a "boneyard" for worn-out equipment, thus allowing the Key to better utilize space in Oakland and Emeryville.

Still, the line didn't last long, for on November 7, 1933, all streetcar service in Richmond was ended.

Sacramento Northern Streetcars

The Sacramento Northern and predecessor Northern Electric operated a series of streetcar lines in Chico and Sacramento as well as the line from Marysville to Yuba City. While these lines were run in order to satisfy franchise demands, they interestingly enough predated the N.E.'s interurban service, and the S.N.'s last passenger service, over the Marysville-Yuba City streetcar line, actually postdated the interurbans by some six years! This line maintained a five-cent fare to the very end, and in so doing became the last streetcar service in California to charge a nickel a ride.

Utilizing former United Railroads of San Francisco single-truck cars, single-truck Birney Safety Cars, open cars (to take advantage of the warm climate) and suburban cars (heavier than city cars but not as ponderous as the interurbans), the Sacramento Northern's array of streetcar equipment over the years merits a study in itself. A roster of these cars appears with the other S.N. rolling stock.

The South End of the Sacramento Northern never maintained streetcars at any time. Since these lines were strictly North End, all servicing of the S.N.'s streetcars was done at the Mulberry Shops in Chico, and it was not unusual to see a diminutive Birney, for example, rolling along the right-of-way shared by S.N. freight drags and interurban cars.

Sacramento & Woodland Railroad

The Sacramento & Woodland Railroad began on July 15, 1912, as a branch line of the Northern Electric Railway from Woodland to Sacramento. However, in all respects of railroading, it was part of the main line. N.E. motor No. 107 was lettered Sacramento & Woodland No. 1, but later reverted to Sacramento Northern logo and numbering.

Sacramento Terminal Company

The Sacramento Terminal Company was not actually a railroad, but rather a single track, 5.73 miles in length, owned jointly by the Sacramento Northern and Central California Traction. Located in Sacramento, it was used for switching operations. Incorporated on September 17, 1908, it owned no equipment. The original charter called for an additional line to be built from 31st Street west between L and X Streets to and across the Sacramento River to Broderick, but this track was never laid.

Sacramento Valley West Side Railroad

Known as the Dixon Branch of the Oakland, Antioch & Eastern, this road was promoted by a group of wealthy farmers and ranchers in the Sacramento Valley to insure railroad service in the Dixon area. All operations were carried out by the O.A. & E. Running some 11.8 miles due north from Dozier to Dixon, the line consistently lost money and was abandoned after running from October 10, 1914, to August 9, 1917.

San Francisco-San Jose Service (Southern Pacific)

Railway service between the City by the Golden Gate and San Jose had its inception with the incorporation on August 18, 1860 of the San Francisco and San Jose Railroad. However, it was not until October 18, 1863, that regular service commenced—a service which continues today under the ownership of the Southern Pacific and ranks as one of the oldest continuously operating passenger runs in western railroading.

Coming under the ownership of the Central Pacific in 1868, the rail line from San Francisco to San Jose had a monopoly of rail passenger service on the San Francisco Peninsula until 1902 when the San Francisco and San Mateo Electric Railway began to compete for the patronage between San Mateo and San Francisco.

On January 22, 1957, at 5:45 P.M., locomotive No. 4430, a GS-4 Class refugee from the *Daylight*, headed Train 146 from San Francisco to end steam-powered commute service on the San Francisco Peninsula. Today the San Francisco-to-San Jose commute trains are headed by diesel-electric locos on the 49.5-mile trip.

For years the peninsula trains formed a connection with the Peninsular Railway, and passengers found it convenient to utilize the Peninsular as a feeder to the Espee. Today, the commuters are a consistent money loser and studies are underway to ascertain the feasibility of better utilizing the roadbed for rapid transit.

San Jose Railroads

The San Jose Railroads were the local streetcar arm of the Peninsular Railway, and served the City of San Jose for some time after abandonment of the interurbans, finally succumbing to the automobile in 1938. The exception was the streetcar service in Palo Alto which came under the purview of the Peninsular Railway, and the cars in Palo Alto service were lettered "Peninsular Railway" and had their own carbarn.

A number of cars were interchanged between the Peninsular and the San Jose Railroads as needs and abandonments demanded, thus creating a streetcar line served by interurban equipment.

San Rafael-Petaluma Service (Northwestern Pacific)

The Petaluma & Santa Rosa Railroad had long had its connections with the Northwestern Pacific at both Petaluma and Santa Rosa. The Northwestern Pacific's steam trains connected Petaluma with San Rafael, and passengers who wanted to go directly into Sonoma County from San Francisco or Marin would catch the N.W.P. trains in either Sausalito or San Rafael. After abandonment of the P. & S.R.'s electrics, the Petaluma-Santa Rosa area's passengers continued to be served by the Northwestern Pacific until the end of passenger service.

For many years, the N.W.P. advertised what it called the "Triangle Trip." This trip began in Sausalito at the ferry docks where one would board the special trains for the Russian River resort areas. The train would travel on the western side of the triangle via San Anselmo, Pt. Reyes, Tomales, Camp Meeker and Monte Rio. Forming the west to east side of the triangle were the rails between Monte Rio, Rio Campo, Guerneville, Eagle Nest (Rio Nido), Green Valley, and Fulton. From Fulton to Sausalito via Santa Rosa, Petaluma, and San Rafael the rails formed the eastern side of the triangle.

Southern Pacific Service in the Napa Valley

For sixty-four years and two days, the Napa Valley was served by the steam-powered trains of the Southern Pacific in competition with the Napa Valley Route's interurbans. On July 11, 1865, the Napa Valley R.R. opened for service from Suscol to Calistoga. Adding trackage section by section, the intent of its organizers was fulfilled when the North Pacific R.R. Company was sold to the Central Pacific R.R. and the rails reached from Vallejo to Calistoga. The road came under the ownership of the Central Pacific on August 1, 1871. The C.P.R.R., and later the S.P., ran branch line trains for Napa Junction from Santa Rosa.

For years, passengers on the S.P.'s Napa Valley trains who wanted to go to San Francisco had to take the S.P. ferry from Vallejo to Crockett, and then transfer to trains bound for the Oakland Mole. Another ferry ride and passengers arrived in San Francisco. Steam-powered passenger service by the S.P. ended in the Napa Valley in 1929, the trade being left to the San Francisco, Napa & Calistoga interurbans.

Tidewater Southern Railway

A subsidiary of the Western Pacific, the Tidewater Southern was incorporated October 4, 1910. The main line ran between Stockton and Modesto with branches to Turlock and Hilmar, giving the T.S.Ry. a total of 32.23 miles of main line. It was the hope of the Western Pacific to eventually run to Bakersfield via Fresno but the plans never materialized.

The road, which worked closely with the Central California Traction (to the point of sharing the passenger station at Stockton), used trolley poles to collect power rated at 1200 volts, d.c. Both freight and passenger service was provided. The three Niles-built interurban cars ended interurban service on May 26, 1932, although passenger service continued for a while thereafter in mixed consist with steam power. With abandonment of the interurbans, the overhead trolley wire was taken down except for 2.1 miles in the city of Modesto where franchise requirements prohibited the use of steam locos. All electric service ceased in 1947 and the road serves today as a feeder to the Western Pacific behind diesel-electric motive power.

Vallejo & Northern

The Vallejo & Northern Railway Company was incorporated on November 8, 1906, with the intention of building a railroad from Vallejo to Sacramento. Never progressing much beyond the drawing board, it was sold on October 20, 1909, to a newly formed corporation, the Vallejo

& Northern Railroad Company. Experiencing financial difficulties, the railroad never accomplished more than some grading and the laying of a few miles of track except to establish a minor streetcar operation in Sacramento.

On December 31, 1912, the entire V. & N. was taken over by the Northern Electric Railway (later the Sacramento Northern) and in N.E. and S.N. operations it became known as the Vacaville Branch. The S.N. continued the Sacramento streetcar service using the S.N. herald.

At one time it was hoped that the V. & N. rails would be the connection between the Sacramento Northern and the Petaluma & Santa Rosa R.R. However, sale of the P. & S.R. to the Northwestern Pacific ended that idea.

Later, portions of the V. & N. franchise were used by the San Francisco, Napa & Calistoga for both passenger and freight service, and when the old Napa Valley Route passed into U.S. Navy ownership, so did portions of the old V. & N. trackage which were sold at the same time by the Sacramento Northern.

West Side Railroad Company

The West Side Railroad Company was organized by the West Sacramento Company, a group which owned some 7,000 acres of rich farm and industrial land on the west side of the Sacramento River, across from the city of Sacramento. The railroad company was incorporated on August 31, 1911, and operated as a belt line with all operations handled by the Northern Electric, and later the Sacramento Northern, using N.E. and S.N. locomotives.

Chapter Twelve
The Survivors

The cars of the Bay Area's interurban lines tended to have quite long and useful lives, provided they survived such catastrophes as fire, collision, premature scrapping, and sales to other railroad companies which abandoned operations in advance of a car's full depreciation. Another hazard to the interurban cars was the problem of what to do with them when their rails were abandoned. As a consequence, they were, for the most part, scrapped.

A few fortunate survivors still remain for public viewing, however, thanks to the earnest efforts of such organizations as the Bay Area Electric Railroad Association, the Orange Empire Trolley Museum, and the Pacific Coast Chapter of the Railway and Locomotive Historical Society. Members of these groups, and other railfans as well, have made it possible for California to have three railway museums: California Railway Museum, located at Rio Vista Junction, Solano County; Orange Empire Railroad Museum, located at Perris, Orange County; and Traveltown, located in Griffith Park, Los Angeles.

Traveltown, the senior of the three, was established in 1952 with the donation of old steam locomotives from the Southern Pacific, and has expanded continously since. A single track encircles the outdoor exhibit and a former Los Angeles open trolley car, powered nowadays by a gasoline engine, makes the circuit, giving passengers a guided tour by rail. Traveltown is open daily, charges no admission, and is under the ownership and supervision of the Los Angeles Recreation and Parks Department.

In 1956, the Orange Empire Trolley Museum was formed by a group of trolley lovers in order to preserve from the junk pile many of the trolley cars which once traversed Southern California. Two years and several acquisitions later, a permanent home for these cars was opened at Perris, on U.S. Highway 395, about eighty-five miles from Los Angeles. Today the O.E.R.R.M. houses one of the finest collections of railway equipment to be found anywhere, including steam locomotives, steam railroad cars, and city trolley cars from across the nation, British Columbia, Canada, and even Hill of Howth, Ireland, as well as work cars, electric freight locomotives, and interurbans. Unlike many operating railway museums, the tracks at Perris are dual gauge: standard (4'8½") for most cars, and narrow gauge (3'6") for ex-Los Angeles Railway streetcars. The museum is open to the public on weekends all year long. There is a souvenir counter and bookstore and the public may ride whichever cars are running that day.

The Bay Area Electric Railroad Association was formed in April of 1945, and immediately acquired car No. 53 of the San Francisco, Napa & Calistoga Railroad. As the group grew, so did its roster of dispensable cars of the Bay Area's electric lines. The cars were used for railfan excursions over the remaining traction lines, including the Municipal Railway of San Francisco, Sacramento Northern, and Key System. However, there was as yet no permanent place for the cars, and storage tracks had to be borrowed. In 1959, No. 53 was wantonly burned beyond repair by vandals. This, more than anything else, spurred the B.A.E.R.A. into establishing its own museum for safeguarding of the cars, not only from vandalism but from weather and other hazards as well. Thus in November of 1960, under sponsorship of the B.A.E.R.A., the California Railway Museum was opened alongside the Sacramento Northern's mainline at Rio Vista Junction on Highway 12 in Solano County. A spur from the S.N.'s rails connects to the museum's operating tracks, and this has facilitated the donations of more equipment which has been retired from active service by California's electric railways. Some steam railroad equipment also adorns the museum.

There is no admission charge, but donations to help defray expenses for restoration of antiquated equipment are welcome. The public is invited to visit on weekends and on some holidays, and rides are available on the restored cars on Sundays between 2:00 and 4:00 P.M.

In addition to the forgoing, the State of California maintains a museum at the Hyde Street Pier in San Francisco, where historical vessels of the Bay are maintained in floating condition. Of interest to this volume is the preservation of the *Eureka*, kept in her Northwestern Pacific livery, with an exhibit of vintage autos on her main deck to enable visitors to envision Bay travel from Marin County to San Francisco in past years. The museum is open daily and an entrance fee admits visitors to all boats.

In the hopes that this volume has kindled a latent interest in the interurbans of the Bay Area, and in recognition of the many railfans who have worked uncounted hours to restore these monuments to a significant period in the development of rapid transit, a complete roster of former Bay Area interurban cars at these museums is hereby given.

Traveltown

North Shore R.R. *Electra*, displayed as Pacific Electric No. 1544.

Interurban Electric Railway No. 379, displayed as Metropolitan Transit Authority No. 1543.

Orange Empire Railroad Museum

Interurban Electric Railway No. 344, displayed as Pacific Electric No. 314.

Interurban Electric Railway No. 672, displayed as Pacific Electric No. 498.

Key System Transit Lines, No. 167, displayed in Key System livery.

Northwestern Pacific No. 384, displayed as Pacific Electric No. 384.

Sacramento Northern No. 653, displayed in S.N. colors.

California Railway Museum

Central California Traction No. 7, an express motor displayed in C.C.T. colors.

Interurban Electric Railway No. 332, displayed as Southern Pacific No. 332 (undergoing restoration).

Key System No. 182. All former Key System equipment, except for Nos. 495, 561, and 563, is displayed in Key System livery and number.

Key System No. 186.

Key System streetcar No. 271.

Key System No. 495, displayed as Sacramento Northern No. 1005.

Key System No. 561, displayed as Interborough Rapid Transit No. 844.

Key System No. 563, displayed as Interborough Rapid Transit No. 889.

Key System streetcar No. 987, a streetcar used on interurban tracks.

Key System No. 1001, a freight locomotive displayed as Oakland Terminal Railroad (Key System) No. 1001.

Key System wrecker car No. 1011.

Key System line car No. 1201.

Key System shop switcher No. 1215.

Key System line car No. 1218.

Peninsular Railway No. 52 (undergoing restoration).

Peninsular Railway No. 61 (undergoing restoration).

Petaluma & Santa Rosa R.R. No. 63.

Sacramento Northern No. 62, a streetcar used in intercity service.

Sacramento Northern express motor No. 602, in S.N. colors.

Sacramento Northern No. 1005, former Key System No. 495, displayed as S.N. 1005.

Sacramento Northern No. 1019, in S.N. colors but de-motorized.

Sacramento Northern No. 1020, in S.N. colors but de-motorized.

Sacramento Northern freight locomotive No. 652, in S.N. colors.

Sacramento Northern freight locomotive No. 654, in S.N. colors.

Chapter Thirteen
Epilogue

Justified or not, the remark "The Public be damned" was attributed to New York Central magnate William H. Vanderbilt, and ever since, that attitude has been attributed, justified or not, to any railroad which attempts to reduce or abandon service. The question persists: was abandonment of interurban passenger service in the Bay Area the result of parsimonious ownerships or was that service a luxury which private industry could no longer justify to its stockholders?

In order to analyze properly the events which followed—in which the once interurban-riding public resorted to the private automobile for transportation and eventual disillusionment with same—we have to examine the years 1930 to 1940. The abandonments of the Key System's rails in 1958 and of the #40 Line in 1949 were due in large part, we believe, to other factors.

First, those were the years of the Great Depression. Money was unavailable for luxuries, and this included trolley rides for pleasure. Jobs were scarce, which helped curtail the number of commute riders while commute schedules were nonetheless maintained. Due to lack of cash box revenue, the railroads had to dip into capital funds for operation. This forced many repairs and modernizations to be deferred (much of which would have helped only on a long-term basis), and many essential improvements never took place.

Even if money for modernization of cars were available, it must be noted that carbuilding by 1930 was greatly curtailed, and many honored names in the business had passed from the scene. As evidence, the Napa Valley Route's Nos. 62 and 63, when delivered from St. Louis in 1933, were *the last conventional interurban cars built in America.*

By 1930, the internal combustion engine had proved its worth, and the interurbans faced competition for freight hauls from the relatively new trucking industry. The advantages of trucks over railcars for short hauls were several, among them the ability to deliver to the receiver's front door, one-man operation in contrast to full crews for less-than-carload manifests, and probably of equal importance, no maintenance costs for the roadbed.

Railroads, by their very nature, can only deliver from stationary point to stationary point. And the manifests—whether they be people or goods—must first be delivered to that stationary point. A truck or bus can vary its route as needs demand, even on a daily or hourly basis.

A single interurban car, whether it be box motor, passenger-baggage combo, or freight trailer, still required at least two men and sometimes three to operate. Add to this the yard hands necessary to assemble and load the train, and it is easy to see why a single driver of a truck could reduce freight costs.

Interurbans, generally, in contrast to their big brothers of transcontinental railroading, did not construct their roads with land grants and government-backed bonds. Yet when they did build their often undercapitalized railroads—witness the number of reorganizations of the Bay Area's interurban companies—they were subject to taxation and street maintenance in much the same manner as the steam roads. Local railways, in assuming the attitudes of big-time railroading, often found themselves fair game for the local tax assessor, and it must be pointed out that by tradition local communities rely on the property tax for survival.

The interurbans also bore an additional cost which the steam roads did not, and that was the electric overhead. For fiscal purposes, the overhead constituted, in effect, an additional roadbed with its own army of maintenance men: highly

Racing southbound toward Daly City in what was once #40 Line territory, this modern train of the Bay Area Rapid Transit District—better known as BART—is competing with a fifty-five-mile per hour freeway. It was freeways such as this one which helped to doom the interurban railways of the San Francisco Bay Area. (Bay Area Rapid Transit District Photo/Author's Collection)

skilled electricians. Moreover, electric railroads had to maintain their own power plants and substations. Thus, when diesel-electric locomotives became available in sufficient quantities after World War II, the electric railroads converted as soon as finances and available equipment would permit.

As autos supplanted the interurbans insofar as pleasure travel was concerned, and as trucks made their inroads into short-haul and l.c.l. freight business, the only trade left to the big electrics was that which had proved to be nothing but a money-losing operation: commuters. Nobody in positions of responsibility seemed to want to tackle this thorny problem, either because it was fiscally a monumental headache, or through lack of foresight for the demand for large scale commuter services in the 1960s and beyond. Yet in fact commuters were the best public relations program that electric railroads had to offer; here were hundreds or thousands of patrons, or potential shipping customers, being transported daily by the shipper and being shown every courtesy that the railroad had to offer.

All eight of the Bay Area's interurban lines were privately owned and therefore each one faced at least some of the disadvantages mentioned above. Yet, only three of these railways were not owned by a major transcontinental railroad. The Western Pacific owned the Sacramento Northern, while the Interurban Electric Railway, the Northwestern Pacific, the Peninsular Railway, and the Petaluma & Santa Rosa were under the ownership of the Southern Pacific. The Key System and the San Francisco, Napa & Calistoga remained in private ownership until cessation of operations while the Market Street Railway did not come under public ownership (the only one of the eight to eventually do so) until 1944, and that was the result of the long-standing policy of San Francisco regarding privately owned streetcar companies rather than the desire to salvage a failing interurban line.

Could not the major railroads subsidize their

interurbans out of their corporate largesse for the public good? Perhaps so, but at what price to the stockholders? It might well be argued that the awarding of a franchise to operate over public lands such as city streets included the responsibility to accept losses as well as the right to glean profits. The Southern Pacific, while dropping unprofitable passenger service on the Petaluma & Santa Rosa and on the Peninsular Railway, did upgrade equipment when it assumed full control of the Northwestern Pacific and did extend its East Bay interurbans directly into San Francisco when the San Francisco-Oakland Bay Bridge was built. Further, the S.P. for many years had to subsidize its Pacific Electric Railway in Southern California. The Western Pacific likewise extended its Sacramento Northern over the Bay Bridge to San Francisco even though the W.P. was in the process of reorganization caused by the declaration of bankruptcy in 1935.

Was this direct trackage to San Francisco given a chance to prove its worth? The only comparison that can be made is with the Key system, and the Key System steadily lost money. The Key did experience a few boom years during World War II when automobile gasoline and tires were rationed and it provided public transit to the naval station at Treasure Island.

In the matter of the Napa Valley Route, it was simply a case of being too overburdened with fiscal setbacks for a local railway to be able to hold out under private ownership.

When the Market Street Railway, including its #40 Line, passed to municipal ownership in 1944, the cars—though still serviceable—would be due for replacement in a few years, some kind of off-street trackage in the city would have been required, and it is doubtful that the citizens of San Mateo County would have cared to stand the cost of upgrading San Francisco's property.

The concept of public ownership of interurbans had not yet gained public acceptance. Indeed, the National Railroad Passenger Corporation, or Amtrak, would not come into existence until May 3, 1971. It should be noted that during World War I the Federal Government took control of the nation's railroads under auspices of the United States Railroad Administration. The management of the U.S.R.A. left so much to be desired that the railroads were quickly returned to private control and the experiment was not repeated during World War II.

In a statement which would make the ghosts of James J. Hill, Commodore Vanderbilt, and the Big Four writhe in agony, the president of the Illinois Central Gulf Railroad and former Secretary of Transportation, Alan Boyd, said he expected to see nationalization of America's railroads unless something is done to ease their current financial plight. While not an advocate of nationalization, Boyd was quoted on April 23, 1974 by the Associated Press as saying, "That idea doesn't bother me at all. It's certainly one answer, and it may be a logical one. The government could own the rails and charge the railroad companies a user charge, much like they do trucking companies on the highways."

By 1941, six of the eight interurban lines had passed into memory. What were the results? Minus the interurbans, substitutes would have to be found. World War II had ended the Great Depression and substituted the boom economy of wartime. With prosperity came the demand for automobiles, but large scale production did not resume until after the war. When it did resume, the State of California embarked on a massive highway construction program, based on the premise that *public transportation was for the public good, and therefore justified public expenditures*. Yet there was no money to restore the six lost interurban lines, while huge sums were spent not only on the aforementioned highways but on airline facilities as well.

In June of 1973, *Railroad Magazine* noted the following: "United Transportation Union's News comments on this year's $8.5-billion budget of the U.S. Department of Transportation: 'Note that more than 71 per cent of the budget...is for highways, while the Federal Railroad Administration gets only 9 tenths of one per cent, only one tenth of 1 per cent more than the Office of the Secretary of the Department.' The budget breakdown reveals once more just how Uncle Sam's transportation priorities are aligned. Railroads apparently rank just a cut above the DOT typing pool!"

The Key System alone would continue to run until 1958, finally succumbing to a combination of fiscal and labor troubles which in themselves could have spelled disaster even if National City Lines had not taken such a belligerent attitude toward the concept of rail transit. Moreover, the Key System, and also the Market Street Railway, was saddled with a number of unprofitable city lines, both streetcar and bus.

What happened in the years between 1940 and 1962? In 1962 the voters of San Francisco, Alameda and Contra Costa Counties voted to restore interurban service. Marin County was willing, but repeated studies failed to ensure that trains could be run on the Golden Gate Bridge. Santa Clara County was apparently willing to join in the formation of BART, but reluctance on the part of San Mateo County precluded Santa Clara's participation. Despite pockets of protest, it had become apparent that a dramatic change in attitude had taken place concerning interurban rail service. Why?

The postwar years in the United States, and particularly in California, witnessed a massive migration to what sociologists refer to as suburbia, or newly developed areas outside of the boundaries of a central city. This migration was particularly noticeable in California where a prodigious statewide growth in population—due largely to immigration from other states—forced the growth of suburbs at an unprecedented rate. (Census figures for the nine counties of the San Francisco Bay Area can be found in Appendix "C.") Principal causes of heavy suburban growth in the Bay Area can be attributed to several factors, among them a lack of land area for new individual homes in the City of San Francisco,* a more desirable climate outside of San Francisco, and a need for local services and merchandising.

Historically, large portions of the labor force of San Francisco have been suburbanites. But this is, in fact, a direct result *of* and not a cause *for* interurban transit. Even within the city itself, it can be shown that the proliferation of cable cars on San Francisco's steep hills from the 1880s onward effected an immediate rise of property values and development.

If we have an unprecedented rate of suburban growth accompanied by a lack of public transportation, how do commuters get to the central city? Again we return to discussion of the family automobile. Whereas the local streetcar or interurban once symbolized a town's sophistication, prosperity or growth, the automobile in America has always symbolized sophistication or prosperity to the individual. While the ownership of an automobile once indicated that the individual could afford the luxury of private transportation, with a lack of public transit it had become a necessary substitute for the mass transportation which the new suburban communities had failed to provide. Large shopping centers in suburban communities were designed with parking lots, not with streetcar or railway waiting stations. As intercommunity freeways were built, no provision was made for additional public transit rights-of-way.** In Los Angeles, former roadbeds of the Pacific Electric were converted to freeways.

Yet for all the heavy freeway construction, the growth of automobile traffic outstripped the capacity of the governing agencies to either maintain or construct new roadways. And once the automobiles from suburbia had reached the central city, it was discovered that conventional city streets were incapable of handling them, causing monumental traffic problems. Indeed, in 1963 the automobile traffic on four of the transportation arteries once served by the interurbans was as follows:

Route	Daily	Peak Period
Bay Bridge	117,000	10,500 cars per hour
Nimitz Freeway	108,000	9,700 cars per hour
East Shore Freeway	121,000	10,900 cars per hour
Bayshore Freeway	174,000	15,700 cars per hr.***

Then there was the environmental byproduct of excessive automobile use: smog.

Smog, a term used loosely to define air pollution from internal combustion engine emissions and industrial smoke and gases, had long been accused of being a health hazard, but so long as there was the feasibility of moving away from the smog areas, the problem was ignored. Eventually, it had to be faced, as residents of smog-infested areas intensified their demands for clean air. These complaints were supported by both health and environmental groups. As drawbacks to the ubiquitous automobile began to become more and more apparent, people began to wonder whatever became of the interurbans of the "good old days." As if in answer to prayers, the San Francisco *Chronicle*, on February 2, 1973,

---

*Geographically, San Francisco is a city of about forty-two square miles surrounded on three sides by water and on its southern boundary by San Mateo County.

**A notable exception is in Chicago, Illinois, where rapid transit trains operate in center strips of the freeway network.

***Source: *California Information Almanac*, 1966 edition.

Southbound toward Fremont, this BART train is providing electric railway service which was lost when the Key System's rail service was abandoned in favor of buses. Ironically, BART is close to reaching "Borax" Smith's goal of electric railway service between Oakland and San Jose. (Bay Area Rapid Transit District photo/Author's Collection)

reported that the United States District Court of Appeals for the District of Columbia had ruled that California and seventeen other states had until 1977 to comply with Clean Air Act standards as adopted in 1970.

In 1964, citizens of San Francisco staged what has become known as the "Freeway Revolt." Disenchanted with freeways crossing the city, quickly formed *ad hoc* committees applied political pressure on the city's Board of Supervisors to prevent their granting the authorizations for further freeway construction in the city. The Board of Supervisors bowed to this pressure, and as of this writing it is unlikely that any further freeways will be built in San Francisco for another generation to come.

Still, the demand for some kind of public transportation continued unabated, centered around the growing ranks of commuters. During the early morning and later afternoon hours when large masses of people were traveling to and from places of work, transportation facilities, whether bus, train, or freeway, were strained to the utmost. Here was one of the basic commuter problems. For only about four hours out of the day, there would be a heavy influx of people using the various systems, but throughout the remainder of the day these systems would remain relatively idle. This meant that huge investments (particularly in the privately owned transit sector such as interurbans and buses) were failing to yield a substantial return. In the public transit field, manpower costs were accelerated due to the concept of a day's pay, rather than an hour's pay. Translated, this means that when an employee reports for work he is entitled to the rate of pay for the entire day, and it is up to the employer to utilize the number of hours for which the employee has contracted himself. If the employee is not assigned to work the full number of hours in the work day, he is still entitled to the full day's pay. Any hours worked beyond the normal number in the work day calls for payment at the overtime rate. As a consequence, since the hours of commute were staggered by the number

The East Bay Terminal in San Francisco is no longer one of the nation's major interurban terminals, but rather is a vital bus terminal serving the Alameda-Contra Costa Transit District's buses (shown here) which are successors to the Key System, Sacramento Northern, and Interurban Electric Railway. The Terminal also acts as San Francisco host to the buses serving Marin and Sonoma Counties—latter day successors to the Northwestern Pacific's passenger service.

of hours in a work day, it meant that two shifts of crewmen were needed to carry one shift of commuters to work and return if payment for overtime were to be avoided.

This problem was not restricted to the interurbans. Commuters are the bane of every transit service in the United States, ranging from city bus and streetcar lines to major railroads. In fact, it has been alleged that commuter service was the downfall of such heavily traveled eastern railroads as the Long Island Railroad, the Reading Railroad, and the New York, New Haven and Hartford as well as contributing to the financial demise of the Penn Central, the Chicago & Northwestern, and the Boston & Maine. It is no secret that the Southern Pacific would dearly love to abandon its commuter service on the San Francisco Peninsula.

Now we must, on the basis of evidence submitted, try to answer our own questions. Were the major railroads guilty of taking a "public be damned" attitude? Were the regulatory bodies failing to take the public interest into consideration when they gave permission for abandonment? Our answer is a qualified negative.

Public ownership of intercity transit lines was not a fully accepted concept in the years 1930 to 1940. San Francisco voters, in fact, had rejected bond issues to purchase the Market Street Railway in 1925, 1938, again in 1938 during a special election, 1942, and 1943. Then too, many people sincerely believed that a government agency had no business interfering in what the interurbans were: a business. If the people chose not to subscribe to the service offered, why should a business be forced to provide it? Therefore, when the ownerships were able to supply figures demonstrating their continually decreasing ridership—and attendant fare box receipts—it could then be shown that a business was failing to meet its obligation toward its investors.

As for the role of the public regulatory bodies, any decisions made had to be placed on record. Since public records are subject to public scrutiny (assuming those who no longer cared enough to ride the interurbans cared to scrutinize public records), a decision could not be based on such evidence as handsome paint jobs, courteous conductors, and the fun and pleasure of riding an electric interurban train. Needless to say, the railways' evidence was, for the record, convincing.

The #40 Line of the Market Street Railway, whether or not it realized it, was living on borrowed time after the M.S.Ry. was purchased by the City of San Francisco. Yet it, also, is having a portion of its route encompassed with the new trackage of BART. Perhaps this is in some measure indicative of a changing attitude toward Bay Area interurban transit.

It has been noted that the northern terminus of the #40 Line was at the intersection of Fifth and Market Streets, San Francisco, and that the #40 Line was the only interurban line ever to run on San Francisco's streets. True, the I.E.R., Key System, and Sacramento Northern did enter and terminate in San Francisco, but their lines never ran on the city's streets and their rails never connected with any other rails within the city. Oddly enough, the Transbay Terminal was a scant five city blocks away from the #40 Line's San Francisco terminus!

Suppose that the necessary government agencies had had the foresight to acquire, under powers of eminent domain, all eight interurban electric railways. This could include an option for the passenger-carrying rights of certain connecting roads such as the Central California Traction and the Tidewater Southern. Had this been done, would the interurbans have been condemned? At this time let us explore the possibilities of what might have been.

Since both the Petaluma & Santa Rosa and the Northwestern Pacific were under Southern Pacific ownership after 1932, the P. & S.R. passenger cars should have been retained and the N.W.P. electrification should have continued north from San Rafael to Petaluma. This would have permitted passengers a continuous journey from Sausalito to Forestville, forty-six miles as the crow flies. Instead, the eighteen miles between Petaluma and San Rafael had to be served by the steam trains.

Another possibility was the annexing of both the Petaluma & Santa Rosa and the San Francisco, Napa & Calistoga by the Sacramento Northern. The S.F.N. & C., in all probability, would have had to be converted from alternating current to direct current. This alignment, coupled with potential connections with the Northwestern Pacific, might have saved the Napa Valley Route and the P. & S.R. as well as formed the nucleus of a viable interurban network linking the entire North Bay Region.

Francis M. "Borax" Smith envisioned his San Francisco, Oakland & San Jose Railway running to exactly those places. While Smith's Key Route did extend as far as Richmond, it never reached San Jose thanks mainly to financial difficulties. However, interurban service from Richmond to San Jose would have provided a valuable link had that service been joined to the Peninsular Railway. It remains questionable why the Southern Pacific failed to electrify its own rails between Oakland and San Jose, providing through trains on all-S.P. rail and beating Borax Smith to the punch.

There is no apparent reason why the Peninsular Railway and the Market Street Railway should not have connected. Approximately twelve miles of track, mostly over level bayshore land, separated the northern tip of the Peninsular from the southern tip of the Market Street Railway's #40 Line.

Had all these lines been brought together under unified management, the nagging question for North Bay riders would persist, "How could trains from the Northwestern Pacific have effected a Bay crossing?" Since Petaluma & Santa Rosa passenger service was ended in 1932, and since the Golden Gate Bridge was not completed until 1937, it would therefore stand to reason that the original specifications and construction of a Golden Gate crossing would have provided for interurban transit over the water. Potentially, interurbans from the North Bay could have used the Municipal Railway's Geary Street "B" Line tracks which were to make their inbound terminus the Transbay Terminal, thus connecting with Key System, I.E.R. and Sacramento Northern trains.

Having placed all eight interurbans which ran in the Bay Area under a single management, and having connected them all, we would then have had a service which would have transported passengers from San Jose to Chico, from San Francisco to Modesto (had this hypothetical railway been able to incorporate the Central California Traction and the Tidewater Southern), from Forestville to San Jose, and from Sausalito to Oakland via Napa, Vallejo, or San Francisco. With such a network in existence, and with public ownership no longer a bogeyman, it seems unlikely that abandonments would ever occur, particularly if a tax resource would be found to subsidize such a network. With taxing power to subsidize unprofitable runs—and today every run would most likely fall into the subsidy category—not to mention public bonds to finance new equipment from time to time, the interurbans would likely have ended the need for ferryboat service but at the same time strengthened their position to such an extent that there would have been no limit to the length of time they could continue to serve the Bay Area.

Nevertheless, if such a system were to be established, it could only be effectual if accompanied by compatible city/county planning. It would do no good, for example, if a high speed interurban deposited a passenger several miles from his home, as he would still need transportation to complete his journey. The sprawl type of suburban communities are, by design, automobile-oriented, while public transit is invariably high population density-oriented. It is worthwhile to note that the Golden Gate Bridge, Highway and Transportation District recognizes this in its routing of Marin County bus lines, and commuter service to such "bedroom" communities as San Marin, Lucas Valley, Terra Linda and Tiburon is tied into trunkline runs. The success of this program is evidenced by the fact that in less than two years after the District assumed the transit responsibilities of Greyhound in Marin and Sonoma Counties, the ridership more than doubled.

A strong case against indiscriminate abandonment of railway trackage was made by John E. Ullman of Hofstra University, Hempstead, New York, in the November 1973 issue of *Trains*, an excellent magazine on railroading which is not noted for its coverage of trolley lines. Ullman advocated placing unneeded railway roadbed aside without tearing it up, so that it could later be revived at minimum cost, thereby eliminating the expense of reacquisition and grading. Ullman's classic example offered was the abandonment of the Bay Area's interurban trackage.

On April 22, 1974, Bill Dorais, coordinator of the Transit Improvement Program for the San Francisco Municipal Railway, was quoted in the San Francisco *Examiner* as saying, "Rail is the proven technology—the most effective mode of public transportation." However, he went on to note the potential outcry of residents to having streets torn up to install new tracks. Yet what has been the public inconvenience from freeway construction? D. R. Neuzil of the Institute of Transportation and Traffic Engineering, University of California, estimates that 15,000 people per year are displaced by highway construction. This does not take into consideration the pollutants emitted into the air from the automobiles themselves.

During the 1930s, California constructed 14,000 miles of paved roads, largely as an anti-Depression public works project. In 1940, the Pasadena Freeway became the state's first freeway, but the major impetus to California highway construction came in 1956 with the enactment of the Interstate Highway System. Financed through taxes on gasoline and automobile-related merchandise as well as through licensing fees, California's highway mileage soared to 3,179 miles by 1972. This is only a fraction of the master plan's 12,500. What would be the cost of this undertaking? Freeway construction runs as high as $8,000,000 or more per mile, not to mention periodical repairs, general maintenance, and police.

With freeway construction came the problem of what to do with the cars when they left the freeways and entered city streets. Parking, the largest single problem, grew to such proportions that by 1969 it was estimated that one-third of the downtown land area of the city of Los Angeles was devoted to parking lots and garages!

In July of 1973, it was announced that the State of California had entered into a joint study with Alan M. Voorhess and Associates, a transportation consulting firm, to re-examine the transit corridor between Sacramento-Stockton and the Bay Area.

Now is the time to raise another question. In view of past, present, and possible future intercity rail transit restoration, what did it cost the public to abandon the original interurbans? A fair question, so let us use BART and the latest attempts to rebuild a rapid transit network in Los Angeles as examples.

The situation in Los Angeles was reported in *Railroad Magazine* in December 1973, as follows:

"Los Angeles, hoping to install rapid transit, has planned a 250-mile system to be operating by the turn of the century. Immediate priority is 140 miles of subway-surface rapid transit and bus routes in eight of the most heavily traveled corridors in the L.A. basin.

"The 140 miles would be developed as 116 miles of fixed guideway lines and 24 miles of bus routes, but it is not clear to us what is meant by 'fixed guideway lines,' whether rapid transit or some untested operation such as Skybus. A final decision may well depend upon how effectively the bus-rubber-cement-gasoline interests lobby against the rail proponents. The 140-mile priority system would be completed in 12 years at an estimated price of $6.6 billion—more than $47 million a mile!—and such jobs usually exceed the original cost estimates. Wow!"

And this is merely to *replace* portions of the Pacific Electric Railway which once was able to boast over 1,100 miles of track!

In the Bay Area, despite grants from the Federal Government and revenues from a special sales tax, the cost for BART has swelled to $1.2 billion for a seventy-five-mile system, or sixteen million dollars per mile. Included is an interesting sum of $1,700,000 to construct a stone and concrete protective blanket over the underwater tube which carries the trains under San Francisco Bay. This blanket is to protect the tube from the ships' anchors. Now the point of the item is that there were already transbay rails on the bridge as late as 1958. To the cost of BART must be added $30,000,000 to remove the interurban rails from the Bay Bridge and convert the roadbed, as well as the Transbay Terminal, to all-motor vehicle use. While the removal of the tracks was a separate project from BART, cost comparisons show that approximately $3,750 per mile was spent to *destroy* what is now costing some sixteen million dollars per mile to *build*.

Nor is that all. Is the aforementioned Sacramento-Stockton and Bay Area corridor study going to recommend restoration of more Sacramento Northern routing, along with Central California Traction? The author predicts so.

A final quote from the Los Angeles *Times*, as reported in *Railroad Magazine* of June 1973:

"Nearly all the studies and surveys conducted into the area's transportations problems since the 1920s have emphasized the need for mass transit, preferably high-speed rapid transit, Those several million dollars worth of plans and proposals underscore what everybody knows from personal observation—that buses cannot move large numbers of passengers over streets and freeways congested with some of the heaviest traffic in the country."

In conclusion, let us say that only after having forfeited the interurbans in the past through neglect, shortsightedness, and almost total lack of city/county planning have we been able to prove their value beyond a doubt, and now future generations will have to bear the cost in no less a manner than as many as five or six generations paying for the folly of a single war.

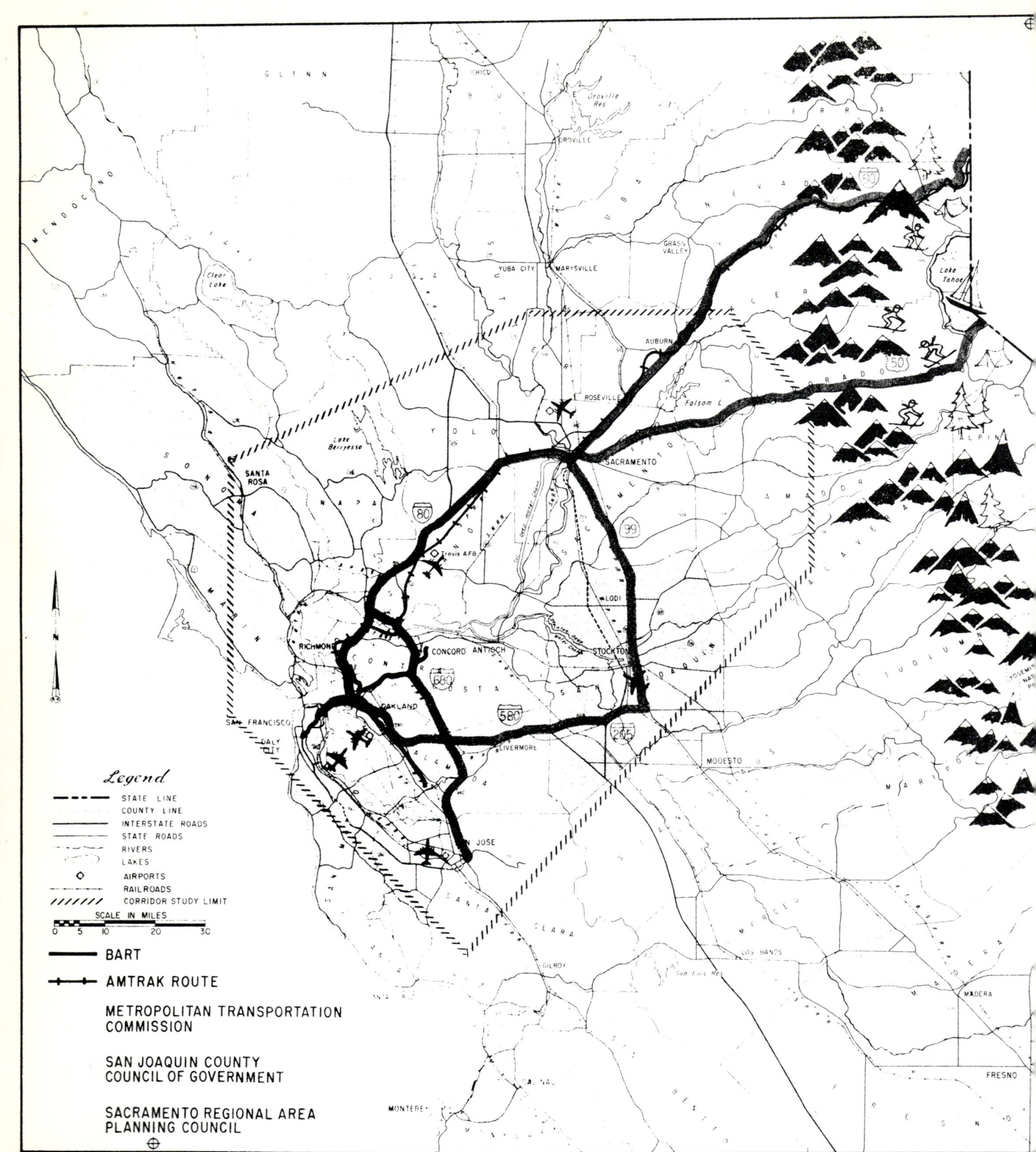

SACRAMENTO-STOCKTON-SAN FRANCISCO BAY AREA CORRIDOR STUDY

Appendix A

Index of Carbuilders

Listed below are the various known carbuilders which participated in the building of interurban cars for the Bay Area. Due to a decline in interurban carbuilding, most of these shops have passed from the scene or have concentrated on the building of other railroad equipment.

AMERICAN CAR COMPANY, St. Louis, Missouri. Purchased by J. G. Brill in 1902.
AMERICAN CAR AND FOUNDRIES, headquarters at New York, New York.
BALDWIN-WESTINGHOUSE, Philadelphia, Pennsylvania.
BARNEY & SMITH, Dayton, Ohio.
BETHLEHEM STEEL COMPANY, Bethlehem, Pennsylvania (built Key System units at plant in Wilmington, Delaware).
J. G. BRILL, Philadelphia, Pennsylvania.
CARTER BROTHERS, San Francisco, Sausalito, and Newark, California.
CENTRAL PACIFIC RAILROAD COMPANY CAR SHOPS, Sacramento, California.
CINCINNATI CAR COMPANY, Cincinnati, Ohio.
DIAMOND MATCH COMPANY, Chico, California.
GENERAL ELECTRIC, Schenectady, New York.
HALL-SCOTT MOTOR CAR COMPANY, Berkeley, California.
HAMMOND CAR COMPANY, San Francisco, California.
HOLMAN CAR COMPANY, San Francisco, California.
JEWETT CAR COMPANY, Jewett, Ohio.
KEY SYSTEM SHOPS, Emeryville, California.
LACLEDE CAR COMPANY, St. Louis, Missouri. Acquired by St. Louis Car Company in 1903. Sometimes spelled LaClede.
MAGUIRE CUMMINGS, Chicago, Illinois.
MAHONEY BROTHERS, San Francisco, California.
MARKET STREET RAILWAY COMPANY SHOPS, San Francisco, California.
McKEEN MOTOR CAR COMPANY, Omaha, Nebraska.
MORAN SHIPBUILDING COMPANY, Seattle, Washington.
NILES CAR COMPANY, Niles, Ohio.
NORTH SHORE RAILROAD COMPANY SHOPS, Sausalito, California.
NORTHERN ELECTRIC RAILWAY COMPANY SHOPS, Chico, California.
OAKLAND, ANTIOCH & EASTERN RAILWAY COMPANY SHOPS, Oakland, California.
OCEAN SHORE RAILROAD COMPANY SHOPS, San Francisco, California.
PENINSULAR RAILWAY COMPANY SHOPS, San Jose, California.
PENNSYLVANIA RAILROAD COMPANY SHOPS (division unknown).
PETALUMA & SANTA ROSA RAILWAY COMPANY SHOPS, Petaluma, California.
PULLMAN COMPANY OF CHICAGO, Chicago, Illinois.
SACRAMENTO ELECTRIC, GAS & RAILWAY COMPANY SHOPS, Sacramento, California.
ST. LOUIS CAR COMPANY, St. Louis, Missouri.
SAN FRANCISCO, NAPA & CALISTOGA RAILROAD COMPANY SHOPS, Napa, California.
WASON MANUFACTURING COMPANY, Springfield, Massachusetts.
WESTINGHOUSE ELECTRIC CORPORATION, Pittsburgh, Pennsylvania.

MARKET STREET RAILWAY CO.
#40 LINE INTERURBAN

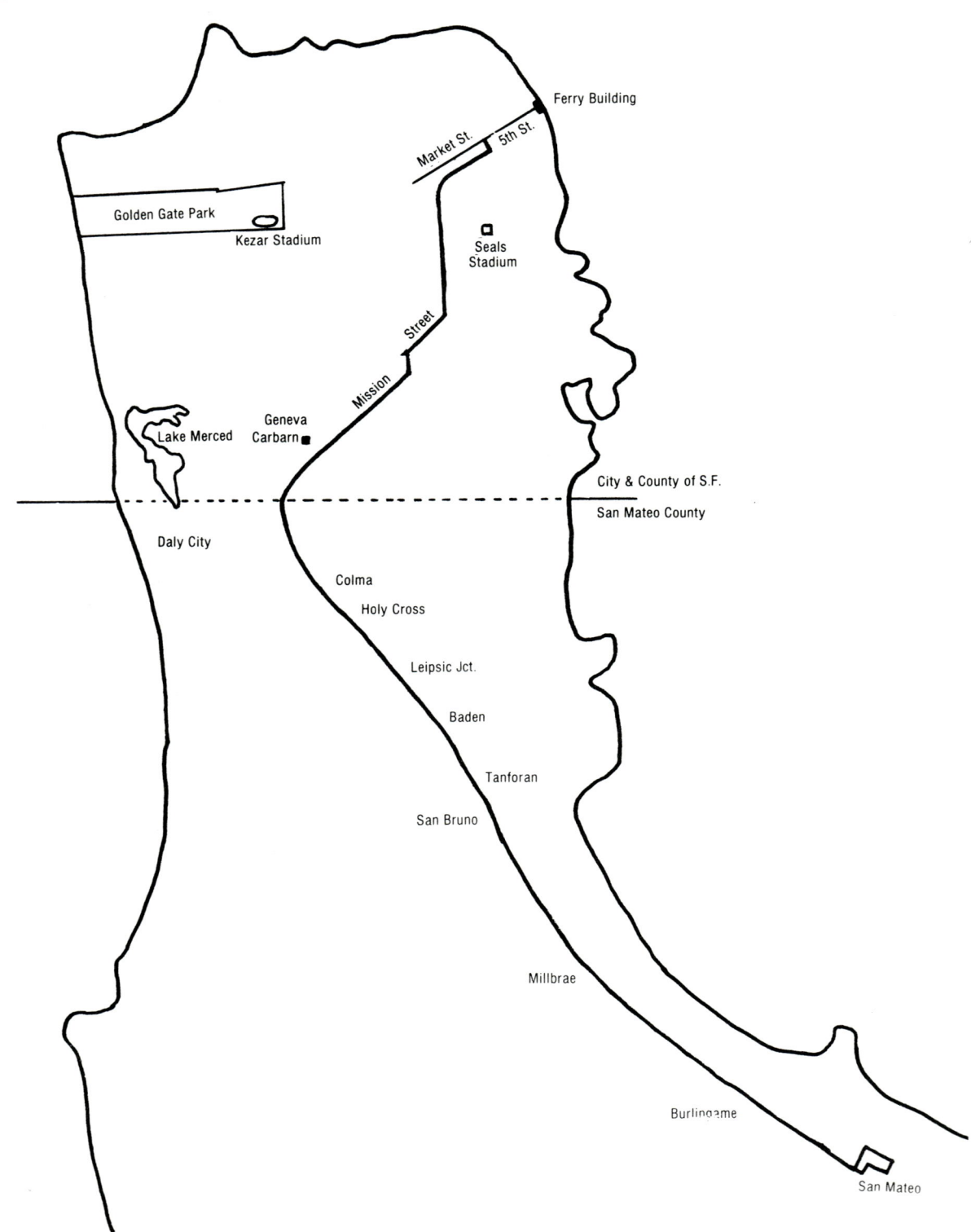

Appendix B

Index of Ferryboat Builders

BETHLEHEM STEEL COMPANY, UNION YARD, San Francisco, California (formerly the Union Iron Works).
CENTRAL PACIFIC RAILROAD, Oakland, California.
WILLIAM COLLYER, San Francisco, California.
WILLIAM CRAMP & SONS, Philadelphia, Pennsylvania.
JOHN W. DICKIE, Alameda, California.
GENERAL ENGINEERING & DRYDOCK COMPANY, Alameda, California.
MARUCCI, San Francisco, Stockton, California.
MARYLAND STEEL COMPANY.
MOORE & SCOTT IRON WORKS, Oakland, California.
MOORE DRYDOCK COMPANY, Oakland, California.
OAKLAND, ANTIOCH & EASTERN RAILWAY, Pittsburg, California.
PATRICK TIERNAN, San Francisco, California.
JAMES ROBERTSON, Alameda, Benicia, California.
SAN FRANCISCO & NORTH PACIFIC RAILWAY, Tiburon, California.
E. SORENSON, Ballard, Washington.
SOUTHERN PACIFIC RAILROAD, Oakland, California.
MATTHEW TURNER, Benicia, California.
UNION IRON WORKS, San Francisco, California (later sold to Bethlehem Steel).
G. R. WHIDDEN & COMPANY, New Whatcomb, Washington.

In addition, the *Gold II* was built at Fort Bragg, California, for the California Transportation Company, but her builder is unknown. The *Arrow* was built at Puget Sound, builder unknown.

Appendix C

Population Growth in Bay Area

County	Years of Census							
	1900	1910	1920	1930	1940	1950	1960	1970
Alameda	130,197	246,131	344,177	474,883	513,011	740,315	908,209	1,064,049
Contra Costa	18,046	31,674	53,889	78,608	100,450	298,984	409,030	553,415
Marin	15,702	25,114	27,324	41,648	52,907	85,619	146,820	204,046
Napa	16,451	19,800	20,678	22,897	28,503	46,603	65,890	76,819
San Francisco*	342,782	416,912	506,676	634,394	634,536	775,357	740,316	706,546
San Mateo	12,094	26,585	36,781	77,405	111,782	235,659	444,387	551,027
Santa Clara	60,216	83,539	100,676	145,118	174,949	290,547	642,315	1,057,032
Solano	24,143	27,559	40,602	40,834	49,118	104,833	134,597	165,949
Sonoma	38,480	48,394	52,090	62,222	69,052	103,405	147,375	199,360

*San Francisco is both a city and a county.

PETALUMA AND SANTA ROSA ELECTRIC RAILROAD

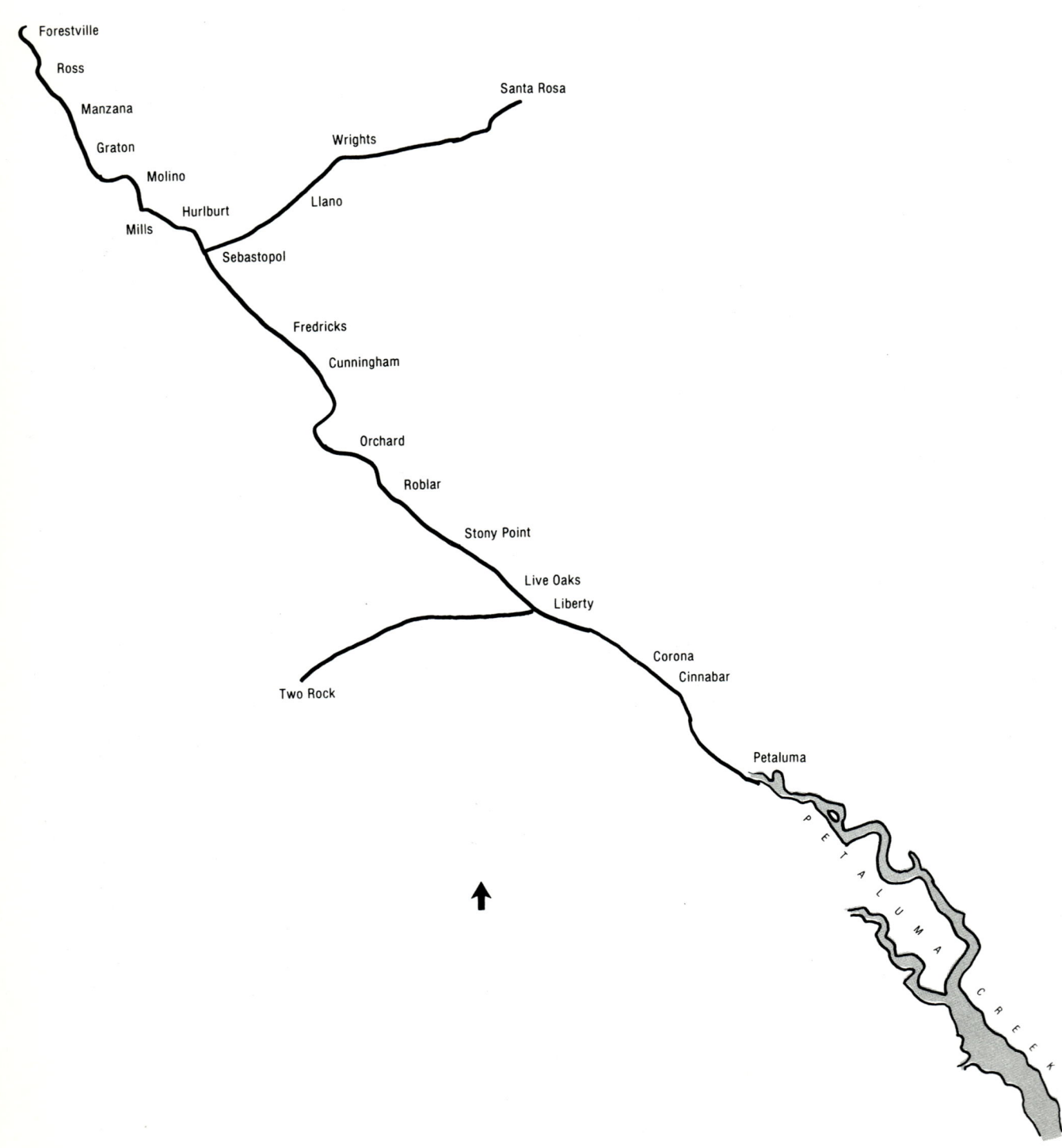

Appendix D

Motor Vehicle Growth in Bay Area

County	Years of Census							
	1914-15	1920	1930	1940	1950	1960	1970	
Alameda	8,449	36,139	139,885	182,383	265,183	375,379	511,764	Cars
		2,111	5,811	11,188	25,685	44,557	81,446	Trucks
Contra Costa	930	5,815	24,329	37,468	99,992	170,450	281,929	Cars
		371	1,066	2,520	9,075	18,914	43,062	Trucks
Marin	686	2,638	10,836	16,753	30,747	62,401	108,072	Cars
		164	512	1,226	3,171	6,493	12,273	Trucks
Napa	687	2,766	7,604	10,183	16,546	25,246	39,285	Cars
		166	484	1,158	2,583	4,621	8,997	Trucks
San Francisco*	12,081	47,969	146,182	176,290	237,574	264,723	288,056	Cars
		4,894	9,706	16,108	30,297	44,918	48,866	Trucks
San Mateo	1,258	4,138	24,427	41,799	90,700	195,780	308,460	Cars
		335	1,233	2,412	7,137	20,367	39,243	Trucks
Santa Clara	3,941	16,605	53,948	70,248	115,532	277,960	542,650	Cars
		1,013	2,751	6,183	15,063	36,077	79,020	Trucks
Solano	848	5,059	13,334	18,333	36,657	51,386	81,427	Cars
		301	617	1,415	3,908	7,142	13,937	Trucks
Sonoma	1,913	9,418	25,376	28,558	43,259	64,733	104,213	Cars
		659	1,709	3,555	8,323	15,661	27,530	Trucks

These figures reflect the growth of automobile and truck registrations in census years during the life of the interurbans with the exception of the years 1914-1915, the earliest county-by-county statistics available.

The figures for truck registration include all trucks, regardless of type.

Just as the figures on automobile registrations are not broken down into use categories, neither are those for trucks; it remains impossible to determine exactly how many automobile or truck trips actually caused the interurban railways to lose revenue.

Source: State of California Department of Motor Vehicles

*San Francisco is a city and a county.

SAN FRANCISCO, NAPA & CALISTOGA RAILWAY

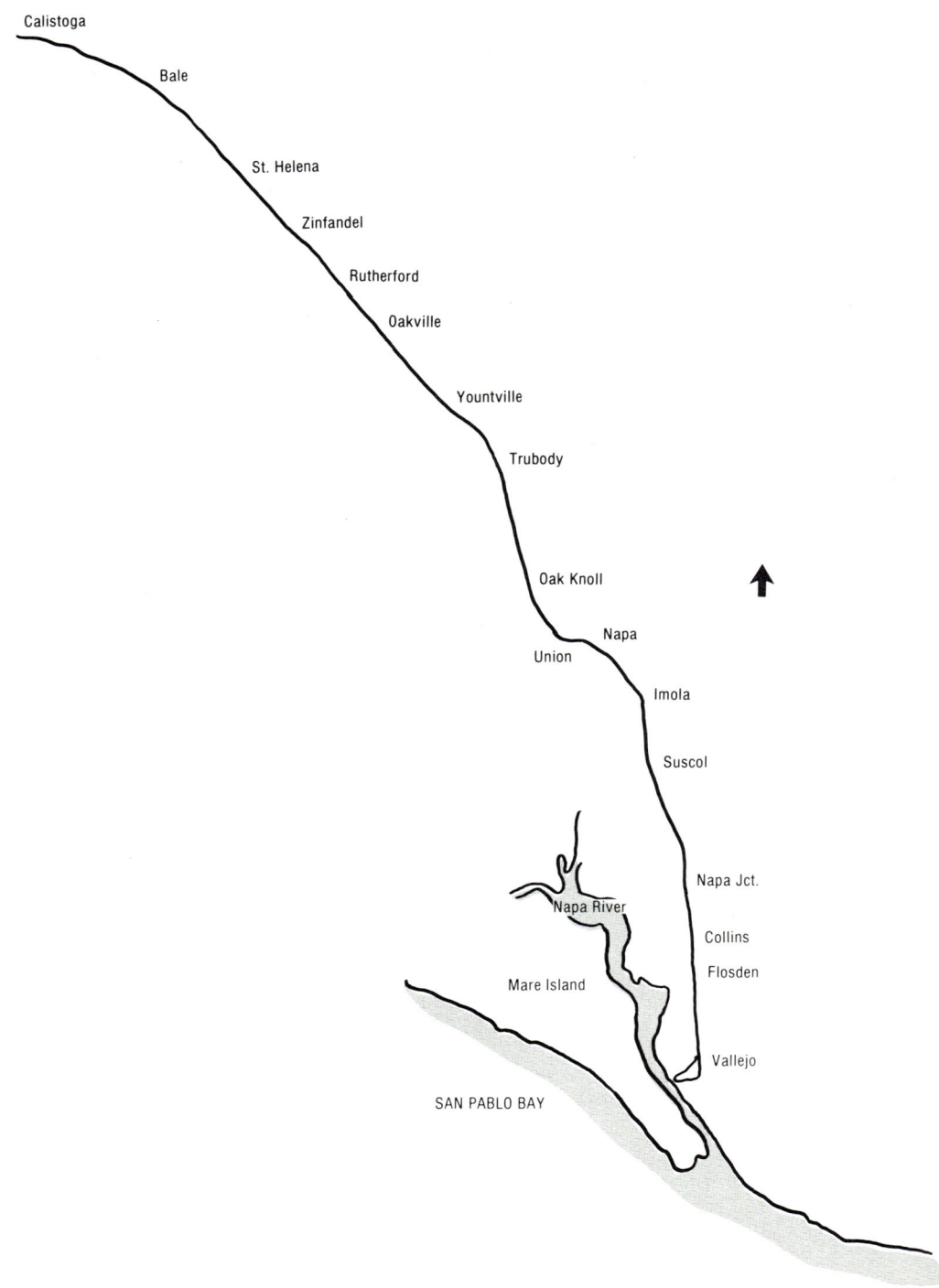

Bibliography

Aitken, Harry C., Jr., and Swett, Ira L. *The Napa Valley Route.* Glendale: Interurbans, 1975.

Arnold, Bion J. *Report on the Improvement and Development of the Transportation Facilities of San Francisco.* San Francisco: 1913.

Beebe, Lucius. *The Central Pacific & The Southern Pacific Railroads.* Berkeley: Howell-North, 1963.

Carper, Robert S. *Focus: The Railroad in Transition 1947-1967.* Cranbury, New Jersey: A. S. Barnes and Co., 1968.

Dickenson, A. Bray. *Narrow Gauge to the Redwoods.* Los Angeles: Trans-Anglo Books, 1967.

Dunscomb, Guy L. *A Century of Southern Pacific Steam Locomotives.* Modesto, Calif.: 1963

Dunscomb, Guy L., and Stindt, Fred A. *The Northwestern Pacific Railroad.* Modesto, Calif.: 1964.

Harlan, George H. *San Francisco Bay Ferryboats.* Berkeley: Howell-North, 1967.

Harlan, George H. and Fisher, Clement, Jr. *Of Walking Beams and Paddle Wheels.* San Francisco: Bay Books, 1951.

Hilton, George W. *The Cable Car in America.* Berkeley: Howell-North, 1971.

Hilton, George W., and Due, John F. *The Electric Interurban Railways in America.* Stanford: Stanford University Press, 1960.

Hitt, Rodney. *Electric Railway Dictionary (1911).* New York: McGraw, 1911. Reprint. Novato, Calif.: Newton K. Gregg/Publisher, 1972.

John Stephenson Company. *Electric Railway Cars & Trucks.* Elizabeth, New Jersey:1905. Reprint. Felton, Calif.: Glenwood Publishers, 1972.

Kneiss, Gilbert H. *Redwood Railways.* Berkeley: Howell-North, 1956.

MacMullen, Jerry. *Paddle Wheel Days in California.* Stanford: Stanford University Press, 1944.

McGregor, Bruce A. *South Pacific Coast.* Berkeley: Howell-North, 1968.

Middleton, William D. *The Interurban Era.* Milwaukee: Kalmbach, 1968.

Middleton, William D. *When the Steam Railroads Electrified.* Milwaukee: Kalmbach, 1975.

Mowbray, A. Q. *Road to Ruin.* Philadelphia and New York: J. B. Lippincott, 1969.

Nicholas, Frederic, ed. *McGraw Electric Railway Manual 1914.* New York: McGraw Publishing Co. 1914.

Rowsome, Frank. *Trolley Car Treasury.* New York: McGraw-Hill, 1956.

Smallwood, Charles A. *The White Front Cars of San Francisco.* South Gate, Calif.: Interurbans, 1971.

Swett, Ira, ed. *Cars of Sacramento Northern.* South Gate, Calif.: Interurbans, 1972.

Swett, Ira, ed. *Market Street Railway Revisited, the Best of "The Inside Track."* South Gate, Calif.: Interurbans, 1972.

Swett, Ira, ed. *Sacramento Northern.* Los Angeles: Interurbans, 1962.

Swett, Ira, ed. *Sacramento Northern.* Los Angeles: Interurbans, 1962.

Swett, Ira, ed. *Sacramento Northern Album.* Cerritos, Calif.: Interurbans, 1973.

Wurm, T. G., and Graves, A. C. *The Crookedest Railroad in the World.* Berkeley: Howell-North, 1954.

Booklets

Arnold, Ian. *Locomotive, Trolley, and Rail Car Builders—An All-Time Directory.* Los Angeles: Trans-Anglo Books, 1965.

Best, G. M. *Traveltown.* San Mateo: The Western Railroader, 1956.

Borden, Stanley T. *Petaluma & Santa Rosa Electric R.R.* San Mateo: The Western Railroader, 1960.

Brandt, Rudolph. *Ocean Shore.* San Mateo: The Western Railroader, 1965.

California General Information Almanac, 1966 ed. Lakewood, Calif.: California Almanac Company, 1965.

Early Day Trolleys of the East Bay. San Mateo: The Western Railroader.

The 40 Line. San Mateo: The Western Railroader.

IER "The Big Red Cars." San Mateo: The Western Railroader.

Illustrated History of Rail Transit in the East Bay, 1865-1960. Oakland: Alameda-Contra Costa Transit District, 1960.

Interurban Lines, Northwestern Pacific. San Mateo: The Western Railroader.

Jenkins, Arthur C., ed. *Report on Prospective Participation in a Public Transit Bus System by the Golden Gate Bridge and Highway District.* Berkeley: 1968.

Key System Interurban Lines. San Mateo: The Western Railroader.

Market Street Railway 1934-1944. San Mateo: The Western Railroader.

Napa Valley Route. San Mateo: The Western Railroader, 1953.

Niles Car and Manufacturing Co. 1910. Chicago: Electric Railway Historical Society, 1958.

1971 California County Fact Book. Sacramento: County Supervisors Association of California, 1971.

Orange Empire Trolley Museum. Perris, Calif.: Museum guidebook.

Peninsular Railway. San Mateo: The Western Railroader, 1969.

Reconstruction of the San Francisco-Oakland Bay Bridge. Berkeley: Division of San Francisco Bay Toll Crossings, 1957.

Renovich, Steve. *Fresno Traction and Fresno Interurban.* San Mateo: The Western Railroader.

Sacramento Northern's 50th Anniversary. San Mateo: The Western Railroader, 1955.

Sacramento-Stockton-San Francisco Bay Area Corridor Study. A proposal for a corridor study jointly sponsored by Business and Transportation Agency, State of California; Senate, State of California; United States Department of Transportation; Metropolitan Transportation Commission; Sacramento Regional Area Planning Commission; San Joaquin Council of Government, 1973.

San Francisco Municipal Railway 1912-1944. San Mateo: The Western Railroader.

San Jose-Los Gatos Interurban Railway. San Mateo: The Western Railroader.

Sappers, Vernon J. *From Shore to Shore, The Key Route.* Oakland: Peralta Associates, 1948.

Selections from 1920 Electric Railway Journal. Indianapolis: Traction Heritage, 1971.

Sievers, Wald. *Steam Dummies of San Francisco.* San Mateo: The Western Railroader.

Sievers, Wald, and Stindt, Fred A. *N.W.P. Narrow Gauge.* San Mateo: The Western Railroader.

Stindt, Fred A. *Peninsula Service.* San Mateo: The Western Railroader, 1957.

Street Railways of Sacramento and Stockton. San Mateo: The Western Railroader.

Swett, Ira, ed. *Official Car Records, Pacific Electric Railway Co.* Los Angeles: Interurbans, 1964.

Tenney, Will, and Reynolds, Richard. *California Railway Museum.* Rio Vista Junction, Calif.: Bay Area Electric Railroad Association.

Tidewater Southern. San Mateo: The Western Railroader, 1950.

Periodicals

American Heritage. April 1966.

Bulletin, The. Vol. 37, no. 6. National Railway Historical Society, 1972.

Commonwealth, The. Commonwealth Club of California, November 17, 1931.

Pacific News. February 1965; April 1972; May 1973; March 1974.

Railroad Magazine. January 1941; April 1945; July 1948; December 1953; August 1955; May 1973; June 1973; December 1973.

San Francisco *Chronicle.* February 2, 1973.

San Francisco *Examiner.* April 20, 1973, April 22, 1974.

Trains. July 1953; August 1953; July 1955; November 1973.

Western Pacific Mileposts. Western Pacific Railroad, Fall 1974.

Western Railroader, The. November 1957; January 1958; December 1971; April 1972; May 1974.

Miscellaneous

Annual reports of construction of the San Francisco-Oakland Bay Bridge by the California State Toll Bridge Authority, July 1, 1934; July 1, 1935; July 1, 1936; July 1, 1937; July 1, 1938; July 1, 1939.

Company records of rolling stock of the Key System, courtesy of Vernon J. Sappers.

Company records of rolling stock and marine equipment of the Northwestern Pacific Railroad, courtesy of Fred P. Codoni.

Company records of the San Francisco & San Mateo Electric Railroad Company and the Ferries & Cliff House Railroad, courtesy of Charles A. Smallwood.

Company records of the San Francisco & San Mateo Electric Railroad Company and the Ferries & Cliff House Railroad, courtesy of Charles A. Smallwood.

Opinions of the Railroad Commission of California. Decision No. 8482. California State Printing Office: 1920.

Index

Aberdeen, Maryland, Proving Grounds 21
Agler, James 71-72
Alabama 117,123,130
Alameda II 147,151
Alameda 8-10,13,21,117,165
Alameda Belt Line 165
Alameda-Contra Costa Transit District 37,180
Alameda County 7-8,11,26-27,37,73,177
Alameda Mole 9-10,12-13,150-151
Alameda, Oakland & Piedmont Electric Railway 25
Albany 14,16,48
Alden, S. F. 67
"Alligator, The" 129
Alten 95
Alto 71
Alum Rock Park 84-85
Amador 151
Amador Central Railroad 137
American City Lines 32-33
Amtrak 167,177
Anderson, Frank B. 59
Antioch 119
Antler 149
Arcade Trestle 119
Argentina 163
Army Transport Service 163
Arnstein, Walter 117
Arrow 151
Asbury Park 151,153
Associated Press 177
Atcheson, Topeka & Santa Fe Railway 8,27, 67,71-72,103-104,117,124,162,165-168
Atlanta, Georgia xiv
Auburn 115,165
Auto Stages 100,136,165

Babcock, A. H. 67
Baden 51
Bakersfield 170
Baltimore, Maryland xiv,32
"Baltimore Syndicate" 49
Bamberger Electric 21,23
Bay & Coast Railroad Company 9
Bay Area Electric Railroad Association 32,47, 48,123-124,128,131-132,143,173
Bay Area Rapid Transit District (BART) 17-19,33,37,56,118,120,124,176,178-179,183
Bay City 151
Bay Counties Power Company 67
Bay Counties Transmission Company 71
Bay Point 119,128
Bayshore Freeway 178
Benicia 7
Berkeley 6,8,10,12-16,20,26-30,48,50,145-146
Berkeley 13,117,147,151,163
Bidwell 117,123,128,131
Bidwell, General John 131
"Big Subs" 53,55-57,59,61,65
Birney, Charles O. 132
Birney Safety Car 91,116,123,132,169
"Blossom Line, The" 85
Blossom Valley Trip 85

Bonnie Brae Trestle 85
Boston & Maine Railroad 181
Boston Elevated Railway Company 67
Bowen, Alfred 96-97
Boyd, Alan 177
Brandon, Vermont 2
Braswell, E. L. 67
Bremerton, Washington, Navy Yard 22
Bridget 119,149,153,156
British Columbia (Canada) 173
Brooks, F. E. 117
Brown, Clyde E. 137
Brown Roller Pantograph 128
Brush, Frank A. 95,99
Buenos Aires (Argentina) 32
Burlingame 54,56,60
Burlingame Railway 56,165
Burton 121
Butterfield, Walter 124
Butters, Henry A. 113
Byllesby Engineering and Management Corp. 59-60

Cable cars xiv,1-4,51,54,62-63,146,167,178
Calhoun, Patrick 55
California & Nevada Railroad 25
California Gas & Electric Corporation 101
California Midland 115
California Northwestern Railway 67,71,82, 95-99,103
California Railway and Power Company 51
California Railway Company 25,48
California Railway Museum 21,26,47-48,63, 66,87,89,107,123,128,131-132,168,173-174
California Street Cable Railroad Company 3, 8,62-63,167
California Transportation Company 148,151, 153,155
California Wine Association 166,168
Calistoga xiii,133,137,139,142,170
Calistoga 150,153
Calistoga Flyer 134-135
Cambria Steel Company 8
Camp Lejune, North Carolina 18,22
Camp Meeker 170
Campbell 84,87
Canyon 121
Capetown (South Africa) 113
Capital City 148,153,155
Carew (conductor) 48
Carquinez Bridge 137
Castro Point 149
Cattwell, W. A. 95
Cazadero 152-153
Central Avenue Street Railway Company 25
Central California Traction Company 6,37, 57,117-119,166,169-170,174,182-183
Central Pacific Railroad xiii,2,3,6-10,82,146-147,167,170
Central Street Railway 95
Charing Cross Station, London (England) 145
Charles van Damme 149,153
Cherry 95

Chetzemoka 157
Chicago, Illinois 1,3,32,55,61,178
Chicago & Northwestern Railway 181
Chico xiv,55,113-114,119,121-123,127,130-131,169,182
Chico Electric Railway 113,132
Chipps Island xiv,119,149
Christensen, Chris 99
Chronicle, San Francisco 178
Chrysopolis 159
City of Berkeley 27,46,48
City of Richmond 149,153
City of Sacramento 151,153
City of San Francisco 167
City of San Rafael 149,153
Civil War xii,7
Clara 118
Claremont 153,157
Clean Air Act of 1970 179
Clear Lake 136
Clement, Alpheus W. 113
Coast Daylight 169
Coast Guard, United States 124
Colgate, R. R. 67
College Park 121
Colma 52,62
Colusa 116,127,166
Comet 123
Commonwealth Club of California 58
Concord 119,124
Congress Springs 84-85
Consolidated Piedmont Cable Company 25
Contra Costa County 37,117-118,122,149,178
Coos Bay 149
Corbett, Burke 95
Cotati 103
Creed 119-120
"Creek Route" 9
Crocker, Charles xiii,7
Crocker, William H. 59
Crockett 170
Crowley, John J., Sr. 52-53
Cunningham 95
Cupertino 83-85,87
Cypress Lawn 65

Daft, Leo xiii,2
Daly City 39,53,57,62,65,176
Danville 120
Davenport, Thomas xiii,2
Department of Transportation, United States 177
deSalba, Eugene 67
Diamond Match Company 113,129-131
District Court of Appeal for the District of Columbia, United States 179
Division of Highways, State of California, 149
Dixon 169
Dorais, Bill 182
Dowd, Charles 124
Dozier 169
Dunsmuir 143

195

Eagle Nest (Rio Nido) 170
East Bay Motor Coach Lines 27,168
East Bay Street Railway, Ltd. 26,168
East Bay Terminal (see Transbay Terminal)
East Oakland Street Railroad Company 25
East Shore & Suburban Railway 50,62,168
East Shore Freeway 178
East-West Shrine Game 146
Eastport 118,121
Edinburgh-Glasgow (Scotland) Railway 2
Edison, Thomas A. xiii,2,67
Edith 89
Edward T. Jeffrey 147
Edwards, David S. 113
Eel River & Eureka 67
El Capitan 155
El Dorado 167
Electra 68,73,82,174
Electric Improvement Company 83
Electric Railway Historical Society 137
Electric Railway Journal 17
Ellen 149,155
El Paso 150,155
Elwha 157
Emeryville 46,48,168
Encinal 155
Enetai 162
Erie Railroad 55
Eureka 64,67,72,103
Eureka 145,147,154-155,163
Eureka & Klamath River 67
Ewing Field 146
Examiner, San Francisco 182

Fair, James 9,13
Fairchild, Superintendent of P. & S.R. 98
Fairfax xiii
Fairfield 120
Farmer, Moses xiii,2
Federal Railroad Administration 177
Fernwood 155,157
Ferries & Cliff House Railroad 8,134,141
Ferrocaril Nacional General Urquiza 31
Ferry Building (San Francisco) xiii,8,31,38,52,
  123,145-148
"Ferryboat Series" 146
Fire and Earthquake (San Francisco) of 1906
  54,68,73,82,101,132,165
Firestone Tire & Rubber Company 33
Fisher, B. H. 67
Fleishaker, Herbert W. 59
Florence 89
Flosden 134-135,140,143
Forestville xiii,95,99-101,103-104,156,181-182
Fort Bragg 148
Fort Sutter 148,153,155
49ers xii
Foster, A. W. 71,95-97,99
Fox, Fontaine 85
Francis Bridge 136
"Freeway Revolt" 179
Fremont 179
Fresno 170
Fresno 150,155
Fresno Traction Company 89
Fulton 170

Garden City 155
Gavin 114
Geary Street, Park & Ocean Railroad Company 3,8,62,166
General American Aerocoach 33
General Frisbie 156
General Electric Corporation 12,62,133
General Motors Corp. 33
General Railway Signal Company 15

Geneva (Switzerland) 113
Germania 83,89
Germania Trust Company 83
Giralda Tower, Seville (Spain) 145
Goat (Yerba Buena) Island 25
Gold I 95,101,148,156,158,161
Gold II 148,156,158
Gold Rush xii
Golden Age 156
Golden Bear 156
Golden Coast 156
Golden Dawn 157,161
Golden Eagle 149
Golden Era 155,157
Golden Gate 157
Golden Gate Bridge 74,137,178,182
Golden Gate Bridge, Highway and Transportation District 74,182
Golden Gate Ferry 147-148,150,152-153,163
Golden Poppy 157
Golden Shore 157
Golden State 157
Golden Way 153,157
Golden West 157
Gould, George 101,113
Governor, The 167
Granger 89
Granger, W. S. 83
Graton 95,99,101
Green Valley (Graton) 99,130
Greyhound Bus Lines 30,74,132
Griffin, O. E. 67
Griffith Park, Los Angeles 22,73,173
Grow, C. A. 67
Guarde Republicaine de France 5
Guance, Bob 10
Guerin, John Francis 134
Guerneville 100,170
Hale, O. A. 83
Hamilton City 116
Hammond, John Hays 113
Hannah, Ray 108
Harriman, Edward Henry 11,71
Harry E. Speas 156,163
Hartzell, H. F. 133
Hartzell, J. W. 133
Havens 118,121
Hayward 9,25,168
Hayward 152,157
Healdsburg 101
Heintz, George 67
Heller, E. S. 59
Hempstead, New York 182
Hewitt, R. E. 10
Heyman 116
Highland Park & Fruit Vale Railroad Company 25
Hill, James J. 101,177
Hill of Howth (Ireland) 173
Hilmer 170
Hofstra University 182
Holy Cross Cemetery 52,53,60,65
Hopkins, Mark xiii,7
Horsecars xiv,1-3,51,95
Hotaling, R. M. 67
Humboldt Transit Company 64
Hungerford, Edward 17
Hunt, Judge 99
Huntington & Broadtop Railroad 144
Huntington, Collis P. xiii,7-8,11,25
Huntington, Henry E. 101,130
Hyde Street Pier (see San Francisco Maritime Museum)

Illahee 158
Illinois Central Gulf Railroad 177

Imola xiii
Interstate Commerce Commission, United
  States 30,72,116
Interstate Highway System 183
Interborough Rapid Transit Company 47,174
Interurban Electric Railway 7-23,28,30-31,
  35-38,48,73,78-79,120,123,174,176-177,180-182
Institute of Transportation and Traffic
  Engineering 182-183

James M. Donahue 154,158
Joffre, Marshal Joseph 33
Johnson, Hiram 55,167
Johnstown, Pennsylvania 8
Journal, Marin County 69,71
Journal of Electricity, Power and Gas 52-53

Kalakala 33,159
Kansas City, Missouri 1
Kansas City-Keys Valley Railroad 109
Kehloken 157
Kentfield 78
Key Pier 10,26-35,43,121,129,151-152
Key Route 9,11,25,27,50,118,120-122,135,
  145-147,151-152,167,182
"Key Route Corned Beef Hash" 146
Key System xiii-xiv,4,8,12-13,15,17-19,23-48,
  50,84,87,116,118,121,123,127-128,147,149,
  151-153,155,157,159,161-163,168,173-177,
  179-182
Key System, Ltd. 26-27,168
Key System Transit Company 27
Key Terminal Railway, Ltd. 26-27,168
Kezar Stadium 146
Kidder, Ken 14
"Kitten Cars" 77
Klahanie 156
Klamath 150,158,164
Klickitat 162
Kneiss, Gilbert H. 71,99
Korean Conflict (Korean War) 59

Lafayette 121
La Follette, Robert 167
Lake County 133,142
Lake Temescal 115,121-122
Lake Tahoe 150,158
Leddy 95
Legislator, The 167
Lehigh Valley Transit Company 29,47
Liberty 95,103-104
Lisbon 119
Lisbon (Portugal) 113
Lisbon Trestle 119,123
Loessel, Adolph 113
London (England) 145
Long Beach 73,82
Long Island Railroad 181
Los Altos 87
Los Angeles xiv,1,4,11,18,25,32,73,82,87,173,
  178,183
Los Angeles Railway 173
Los Angeles Recreation and Parks Department 173
Los Gatos 83-84,92
Los Gatos 89
Los Gatos Interurban Railway 83-84,89
Lucas Valley 182

Madera County 133
"Magic Carpet Car" 61,66
Maguire, Stephen D. 33
Malahat 158
Mallard xiv,119,149
Maltry, A. W. 117

Manor 72,80
Mare Island 135,137
Mare Island Naval Shipyard 135,137
Marin 158
Marin County 9,67,73-74,78,80,95,99,145,149, 163,166,170,178,180,182
Marine Band 5
Maritime Commission, United States 18,28, 47,48,161
Market Street Cable Railway 3,4,8
Market Street Railway (horsecar) 2
Market Street Railway (absorbed into United Railroads) 51,63
Market Street Railway (incorporated 1920) 33,38-39,53,57,59-63,102,145,166,176-177,182
Martin, Bert 122
Martin, John 67,71,115,165
Martinez-Benicia Bridge 167
Martinez-Benicia Ferry 162
Marysville 115,123-124,165-166,169
Marysville & Colusa Railroad 127,166
Mason, W. W., Jr. 67
Mayfield 85
McKee, John D. 59
McNear, John A. 95-96
Meinert 114
Melrose 18,150,158
Melrose Station 14
Mendocino 150,152,158
Mercantile Trust Co. of San Francisco 68
Merriam, Governor Frank F. 35
Meteor 123
Metropolitan Coach Lines (Los Angeles) 73,82
Metropolitan Transit Authority 174
Mexico City (Mexico) 113
Millbrae 53,60,62
Mill Valley xiii,69,74,80,166
Minturn, Charles 148
Minerva 1
Mitchell, Harry A. 114,117
Modesto 170,182
Modesto & Empire Traction Company 168
Monte Rio 170
Monte Vista 84
Monticello 158
Monticello Steamship Company xiii,135,138, 148,150-151,153-154,156
Moraga 121
Moraga 114,117,123,131
Mt. Olivet Cemetery Association 64
Mt. St. Helena 136
Mt. Tamalpais 74,78,166
Mt. Tamalpais & Muir Woods Railway xiii, 73-74,166
Municipal Railway of San Francisco 33,38,51, 54,60-66,109,123,133,166-168,173,182
Mutual Engineering 144

Naglee Park Line 91
Napa 101,133-134,136-138,182
Napa 139
Napa County 133,135
Napa Valley xiii,133,136-138,145,148,170
Napa Valley 154,158
Napa Valley Bus Company 136
Napa Valley Railroad (steam) 170
Napa Valley Route xiii-xiv,133-144,148,170-171,174,177,181
Napthaly, J. 117
Napthaly, Sam 117,120
Napthaly, Sara 120
National City Lines 32-33,37,177
National Railroad Passenger Corporation (see Amtrak)
Navy, United States 137,162,166,171
"Navy Yard Freight" 137
Neuzil, D. R. 182

Nevada City 115,165
Nevada Heritage Foundation 32
Newark 9
Newark 149,158,161
Newburgh, Art 96
New Orleans 150,159
New York City, N.Y. 1,29,47,48
New York Central 175
New York, New Haven & Hartford 181
Niles 7
Nimitz Freeway 167,178
Nisqually 158
North Island 157
North Pacific Coast Railroad 67,71,86,148
North Pacific Railroad 170
North Shore Line (Chicago, Ill.) 87
North Shore Railroad 67,71-73,75,79,82,103, 115,165,174
Northbrae Tunnel 8,28,46
Northern Electric Railway 55-56,113-117,119-120,125,127,129,131-132,148,153,155,165-166, 169,171
Northern Pacific Railway 101
Northwestern Pacific Railroad xiii,7,9,11-13, 67-82,85,101,103-104,108,111,145,147,149-153,155,158-159,162-163,166,170-171,174,176-177,180-182
Norton, "Belly" 10

Oakland xiv,1,7-8,12-15,22,25-30,47-48,50,83, 85,87,113,116-121,123-125,128,132,150,153, 159,163,165,167-169,179,182
Oakland II 159
Oakland & Antioch Railway 117-118,120
Oakland & Berkeley Rapid Transit Company 25
Oakland & San Jose Railway 26
Oakland, Antioch & Eastern Railway 114,116-121,125,129-132,149,169
Oakland Mole 9-10,12,13,16,30,147,167-170
Oakland Oaks (baseball) 146
Oakland Railroad Company 25
Oakland, San Leandro & Haywards 25
Oakland Terminal Railroad 27,168,174
Oakland Terminal Railway 27,132,167
Oakland Traction Company 48,168
Oakland Transit Consolidated 25
O'Brien, Bill 50
Ocean Shore Railroad 107,109,111,130,166, 168
Ogden, Utah 23
"Old Maude" 113,131-132
Omaha, Nebraska 1
Omnibus Railroad and Cable Company 8
Orange County 173
Orange Empire Railroad Museum 21,23,32, 80,173-174
Orange Empire Trolley Museum (see Orange Empire Railroad Museum)
Orchard 95
Oregon & Eureka 67
Oregon City, Oregon 2
Oregon Electric Historical Society 32
Oregon Power & Railroad Company 2
Oregonian, The 167
Orinda 25
Oroville 113
Oroville Junction 116
Overland Limited, The 167
Oxford 119

Pacific Coast League (baseball) 146
Pacific Electric Railway 4,11,13,18,73,78-79, 82,84,87-90,93,130-132,138-141,174,178,183
Pacific Fruit Express 105
Pacific Gas & Electric Company 60,115,130

Pacific Limited 167
Pacific Lumber Company 141,144
Palmer, Warren S. 72
Palo Alto 83-87,91,165,170
Parks, Bill 99
Pasadena Freeway 183
Paul, Les 124
Payson, A. H. 72
Peninsular Railway xiv,11,37,70,83-94,149, 169-170,174,176-177,182
Penn Central Railroad 181
Penngrove 103
Pennsylvania Railroad Company 130
Pennsylvania Station (New York City) 26,29
Peralta 30,33,159
Perris (see Orange Empire Railroad Museum)
Petaluma xiii,95-96,99,101-106,112,145,148, 161,165,170,181
Petaluma (interurban) 101,107
Petaluma I (riverboat) 103,148,159
Petaluma II (riverboat) 148-149,158-159
Petaluma & Haystack Railroad 67
Petaluma & Santa Rosa Railroad (also Railway) xiii,95-112,134,148-149,151,156,159, 161,166,170-171,174,176-177,181-182
Petaluma of Saucelito 148
Petaluma Street Railroad 95
Petaluma Transportation Company 103,148
Philadelphia & Western 55,127
Phillips Petroleum 33
Piedmont 28-29,46
Piedmont 159
Piedmont & Mountain View Railway Company 25
"Pig, The" 136,144
Pinehurst 121
Pittsburg 119,123-124
Pittsburgh, Pennsylvania xiv
Point Reyes 170
Pollock, Allan 117
Port Chicago 119
Port Costa-Benicia Bridge 167
Port of Stockton 153
Portland, Oregon 2,22-23
Preison, William M. 67
Presidents' Conference Committee 61
P.C.C. car 4,61,66,166
Presidio & Ferries Railroad 64
Public Utilities Commission, State of California 17,123
Puget Sound, Washington 33,156-159,161-162

Quarry 95
Quinault 159

Railroad Administration, United States 177
Railroad Commission, State of California 59, 74,102,136
Railroad Magazine 33,123,177,183
Railway & Locomotive Historical Society 32, 47,173
Railway Equipment and Realty Company 26, 168
Railway Express Company 105
R.P.O. mail 73,135,137,144,148
Ramon xiv,119,123-124,149,157,159,167
Ramon Junction 120
Rank, William 67
Rea 89
Rea, James 83
Reading Railroad 181
Red Bluff 116
Redwood 67
Redwood Empire 150,152,159
Reed, John 145
Reno Traction Company 64

Requa 158
Resolute 103,148
Rhodes, Cecil 113
Richmond 26,28,47,48,50,149,166,168-169,182
Richmond Railway & Navigation Company 168
Richmond-San Rafael Bridge 149
Richmond-San Rafael Ferry 149,151,153,155, 158-159,162
Rio Campo 170
Rio de la Plata (Uruguay) 163
Rio Vista Junction (see California Railway Museum)
Riversview 119
Robinson, Elmer 33
Roblar 95
Rockridge 121,126
Roosevelt, Theodore 167
Rose, Charles A. 113
Ross 80
Ross, Frank J. 115
Russian River 159

Sacramento xiv,7,32,37,46,101,105,109,113, 115-119,121,124-127,133,145,153,155,166-167, 169-171,183
Sacramento (interurban) 117,123,131
Sacramento II (ferryboat) 158,161
Sacramento & Woodland Railroad 127,169
Sacramento Northern Railroad Company 116
Sacramento Northern Railway xiii-xiv,13,15, 19,29-31,34-39,50,65,104-105,111,113-132, 134-135,137,144,149,151,153,166-167,169,171, 173-174,176-177,180-183
Sacramento Street Railway 115
Sacramento Terminal Company 169
St. Helena 134,136
St. Helena 139
St. Louis Louisiana Purchase Exposition 43,101
St. Louis, Missouri xiv,6,31-32,52-53,73,83, 101,139,174
St. Louis Express 167
St. Mary's College 121,146
Salt Lake & Utah 124
San Anselmo xiii,71,78,170
San Bruno 52,57,60
San Diego 101,126,157
San Diego Electric Railway 132
San Diego Maritime Museum 151
San Francisco xiii-xiv,1,3,7,13,22,25-26,30,31, 33,37,46,48,51-63,68-69,73-74,95,99,105,113, 116,119,122-123,126,132,134-135,137,145-150, 152-155,158,159,163-164,166,168-170,176-182
San Francisco (interurban) 139
San Francisco (ferryboat) 152,157,161
San Francisco, Alameda & Stockton Railroad Company 9
San Francisco & Alameda Rail Road Company 8-9
San Francisco & Napa Valley Railroad 137
San Francisco & North Pacific Railroad 67,71, 82
San Francisco & Oakland Rail Road Company 8
San Francisco & Piedmont Railway 26
San Francisco & San Jose Railroad 169
San Francisco & San Mateo Electric Railway 51-53,63
San Francisco Debris Commission 82
San Francisco Maritime Museum 145,148,154-155,174
San Francisco Municipal Railway (see Municipal Railway of San Francisco)
San Francisco, Napa & Calistoga Railway xiii, 43,133-144,148,170-171,173,176-177,181
San Francisco, Oakland & Alameda Railroad 9
San Francisco, Oakland & San Jose Consolidated Railway 26
San Francisco, Oakland & San Jose Railway 10,25-26,28,32,41,43,182
San Francisco-Oakland Bay Bridge 7,9,12-14, 16,19,20,29-31,33-35,45,121-122,128,137,152, 163-164,167,177,178,183
San Francisco-Oakland Terminal Railway 118
San Francisco-Sacramento Railroad (Sacramento Short Line) 29-30,117,131,153
San Francisco Seals (baseball) 146
San Francisco, Vallejo & Napa Valley Railroad 134
San Jose 7,11,12,19,26,37,51,58,64,83-85,87, 91,94,165,167,169-170,179,182
San Jose 147,161-162
San Jose & Alum Rock Railway 83
San Jose & Santa Clara Railway 83
San Jose-Los Gatos Interurban Railway 62, 83-84,89
San Jose Railroads 83-85,87,89,91,93,170
San Jose Street Railway 83
San Leandro 9-10,25
San Leandro 161
San Marin 182
San Mateo xiv,51-54,57,59-63,65,83,165-167, 169
San Mateo 150,161
San Mateo County xii,51,177-178
San Pablo Bay xii-xiii,134
San Pedro 162
San Quentin 71
San Rafael xiii,69,71-72,74,78,80,99,101,165, 170,181
San Rafael & San Quentin Railroad 67
San Ramon Valley Railroad 120
Santa Clara 83
Santa Clara 147,150,161
Santa Clara County xiv,83,85,87-88,178
Santa Clara Interurban 84,91
Santa Cruz 9,132,168
Santa Rosa xiii,95-106,112,115,156, 170
Santa Rosa (interurban) 101,107
Santa Rosa (ferryboat) 150,152,162
Santa Rosa Street Railways 95
Saranap 120-121
Saratoga 84-85,90
Saucelito 162
Sausalito xiii,71-72,74-75,77-78,80,103,145, 149,153-154,170,181-182
Sausalito 162
Savage, Charles D. 16
Saxon 119
Schellville 72
Schindler, O. H. 124
Sciaroni, Pete 101
Seattle, Washington xiv,1
Seawell, Judge 98
Sebastopol xiii,95,99-101,103-104,106,156
Sebastopol 101,107,112
Sehome 162
Senator, The 167
Severson, Chief of Santa Rosa Police 98-99
Seville (Spain) 145
Shasta 150
Shasta Daylight 167
Shipyard Railway 26,28,48
Sierra 64
Sierra Nevada 150,162
Sievers, Wald 71
Silleman, Lorin 63
Smallwood, Charles A. 89,133,137
Smith, Francis M. "Borax" 10,25-27,83,118, 167,179,182
Smith, F. W. 117
"Snowball" 143

Solano County 173
Sonoma 101
Sonoma County 9,95,100-105,170,180
Sonoma Express Company 103,105
Sonoma Valley 161-162
Sonoma Valley Prismoidal Railway 67
Sonoma Valley Railroad 67
South Pacific Coast Railroad 9,13,147
South San Francisco 61,144
South San Francisco Railway & Power Company 64
South Side Street Railway 95
Southern Pacific-Golden Gate Ferries, Ltd. 135,137-138,147-148,151,154,156-158
Southern Pacific Railroad xiii-xiv,2,6-26,30, 31,47,48,51-55,60,67,71-73,77-79,82-87,94, 101,103-106,111,113,117,120,124,129,136-137, 144-147,149-151,155,158-159,161-163,166-167,170,173-174,181-182
Souza, John Phillip 5
Spanish-American War 83
Spiers Auto Stage Line 136
Spokane, Portland & Seattle Railway 22
Sprague, Frank J. xiii,2,3,47,67
Spreckels, Rudolph 95-96
Standard Gas & Electric Company 57
Standard Power & Light Corp. 57
Stanford, Leland xiii,7
Stanford University 83-84,86-87
Statesman, The 167
Steam dummies 1,3,51
Steamer Special, The 148,155
Stevens, Frank A. 67
Stockton 37,118-119,124,166,170,183
Stockton 150,162
Stony Point 95
Suisun Bay xii,xiv,119,149,157,167
Sun, Baltimore 32
Suscol 130
Sutro Railroad 51
Sutter Street Railway 51
Swanston 116
"Syndicate Railway" 25

Taft, President William H. 48,50
Tamalpais I 148
Tamalpais II 152,162-163
Temescal 121
Terra Linda 182
Texas & New Orleans 94
Thornhill 121
Thoroughfare II 147,150,162
Thousand Oaks Station 10,46
Tiburon 154,182
Tiburon 162
Tidewater Southern Railway 124,166,170,182
Times, Los Angeles 183
Tolf, Albert 54,148
Toll Bridge Authority, State of California (also, Toll Bridge Administration) 18,21-23, 31,41,129
Tomales 101,170
Toonerville Trolley 85
Trains 182
Transbay Terminal (also, East Bay Terminal) 15,20-21,31,36,123,180,182-183
Transit 162
Traveltown 22,82,173-174
Treasure Island 34,177
Treasure Island 162
Tres Vias 116
Turlock 170
Two Rock 95,103-104

Ukiah 147,154-155,163
Ullman, John E. 182

Union Pacific Railroad 11,21
Union Street Railway 95
Union Switch and Signal Company 15
Union Traction Company 132
United Railroads of San Francisco 51-57,59-61,63-66,82-83,127,132,169
United Transportation Union, and U.T.U. *News* 177
University of California (Berkeley) 30,48,146,182
University of San Francisco 146
University of Santa Clara 83,146
Urton, Captain Jack 149
Vacaville 120
Vacaville Junction 120
Vallejo xiii,133-138,142,145,148,170,182
Vallejo & Northern Railway (also Railroad) 120,132,135-137,170-171
Vallejo, Benicia & Napa Valley Railroad 133-136,138,148
Valle Vista 118,121,136
Valpraiso (Chile) 113

Van Depoele, Charles xiii,2
Vanderbilt, Commodore 177
Vanderbilt, William H. 174
Vasona Junction 85
Veterans' Home (see Yountville)
Visalia Electric Railway 133,140-141,143
Voorhees, Alan and Associates 183

Walnut Creek xiv,119,121,124
Washington, D.C. xiv,7
Waterloo, Cedar Falls & Northern 111
Watt, James 1
West Lafayette 124
West Oakland Improvement Club 10
West Side Railroad Company 171
Western Meat Company 73
Western Pacific Railroad (deeded to Central Pacific R.R.) 7
Western Pacific Railroad 27,104,113,115-117,119,124,130,137,165-168,170,176-177
Westinghouse Electric Company 133
Weyerhauser Timber Company 141,143

Wheatland, California 131
White Engineering Company 118
Whittaker, Wilbur C. 12,14,15,163
Wilfred 103
Willapa 155
Willotta 116
Woodland 116
Woodworth 97,101,107
World War I 33,43,83,85,177
World War II xiii,5,18,26,28,31-32,56,61,78,105,132,161-163,166,176-177

Yerba Buena I 147,151,156,163
Yerba Buena II 152,163
Yerba Buena Island 25
Yosemite II 150,163
Yountville xiii,134
Yuba City 116,123-124,169

Zook, Chief Engineer of California Northwestern 99

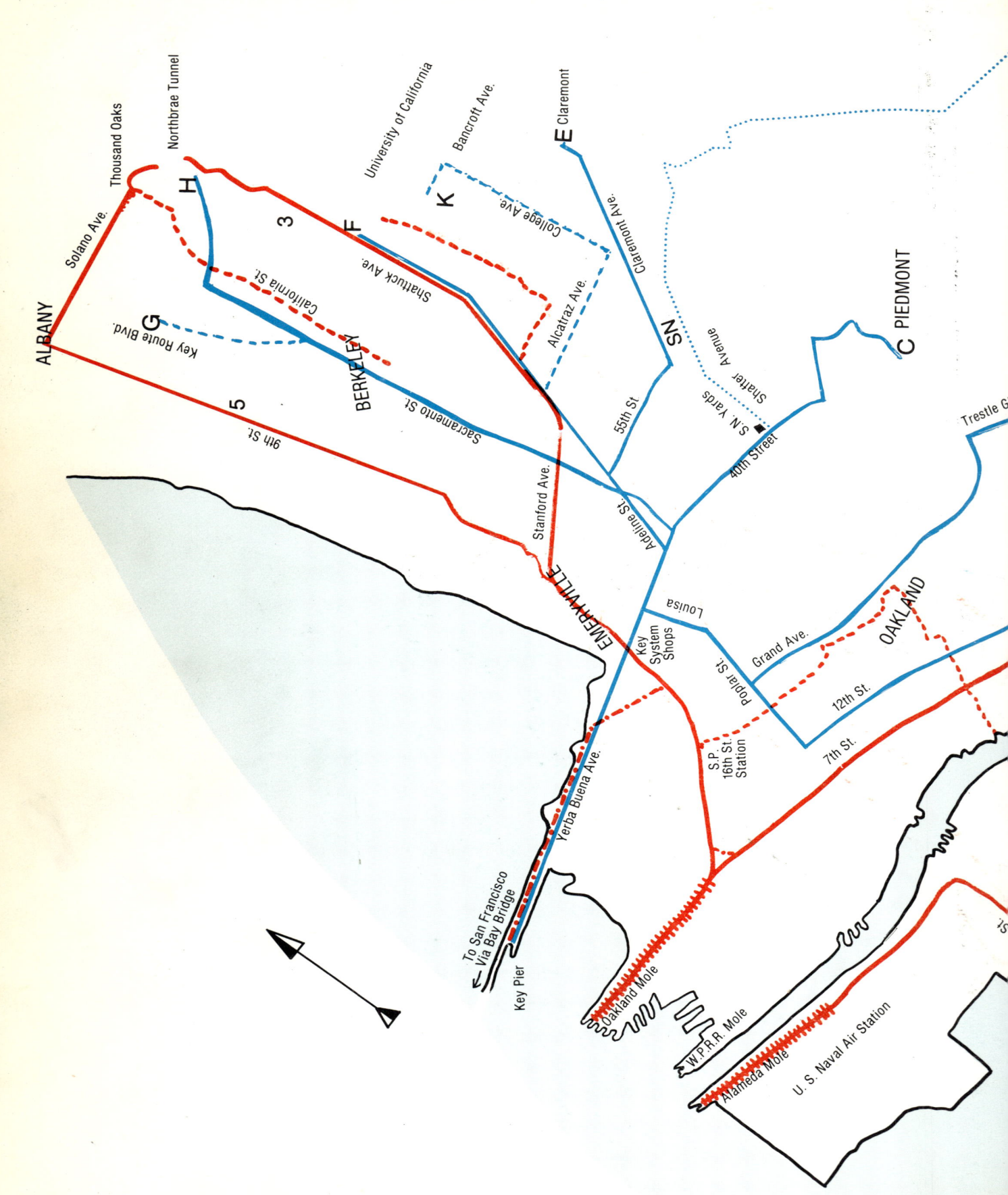